A Beirut Heart
One Woman's War

CATHY SULTAN

SCARLETTA PRESS

MINNEAPOLIS

Another Cathy Sultan book forthcoming from Scarletta Press in 2006: *Israeli and Palestinian Voices: A Dialogue with both Sides.* See www.scarlettapress.com for details

Library of Congress PCN
2005931795

ISBN 13: 978-0-9765201-1-5
ISBN 10: 0-9765201-1-7

Book design by Chris Long
Mighty Media Inc., Minneapolis, MN

Beirut map by Eileen Immerman

First edition | First printing

10 9 8 7 6 5 4 3 2 1

Manufactured in the United States of America

Further information about *Beirut Heart: One Woman's War* and other Cathy Sultan endeavors, including contact information, is available on the author's webpage at the Scarletta Press website. Go to 'authors' at www.scarlettapress.com.

Acknowledgements

I am deeply indebted to my editor, Ian Leask, who, over the years, has constantly pushed me to tackle new writing projects, no matter how challenging. For this project his genius was his ability to unlock memories I had stored in the far reaches of my mind, and help me turn them into coherent stories.

To Colleen McElroy, who thought enough of my writing to award me a spot in her Creative Nonfiction Residency Program at The Loft Literary Center in Minneapolis in 1999. I am grateful for her encouragement and friendship.

To Sarah Harder, for inviting me to sit on her Executive Board at the National Peace Foundation and for the opportunity to expand my work promoting peace between Israelis and Palestinians.

To my friend, Eileen Immerman, who was there when I needed her to design a map, teach me how to cut and paste and make me look good in Photoshop.

To Ed Foreman, for his amazing ability to transform an otherwise ordinary text into something extraordinary.

And finally, to Michel, my husband of nearly 40 years. Through the best and worst of times, we have managed to always come out on top. All my love.

Lebanon Timeline

3000 B.C. – The area known today as Lebanon first appears in recorded history as a group of coastal cities and forested hinterland, inhabited by Canaanites, a Semitic people whom the Greeks call Phoenicians. Each coastal city is an independent kingdom: Tyre and Sidon are maritime and trade centers; Byblos and Berytus (Beirut) are trade and religious centers which at various times come under the control of Greeks, Egyptians, Hittites, Assyrians and Persians. In the rubble of postwar Beirut archeologists discovered ruins they believe to be from ancient Phoenicia 8,000 years ago.

332 B.C. – Alexander the Great captures Tyre. After Alexander's death his generals fight over Phoenicia (present-day Lebanon) for more than two centuries.

64 B.C. – Rome adds Lebanon to its Empire. Emperor Augustus grants Berytus colonial status and the city becomes a famous provincial school of Roman law until it is destroyed by a series of natural disasters in the mid-6th Century

634–1258 A.D. – The seeds of Lebanon's religious strife and civil war in the 20th Century are planted during the Middle Ages. Christianity arrives in the 4th Century when Lebanon is ruled by Rome's Eastern Empire, Byzantium. Islam is founded in 634 A.D. Muhammad's successor, Caliph Abu Bakr, brings Islam to Lebanon. In the meantime, Islam splits into

Shiite and Sunni. Around 1021 the Druze settle in Lebanon. The country is governed by the Umayyads, the Abbasids and finally the Mamluks in 1187 A.D. Under Muslim rule Lebanon prospered as a shipping center, producer of glass, textiles and pottery, also becoming known as an intellectual center.

1512–1840 – Rise of the Ottoman Empire which defeated the Mamluks in 1516–1517 adding Lebanon to its Empire. The Ottomans let the Maans, a local Druze family who settled in the Lebanon Mountains, rule the country until their leader Fakhr al-Din starts an independence movement at which time the Ottomans execute him. Bashir Shihab who takes his place, raises taxes and forces men to serve in the military, causing Christians and Druze to revolt.

1840–1860 – The Ottomans and British exile Bashir Shihab. As a way to squelch any ideas of independence, the Ottomans encourage Christians and Druze to hate each another. In 1860 the Druze massacre 12,000 Maronite Christians. When the Ottomans fail to stop the bloodshed, the French intervene on behalf of the Maronites.

1914–1918 – During WWI the Ottoman Empire joins forces with Germany and Austria-Hungry against the allied forces of England, France, Russia and later the U.S. At the end of the war, the Ottoman Empire collapses.

1916 – The Sykes-Picot Agreement, forged by Britain, France and Russia, carves up the Ottoman Empire, giving Britain control over Palestine and France control over the area that is now Lebanon and Syria.

1920 – France declares the formation of the state of Greater Lebanon, knitting together Mt. Lebanon with the regions of Beirut, Tripoli, Sidon, Tyre, Akkar and the Bekaa Valley.

1941 – During WWII British and Free French armies invade Lebanon and capture Beirut from Vichy French forces.

1943 – Lebanon gains its formal independence from France and the last French troops withdraw in 1946.

1948 – Creation of the state of Israel. A Palestinian exodus of displaced persons ensues, flooding Lebanon and Jordan with refugees.

1958 – First Lebanese civil war as Muslims rally to pan-Arab calls by Egyptian President Nasser. U.S. President Eishenhower sends 15,000 Marines to Beirut to stabilize the situation.

1964 – Arab heads of state establish the Palestine Liberation Organization (PLO) in Cairo.

1969 – Yasser Arafat elected chairman of the PLO

1970 – PLO guerrillas driven from Jordan. They set up headquarters in Beirut and increase their raids into Israel from South Lebanon. Frequent clashes between Israeli forces and the PLO unsettle the country and particularly Beirut where the PLO sets up its own fiefdom in the Beirut refugee camps.

1975 – Coupled with the Palestinian problem, Muslim and Christian differences intensify with the Muslims dissatisfied with what they consider an inequitable distribution of political power sharing and social benefits.

1975 – After shots are fired at a church, a busload of Palestinians are attacked by Christian forces. These two incidents are regarded as the spark which touches off the civil war. Palestinians join forces with the leftist-Muslim side and fighting spreads across Beirut.

1976 – Civil war intensifies. Christians massacre Palestinian inhabitants of Karantina and Tel el-Za'atar; Palestinians massacre Christians in Damour. Syrian troops enter the country at the request of the Christians.

1978 – Israeli Army invades South Lebanon. UN forces (UNIFIL) sent to patrol South Lebanon. Israel forms proxy Lebanese militia (South Lebanon Army) in occupation zone. Syrians launch major attack on Christian neighborhoods in Beirut.

1980–1981 – Increase in hostilities with Israel and Israeli-backed Christian militias fighting the Syrians in the Bekaa Valley, Sannine and Beirut.

1982 – Israeli army, led by Ariel Sharon, invades Lebanon, occupies Beirut and besieges the city for 72 days with heavy bombing. Christian Kataeb leader Bachir Gemeyal is assassinated after his election as Lebanon's President. Christian Kataeb militiamen massacre thousands of Palestinians in the Sabra-Chatilla refugee camp in Beirut while Israeli soldiers drop flares to illiminate the camp. U.S., French and Italian forces arrive in Beirut to take part in Multinational Peacekeeping force.

1982 – PLO expelled from Lebanon. Arafat sets up his headquarters in Tunisia.

1983 – U.S. Beirut Embassy destroyed by Islamic Jihad suicide bomber. U.S. and French military headquarters razed by Islamic Jihad suicide bombers slaughtering more than 300 servicemen.

1984 – Multinational force evacuates Beirut after collapse of Lebanese government army which resulted when the Shiite Muslims and Druze in West Beirut launched a revolt against the Lebanese Army.

1984–1987 – Abduction of Westerners in Beirut including CIA station chief William Buckley who dies after being tortured. Abductions of Westerners continues, including that of journalist Terry Anderson of AP. Archbishop of Canterbury's envoy Terry Waite disappears in West Beirut while seeking release of U.S. hostages. Shiite and Druze milita war in Beirut prompts return of Syrian troops. Palestinian camps siege resumes and Syrians settle into Beirut.

1988 – Failure of Lebanese parliament to elect new president; rival prime ministers take office in west and east Beirut

1989 – General Michel Aoun, Christian Lebanese prime minister declares war on Syrian army in Lebanon. East Beirut besieged by Syrians and the Lebanese militia allies. Aoun abandons his war, leaving hundreds of his followers to be slaughtered while he takes refuge in the French Embassy and is later flown to France.

1989 – Lebanese leaders agree on charter of national reconciliation known as the Taif agreement.

1991 – Terry Waite released after 1,763 days in captivity. His first 4 years were spent in solitary confinement.

2000 – Israel withdraws from most of Lebanon after a 22 year occupation. Its withdrawal is due in large part to the guerrilla war conducted against them by Hezbollah.

2005 – Assassination of former Prime Minister Rafic Hariri. This gives rise to Lebanon's "Cedar Revolution" which in turn prompts Syria to withdraw its troops after a 29-year occupation. A UN fact-finding mission arrives in Lebanon investigating the assassination of Hariri. In early September four generals, all heads of Lebanon's intelligence services, are arrested in connection with the assassination. Parliamentary elections take place but results lead to the same powerful leaders once again taking charge.

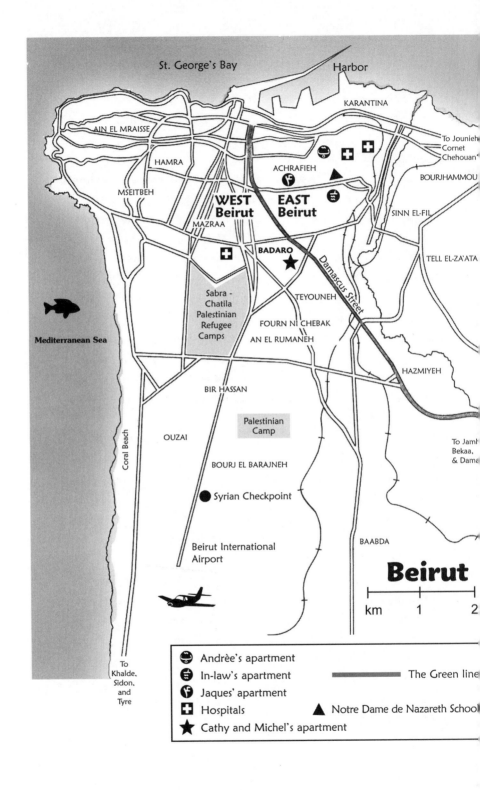

St. George's Bay Harbor

KARANTINA

AIN EL MRAISSE

To Jounieh
Cornet
Chehouan

HAMRA

ACHRAFIEH

BOURJHAMMOU

MSEITBEH

WEST Beirut **EAST Beirut**

SINN EL-FIL

MAZRAA

BADARO

TELL EL-ZA'ATA

Sabra -
Chatila
Palestinian
Refugee
Camps

TEYOUNEH

Damascus Street

FOURN NI CHEBAK

AN EL RUMANEH

Mediterranean Sea

HAZMIYEH

BIR HASSAN

Palestinian
Camp

OUZAI

Coral Beach

To Jamh
Bekaa,
& Dama

BOURJ EL BARAJNEH

● Syrian Checkpoint

BAABDA

Beirut International
Airport

Beirut

km   1   2

To
Khalde,
Sidon,
and
Tyre

Andrèe's apartment
In-law's apartment   The Green line
Jaques' apartment
Hospitals   ▲ Notre Dame de Nazareth School
★ Cathy and Michel's apartment

Contents

Aprons with Bullet Holes

The Syrians have shelled our neighborhood for three days.

After the fighting we return to our apartment to find the windows shattered as usual. I want to sweep up the glass so I go to the kitchen to get my apron and broom. The apron, a long fuchsia one coated with plastic, hangs on its hook behind the kitchen door. As I reach for it I notice a hole right in the middle. I put my finger through the hole and into the splintered wood of the oak door. On the floor nearby, mangled and hardly looking like a bullet at all, lies a three-inch machine gun slug. Across the room I find a round hole in the left hand corner of the window. The bullet ricocheted off the white tile in front of the sink and passed through my apron and the door before falling alongside our daughter's Barbie kitchen set. Nayla often plays there with her pans and utensils spread around her, imitating me as I cook. Our son Naim pushes past me and picks up the bullet, saying, "For my collection!"

I walk to the window and poke my index finger through the hole. In my imagination I can see the bullet entering my back as I stand at the sink, I can feel myself lying on the kitchen floor unable to move, gasping for air, and I can hear the screams of my family gradually fading around me.

My husband slips his hand around my waist to steady me. He does not need to say a word. I know he is thinking the same thing: once again, we were lucky.

And still there is no talk of leaving.

. . .

I now live in Eau Claire, Wisconsin, where aprons hang safely on hooks and bullets rarely shatter kitchen doors. I returned to America in 1983, eight years into Beirut's civil war. While I have come to appreciate the tranquil country living of Wisconsin, after twenty-two years I still anticipate my annual trip to Beirut with the eagerness of a woman about to visit her charming old lover. And I am never disappointed. I delight in the city's warm embrace. I delight in walking the streets, looking at the sights and listening to the sounds of a community rebuilding itself. I love the dinner parties, the elegant lunches with friends at the newly renovated Phoenicia Hotel and catching up on a year's worth of news over great food and local wines. I always intended to move back to Beirut and grow old alongside these same friends. But after all the years in Eau Claire it is hard to imagine going back to a Beirut which has been stalled in its development by fifteen years of war.

The Beirut I carry in my heart is the prosperous city of the late sixties–early seventies with its mansions, city parks, ancient *souks*, its bougainvillea, wisteria, its eucalyptus-lined boulevards – a place that no longer exists.

It was devastating to leave Beirut. The city had worked its way into my soul as great lovers do. Of course what I mean by the city is the people, the culture, the history, and the gracious Lebanese way of doing things. At forty I was forced to abandon it after spending fourteen years in a place I loved. After all this time my heart still beats to the daily rhythms of vibrant, chaotic Beirut. I tell people I cannot help myself, but the truth is I do not want to let it go. I continue to speak French and Arabic. I love the sounds of the words as they come out of my mouth. They make me feel like I am there talking with my friends. Every time I fix hummus and baba ghanouj, savoring the nuttiness of chickpeas and the smoky flavor of eggplant with tahini, garlic and lemon, I feel as if my feet are still firmly planted in the culture and cuisine I continue to call my own.

When the war began I chose for practical reasons to stay and fight. When I say 'fight' I mean fight in the way a housewife does. As the keeper of the hearth you are the heartbeat of your family. You are the mother who comforts her children after a bomb blast shatters part of their bedroom wall. You are the wife who consoles her husband after he has spent his mornings treating wounded civilians and sending mangled bodies to the morgue. Collectively, you are the pulse of a country on the verge of collapse. Your responsibilities are numerous, endless.

You deal with water shortages. You wash your clothes in the wee hours of the night when water finally begins to flow. You fill buckets for doing dishes, watering plants and flushing toilets. You find ways to surmount the daily power outages. Your children finish their homework by candlelight at the kitchen table while you prepare the evening meal. Flashlight in hand you descend eight flights of stairs to walk the dog. In spite of a night-long battle in your street, you have your children dressed and fed in time to catch the school bus at 6:45 A.M. And when the schools close because of war – sometimes for months at a time – you hire a tutor to keep your children's minds usefully occupied.

You stock up on sugar, flour, rice, and canned foods. You store extra gas canisters on your balcony for cooking and hope that a bomb will not fall on them. You no longer walk your streets casually stopping at the green grocery and the bakery. Instead you dodge behind overturned shipping containers in order to avoid the lurking rooftop sniper. Inevitably, he will shoot someone. One morning as you begin your errands you discover a neighbor lying dead in your street, a bullet through her head. You don your black dress and attend yet another senseless funeral. You pray a lot for your family's safety and for the courage to hold it all together.

You retreat to your kitchen. Cooking is like taking a tranquilizer. Most days your table is surrounded by people engaged in lively conversation, which is good for everyone's morale, particularly your children's. You strive to create an atmosphere of connectedness, of community. This helps alleviate the fear, wards off despair and becomes a therapeutic act of resistance.

You try to keep an orderly apartment. The country's leaders do not have your housewifely energy and focus. They cannot keep the streets clean, deliver the mail or collect the garbage. You are able to maintain a peaceful environment inside your home. You have become a skilled negotiator, frequently called upon to act as the peace-maker in your extended family. Your leaders were charged with keeping their Lebanese family together in peace. When they saw the hostility increasing they failed to dissuade the various political factions from turning into vicious militiamen. Either through personal greed, political inflexibility or sheer ineptitude, they have failed to save a nation they were trusted to preserve.

Before the war I led an ideal life. I was accepted and loved as a Lebanese. I lived in a beautiful home surrounded by Roman artifacts, Persian carpets, and Phoenician amphorae, things that I associated with my Lebanese life. I had wonderful friends and I knew my neighbors by name. My husband had a successful medical practice and our children were growing up speaking English, French and Arabic. When you are blessed in so many ways you do not hastily pack up and leave just because there is machine gun fire at the end of the street. At first you persuade yourself that the fighting will stop, that the warring factions will come to their senses. Why would they not when the very existence of their city is at stake? You are naïve. You do not understand how hatred builds up when there are no wise leaders to repair the social ills that fuel this kind of discontent.

. . .

To those who question why I stayed, why I did not do the sensible thing and return to the United States, I have only one thing to say: most people would do as I did. You do not leave an earthquake zone even if a major fault line runs down your street, even when there have been a few shudders. After the next tremor, when your street is destroyed, what do you do? You stay; everyone you know stays. Or you live in South Florida. God decides in his infinite wisdom to sweep it clean now and again. Do you leave after the hurricane has damaged your home? No, you rebuild. People who live along the Mississippi River and have been flooded out two or three times, do they leave? No, they love the valley they live in.

Are our decisions unreasonable? Absolutely! After all, we are human.

1

Beginnings

I had not always stubbornly clung to one place. I was raised in Washington, D.C., a city amazingly similar to Beirut not for its cultural diversity, but for the sharp contrasts between opulence and poverty. One of the reasons I left was youthful rebellion. I blamed my parents for what I thought was a variety of inflexibility and frigidity peculiar to them, and their belief that a father's word was God and mothers rarely, if ever, intervened. In fact their behavior was completely typical of their generation. As it is usually the people who make or break one's impression of a city, I connected Washington with my parents' mind-set. For the longest time I associated the quality of open-mindedness only with Beirut, which swept me up in a lover's embrace. So when the city where I had put down roots and with which I was enamored began turning into something far worse than Washington could ever become, it was one of the worst things which could possibly have happened.

Of course my parents and I were both wrong. Infighting and immaturity are the seeds of unrest as much for individuals as for nations. Families – and countries – are led into war by the lack of enough maturity to take responsibility for disagreements or to resolve conflicts.

. . .

High school was the most dreadful period of my life. The nuns and I shared a mutual dislike. In their opinion, which they shared freely, I was and always would be an academic failure. Imagine everyone's surprise when I did quite well at university once I was out of their clutches.

Unable to decide what to do after I graduated I landed a job as the Assistant Medical Director at Providence Hospital in Washington. My job was to take care of the interns and residents, most of whom were foreign. I helped organize their conferences, their on-call schedules and their housing. I wrote recommendation letters and résumés and helped them improve their English. I enjoyed meeting these people from all over the globe and made many friends. I was introduced to their families and invited to their cultural celebrations. The laughter and joy around the dinner tables, the spontaneous kisses and hugs, the facility with which their children spoke multiple languages, were all so different from my own family.

I began dating a couple of the physicians. I even imagined myself marrying one of them and living abroad. Since my parents and I were engaged in a cold war, the idea had enormous appeal.

For years I had imagined living somewhere in Central Asia. I saw myself behind a strong Tajik on a galloping horse. In other dreams I was sailing the South China Sea on my way to Borneo, the scent of nutmeg and cinnamon in the air. Or I was kidnapped by a sultan and traversing a brilliant star-lit desert atop a camel.

My future in Beirut began in a dream where sheets of sand and waves of dunes rippled across the serene beauty of a boundless stretch of desert. My dream-woman lived in a tent with her Bedouin husband. Like him she was tall and majestic. Her long blue garment embroidered in gold shone brilliantly when she stepped into the sun. Her golden hair hung in two long braids almost touching the ground. She was queen of her husband's tribe in the exotic land of Ali Baba, of Scheherazade's *A Thousand and One Nights*, a place where caravans of laden camels travel along sand highways heading for market at the desert's edge.

I met 'my' Sultan in early December, 1964, not on the sandy desert of my dreams but when he began his internship at the Washington Hospital Center. A mutual friend who had attended the same medical school in Beirut introduced us. Over the next six months when Michel was not on call on alternate nights we spent every minute together. He introduced me to his world of music, art, language, and culture. I saw my first live opera, attended a concert at the National Symphony Orchestra and heard Jean-Pierre Rampal play the flute. Michel took me to charming restaurants in Georgetown where we sat at secluded, candlelit tables and ordered champagne. For my birthday he gave me a pair of gold earrings studded with turquoise stones. Sometimes after a concert at the Washington Cathedral, where I heard Bach and Vivaldi for the first time, we would stroll through Rock Creek Park.

I found the courage to walk out of my parents' Washington home – against their wishes – in this Lebanese man, Michel Naim Sultan, whom I had known for only six months. I loved that he treated me like a lady, opening doors and pulling out chairs. When he took my hand, he kissed it; when he looked into my eyes, his smile was reassuring. In his ongoing effort to speak better English he was willing to be corrected when he made a mistake. I loved everything about Michel. I loved the texture of his slightly darker skin and the way the warmth it gave off in the sunlight made his black eyes glow. There was something special about the way his curly hair lay in tiny ringlets on the back of his neck. I loved the way he kept his nails short and clean; his fine leather shoes and cashmere socks; his Chanel cologne; the way he wore his beautifully-tailored cotton shirts and silk ties with French labels under luxuriously soft woolen suits. There was always a neatly folded handkerchief in his right pants pocket. Sitting beside him in a dark theater I loved the way he took my hand in his, the way he stroked my palm in circles with his thumb. Most of all I loved his gentleness.

. . .

All these years later I still believe the inspiration to leave Washington came from my maternal grandmother, Catherine Sheehan. In 1905 at age eighteen she left poverty-stricken Ireland. After she landed at Ellis Island she boarded a train for Washington where several of her cousins lived. There she met and married William Collins, a widower with six young children; subsequently she bore him six of her own. My mother, also named Catherine, was her first-born, and as the eldest was expected to help care for her younger siblings.

Sixty years later I was not fleeing an impoverished country at age twenty-two. I was escaping my parents' narrow view of the world in search of a much wider one. From early childhood I had been a major source of frustration to my parents. My father had no idea how to handle a stubborn, independent child who challenged his every decree. No doubt open dialogue would have fostered a healthier atmosphere of love and understanding between us, but my parents believed a child should be seen and not heard. Unfortunately I craved attention, and when I did not get it I sought to attract it through rebellion, which only convinced them I was spoiled and self-centered. Once I became too old to be punished physically, I found I had more power to do as I pleased. By the time I turned twenty-two my parents and I had established a hardcore pattern of tension and resistance that teetered on the brink of domestic war.

I know it is wishful thinking – and it was out of the question given the generational misunderstandings – but what if my parents and I had been able to discuss our differences? Would I still have gone looking for someone to take me as far away as possible? If they had welcomed Michel into their home; asked questions about his family, his country and culture; if my father had gone to the trouble of learning a word or two of Arabic and surprising

❤

Michel with them one day, my life might have turned out differently. If my father had taken Michel aside and offered to help him set up his medical practice; or if he had said, 'We'd enjoy having you and Cathy living near us and seeing our grandchildren grow up around us. What do you think of that idea? It might be safer than going back to Lebanon.' Just suppose all that had happened and Michel had come to love my father just as I came to love his. I might not have done something as extreme as leaving the most prosperous nation in the world to live in the turbulent Middle East.

. . .

On a late June morning in 1965 Michel and I left for Boston where he would begin his residency in internal medicine at the Lahey Clinic. There were no promises of marriage, but I knew he had broken off his engagement to a young Lebanese woman. There was no 'I love you,' either. 'Your green eyes have captured my heart,' was as close as he had come to a declaration of love. Perhaps I should have had misgivings, but I was never so certain about anything in my life. I cannot recall determining to win him over to the point of asking me to marry him, but it must have been in my subconscious, because I strove very hard to turn our love affair into something permanent. Later, when Michel opened up and revealed more about himself, I found that he had done the same thing. This is how great relationships come about: both partners decide they are going to make it work. I knew Michel had no intention of staying in the States once he finished his training. He wanted to practice medicine in Beirut, which made the idea of marrying him that much more exciting.

I had a very romantic notion of what life would be like with Michel, so I failed to realize that an essential component of this relationship was that someone had to know how to cook, and it was probably going to be me.

Before we moved to Boston I rarely set foot in a kitchen. This was my mother's domain and I lacked even the most basic cooking skills. Turkey seemed like an easy thing to prepare, so it was one of the first things I tried. One Friday evening before we left for a party I got out a small Butterball® that I had bought on sale at the supermarket. I went into the kitchen early Saturday morning – despite a very late evening – still wearing my white fur slippers. Somewhere I had got the notion that long, slow cooking at a low oven temperature would result in a succulent bird. I wanted the turkey ready to put in the oven by late morning so Michel and I would have the afternoon free to do something fun. As I was taking the plastic off the bird I caught a glimpse of myself in the mirror behind the stove. My hair stuck up at all angles like a rooster. I kept looking at myself, at the muscles on my forearms working as I tore the packaging off and rinsed the bird.

"Look at you, Cathy," I said. "You're a chef and your first turkey is going to be great."

For some reason I thought I knew how to cook stuffing. I sautéed some onions in vegetable oil, burning them only slightly; then I poured the stuffing mix on top. It got very stiff until I consulted the instructions: 'add water.' Of course now I cannot imagine ever being that dumb. When I thought I had poured in enough liquid I stuffed it all inside the bird and closed it up with toothpicks. I put the bird in the oven at 300° just before Michel and I left for a stroll along the Charles River.

When we returned I made mashed potatoes, defrosted peas and opened a can of cranberry sauce. Then I dressed nicely and groomed carefully for the occasion, and when I thought it was time I pulled a perfectly browned bird from the oven, transferred it to a serving platter and proudly set it on the table. It was not until I had already put the cooking pan to soak that I realized I had forgotten to save the juices. Fortunately I had a can of ready-made gravy in the kitchen cabinet.

Blood spurted forth as I cut deeply into the turkey, spotting my dress and the white tablecloth. Michel flung himself back just in time to avoid blotches on his dress shirt. The bird was cooked to a depth of about an inch; the rest was raw. I suddenly felt so hot I thought steam was coming off my face. Michel sat quietly with his eyes lowered and his hands in his lap. I searched over the surface of the bird to find cooked bits to put on his plate; I found no more than a few slivers. I filled his otherwise empty plate with a mound of mashed potatoes and lots of peas, smothering it all with canned gravy.

"You'll like the stuffing," I said, turning the bird on its side to serve him. More blood gushed out, followed by a sac full of inner organs I had neglected to remove before stuffing the bird. Michel stood up, threw his napkin on the table, walked into the bathroom, and locked the door.

The minute I heard the key turn I swooped up the bleeding turkey, took it into the kitchen and threw it in the garbage bin. When he came out I was sitting on the couch.

"Would you be interested in taking a starving lady to dinner?" I asked sheepishly.

The next morning I went out and bought *The Joy of Cooking*, the cookbook my mother used, but my real find was Julia Child's *Mastering the Art of French Cooking*. There I was, the eager, aspiring young cook paging through the recipes, learning about such things as blanching, braising, deglazing, and sautéing. The old me, the one who was brought up feeling very insecure, the one who failed her national tests, might have said: 'Here's something else I'm not good at – I can't even cook.' But my life was changing and instead of accepting that first failure I was determined to become a great cook.

At night while Michel read his medical journals I studied recipes and made lists of things I needed to buy. One evening, much to Michel's delight, I tried something entirely new: scallops. Julia Child called these round silky mouthfuls that felt like wet tongues 'Coquilles St. Jacques.' After simmering gently in white wine the scallops were delicately spooned into a velvety blend of cream and egg yolks, returned to their shells, sprinkled with grated Swiss cheese and briefly placed under the broiler. A glass of *Sauvignon Blanc* and a toasted baguette were all I served on the side. I was amazed at the difference in Michel's romantic behavior when we retired to the bedroom early that night, so different from the night when I served him raw turkey. I could think of no better motivation for becoming an excellent cook.

After enjoying the effects of seafood on Michel I could not wait to try other foods. I could only imagine the delightful pleasures tart and sweet would produce, or spicy and cool on a summer day at a secluded beach on the Cape, or a creamy Camembert or Brie accompanied by the dense earthiness of a red Bordeaux on a crisp autumn night in front of a fire.

With lists of necessary ingredients from Julia's book I visited Boston's open air market each Saturday. I walked from stall to stall discovering foods I had never seen before: eggplants, artichokes, different kinds of lettuce – all this time I had thought it came in only one variety, iceberg. I was buying fresh rosemary and basil and actually knowing how to use them on poultry and beef. I found cheeses with molds on them: white, green, black. "Do people actually eat that," I asked, "or do they scrape it off ?"

There were huge carcasses of beef ready to be cut to order; piles of mouth-watering fruits, none of it canned; arranged on ice beds were whole fish in varieties I never knew existed, things that looked like monsters with huge heads and sea-cat whiskers.

My game of enticement began the minute Michel arrived home from the hospital. By the time I called him to dinner wonderful aromas filled our tiny apartment. He arrived at the table practically swooning in anticipation. As the prelude to the main event I teased and aroused his appetite with something simple like roasted red peppers marinated in fruity olive oil, vinegar, pine nuts, golden raisins, and crushed garlic and served on slices of toasted baguette. It was light, the pepper's rich color evoking the sun, the vinegar's tartness suggesting the earth. This might be followed by a hearty soup of lentils and vegetables spiced with cumin and lots of garlic.

The next time I tried turkey for Thanksgiving it was properly cooked and stuffed with fresh chestnuts and sausage. I swore I would never attempt it again when it took me almost six hours to soak and peel just a few pounds of these tasty nuts. Of course I did

❤

for many Thanksgivings thereafter because the aroma of roasting chestnuts in fatty pork sausage and herbs is so delectable.

. . .

After all these years of gourmet cooking, Michel still joshes me whenever I roast a turkey.

"Don't forget to take out the gizzards," he says, laughing.

I grab a dry sponge and throw it at him but he deftly dodges out of the way; I never get to nail him as he deserves.

. . .

After eight months of eating my good food Michel asked me to be his wife. Out of my great and huge wisdom – I was twenty-three – I accepted.

"Shouldn't we invite your parents to the wedding?" he asked.

At the core of my personality I was an extrovert and an unrepentant attention seeker. In response to his question I replied, "We could, if you want it to go something like this."

Climbing onto the table I did my father's voice alternating with my mother's. My left-leaning head was my father; the right-leaning was my mother. The right began.

"Do you know anything about him?"

"How do you expect me to know anything? I can't understand a word he says."

"Cathy did say he was Greek Catholic."

"Does that mean he's a *real* Catholic?"

"His name is Michel. I thought that was a girl's name."

"I don't care what his name is. I'm going to call him Mike."

At this point Michel was laughing so hard that tears were rolling down his cheeks.

"I wonder if he eats hamburgers and hotdogs?"

"If he eats something called 'kibbeh' I doubt he eats 'real food.' How do you even say 'kibbeh'? It sounds like a barking dog."

By this time Michel had reached for a handkerchief to wipe his eyes and blow his nose. I could hardly breathe myself but I was playing to an appreciative audience and did not want to stop. I inclined my head to my father's side.

"Hell's bells, I bet he doesn't even know what football is."

. . .

Michel and I were married on April 14, 1966, in the presence of a few Lebanese friends. Later that day I called my parents to announce the good news. They knew I was in love with Michel because he was all I talked about when I was home at Christmas. In my excitement I anticipated – if not a spontaneous outburst of joy – at least some measure of enthusiasm. I did not expect my father's only comment to be, 'Did you at least get married in the church?' In my arrogance I expected him to agree with all the views that were current in the sixties, which I shared. I totally ignored his deep faith. Of course I wished he had said, 'Wonderful, I'm happy for you, Cathy,' but that was not my father's way. Had he been better able to express his feelings, he probably would have given me a good scolding for expecting him to change his values just because I ran away with a man and married him without ever asking his permission.

A couple of days later I called home again and this time I spoke with my mother. To my surprise she said, "Oh, I'm so glad you called."

I could hear my father shouting in the background, "Don't forget to tell Cathy ..."

They both sounded like they were taking drugs. Then I realized what had happened: I had called my sisters and pleaded for help. One of them had interceded on my behalf and gotten my parents to respond more positively to our marriage. Perhaps she had sat the parents down and explained to them that a Greek Catholic was not too far from their kind of Catholic and this was a good match for me. Whatever had happened, it resulted in a huge change of attitude for which I was very grateful.

. . .

Over the next few months I was introduced to some of Michel's family. I still remember the first time I saw his brother Jacques towering over me in our doorway, his dark eyes smiling. With his prominent nose and powerful build he looked like some Greek god. He came walking in and the first thing he did was smell the dinner I was preparing, and with a wink at Michel, said, "Yes, you're going to work out just fine. Look what I brought."

From behind his back he produced a bottle of champagne. He looked at Michel and out came fast, rattling French I could not understand. I loved the sound of it and the way it rolled around in his mouth. Michel, whom I had rarely heard speak French before, rattled right back. Suddenly they both looked at me.

"Sorry," Michel said, "we should speak English so you can understand."

"No, no." I laughed. "I love the sound of it, even if I don't understand it."

"But we're speaking about you," joked Jacques, leaning down to kiss me on the cheek. I was trying to think of an appropriate response when I heard a voice say, "My brothers are extremely rude."

Behind Jacques was an elegant looking woman with short dark hair wearing a lovely tailored suit and high heels. Arms crossed and leaning against the wall, she smiled at me.

"They're always like that," she said. "I don't know how you're going to stand living with them."

In fact, Jacques and his best friend Joe Soussou were moving in with us while they pursued advanced degrees at MIT.

Andrée, Michel's sister, came in and kissed me warmly on both cheeks. "I'll speak English with you but I'll also teach you some French and Arabic. Then you can catch these two in their wicked ways."

. . .

Our small dining room was always the center of much laughter. I had food ready to put out on the table at any minute even if it was nothing more than sliced carrots or cucumbers. I knew if I did not, my three men would call out for food like drunken lords. I used to pretend to get angry at being bossed around but I really did not mind. Some days, even when it was snowing heavily, friends would turn up bringing all kinds of wines; occasionally they brought food that only needed to be warmed up. It was never too much work even if I had a whole meal to prepare. I would sip a glass of wine in the kitchen and participate from there.

Most of the people who came were Lebanese and it took me a while to realize what a diverse lot they were: Muslims, Armenians, Greek Orthodox, Maronite Catholics with big chains on their hairy chests, and Greek Catholics like Michel and his brother. They were all professionals, teasing one another and happy to be together.

Occasionally the wonderful times would break down into furious rows, always in Arabic. To me they sounded like dogs fighting. The women would come into the kitchen and cluster around, mostly amused by the arguing, but I got quite alarmed. Then it would stop as quickly as it began and they would be laughing again.

Michel was about to finish the second year of his internal medicine residency when I learned I was pregnant. If we were thrilled at the prospect of becoming parents, my father-in-law in Beirut was ecstatic. He was convinced I was carrying a boy who would be named after him. Every few weeks he sent us money to buy whatever we needed for his grandson. I was relieved when we didn't disappoint my father-in-law's expectations. On January 12, 1967, I gave birth to a healthy seven pound, six ounce boy, Naim Michel Sultan. In Arabic, 'Naim' means 'gracious.'

. . .

Our move to Lebanon was still a little over a year away. When Michel finished his training in Boston we were going to move to Madison, Wisconsin, where he would spend his last year in the States as a Fellow in Gastroenterology at the University Hospitals. I was pregnant again, and while we wanted to have the second child before leaving America, the timing was awful. Michel's fellowship was to begin on July 1, 1968, and I was due any day after that. The time was very busy and very stressful: I was keeping house for three men, caring for a baby and cooking the evening meals for everyone.

My parents were apprehensive because we were planning to move to Lebanon after Michel's residency; they called every week trying to dissuade me from going. On the other hand my grandmother Catherine surprised me by offering to come to Boston to help with our move to Madison. I thought she might have some ulterior motive because she also was constantly trying to persuade me not to emigrate to Lebanon.

Because of all the chaos in our lives I hardly noticed the Arab-Israeli war when it began on June 5, 1967. For me it was something very distant. Michel kept talking about it to his brother because of course they were very emotionally involved. When I saw how it affected Michel, and watched how he was glued to the television and was very upset, when he could not concentrate on anything else, I began to realize how important it was. I had one small child and another on the way. We were moving to the Middle East and the future of my children mattered a great deal to me. I saw Americans backing our government's support of Israel. Was there a legitimate reason for this policy? Were the Arabs the aggressors as the newspaper articles claimed? The official wisdom about the Middle East clashed with what I was hearing from neutral Lebanese observers. When I questioned Michel he suggested I do some research on my own in order to get a better grasp of the regional conflict.

. . .

In late May, 1967, Egyptian President Gamal Abdel Nasser talked of blockading the Strait of Tiran,[1] which would have dramatically affected Israeli shipping. Both the United States and the United

---

1   The Strait of Tiran is located between the southeast coast of the Egyptian Sinai peninsula and Saudi Arabia, where the Gulf of Aqaba joins the Red Sea.

Nations agreed to work out some sort of mutually acceptable compromise between Egypt and Israel. Before this could be accomplished Israel conducted a preemptive strike against Egyptian Army positions in the Sinai. The United Nations urged an immediate cease-fire but Israel fought on, capturing the Golan Heights from Syria, the Gaza Strip from Egypt and East Jerusalem and the West Bank from Jordan.

Over dinner one evening during the war Michel said, "I learned something very interesting today."

"Did it have anything to do with the war?" I asked.

"I was examining a patient," he said. "He asked where I was from. One thing led to another and pretty soon we were discussing the war. He owns a chain of newspapers in the Midwest so I asked him why the news coverage was so biased, why the Arabs were portrayed as the aggressors and not the Israelis.

"'It's all about money,' the man replied. 'My business depends on advertising. If I write what I perceive to be the truth but it offends a certain group of people, word gets out. Pretty soon agencies stop advertising in my newspaper. I can no longer afford to print my paper and I go broke.'"

"But that's political blackmail!" I said.

"That's exactly what I said," replied Michel, "but the patient just shrugged his shoulders as if to say that was how things worked here."

"America's supposed to be a democracy. Why not tell the truth even if it shows Israel in a bad light?"

"Because in this country Jews have more clout than Arabs."

"Even when there is gross injustice? How can that be?" I asked. "Yesterday, Israel sank the USS *Liberty*, killing thirty-four American servicemen. They called it an accident. It was an American electronics ship in the Mediterranean flying an American flag. How could that have been an accident? What's wrong with our government? Why are they so afraid of condemning Israel when they do something wrong?"

"Cathy, you just called it by its name," said Michel, "it's political blackmail."

I read more and I asked more questions. It was embarrassing how little I knew about the Middle East in general and Israel in particular. Most of our American friends in Boston were Jewish. One was a journalist so I had plenty of experts to consult. When I learned why the State of Israel was created I agreed with the 1948 UN resolution proclaiming the legitimate and moral right of the Jewish people to a homeland after the Holocaust. What was less clear to me was why hundreds of thousands of people already living in Palestine had to be displaced to accommodate the Jewish immigrants. Why, after the fact, was there not some sort of mutual recognition of each other's right to self-determination and survival?

I realized that the Arab-Israeli conflict – which grew out of years of intolerance, narrow-mindedness and lost opportunities for peace – was really the same as family conflicts – started and sometimes never ended – because no one was willing to make the necessary compromises.

. . .

Michel did not know this conflict would follow him to Madison, but it did. A few days after he began his fellowship he attended a conference. The resident seated beside him introduced himself.

"Where are you from?"

When Michel told him, the resident said, "I watched your fellow Arabs begging for water in the Sinai. We didn't give them any, of course. It was much more amusing watching them die of thirst."

Michel told me afterward that he was not sure what to do. He was in shock. He wanted to punch the man but knew that would provoke a terrible incident. Instead he got up and left the room without saying a word. He found out later that the resident was an American Jew who had volunteered in the Israeli Army during the June war. He and his fellow soldiers not only let the Egyptian POWs die of thirst in the Sinai, they forced them to dig their own graves.

James Bamford reveals in his book *Body of Secrets* that it was because the *USS Liberty* was doing reconnaissance on this massacre, among other things, that the Israelis attacked the ship with F-16 fighter bombers and torpedo boats.[2]

. . .

I went into labor the day we arrived in Madison. On June 27, 1968, I gave birth to a beautiful six pound, four ounce daughter whom we named Nayla Maria. In Arabic 'Nayla' means 'recipient of a gift.'

Once I had recovered from the delivery and settled into as much of a routine as one can with two small children, I came to appreciate our apartment overlooking Lake Mendota as the ideal place to mentally prepare for Beirut. Decisions had to be made: what to leave behind or sell, what to ship. I began to study French on my own and tried to practice it with Michel. His idea of a lesson was getting into bed and asking me to read. Within minutes, he was fast asleep.

My grandmother Catherine stayed on another two months to help with Naim and Nayla. She editorialized constantly about the wonders of the United States. 'Now, darling,' she would say, 'you can't be leaving America. It is the most glorious place on earth.' The more she talked, the more my eyes glazed over. One particular afternoon as the children slept we sat on the sofa facing the lake, having tea.

"So, Cathy," she said, "are you still bent on giving up America?"

"Grandma, I've told you before. I am not giving up this country. I just want to experience something different."

"Well, I can't imagine what that could be. You know America's been very good to me. I don't know what would have happened to me if I'd stayed in Ireland."

"Your reasons for leaving Ireland were completely different

---

2   Bamford, James: *Body of Secrets, Anatomy of the Ultra-Secret National Security Agency.* Doubleday, NY, 2001, p. 201–202.

from my reasons for leaving America. But I don't want to go into that now."

"I know, darling. Don't think I don't understand how hard it is. Families are like that. My father was difficult, drunk one minute and charming the next. If he came home sober he'd give you the shirt off his back. If he came in all full of drink his belt would be off in a second and he'd tear our hides like you wouldn't believe. Jesus, Mary and Joseph, there were times when I couldn't sit down for a week. So you see it wasn't just the poverty that made me leave. Ah, to be sure it was beautiful and I loved it dearly, but I came here. America is truly the land of milk and honey, Cathy."

"Well, Grandma, it's a larger world that beckons. Maybe I'll come back one day, who knows?" Then, moving in close and puckering my lips, I said, in exaggerated French, "Ma chérie, je cherche quelque chose beaucoup plus exotique."

Catherine looked at me and closed one eye. "Sure and you're speaking one of those silly languages already. I suppose you'll come back with all kinds of other nonsense on your breath, too."

I poured her more of the steaming strong tea she liked with full milk and two sugars. The brown maple syrup color when the milk was added, and the aroma steaming off it, was lovely. She sat back and sipped it.

"Ah," she said. "You're my only grandchild who can make a proper cup of tea. You know, darling, I really don't want you to go but I know you're as determined as I was, so I'll shut up. My prayers will be with you, Cathy dear, and I wish you the very best."

2

Beirut, My Love

*A*s our plane approached Beirut on June 17, 1969, I saw miles and miles of pristine beaches beside turquoise water. Along the *corniche* dozens of white marble buildings glistened like pearls in the late afternoon sun. My heart throbbed with excitement. 'Just as I dared imagine,' I thought, 'only better.' When we landed the passengers applauded. As they stood gathering their belongings they turned to each other, mostly perfect strangers, and said, 'Hamdalah al salame,' which Michel explained means 'Welcome home, thank God you had a safe trip.'

"Why were they cheering?" I asked, "were they relieved we didn't crash?"

An elderly man seated behind us overheard our conversation. "Mais non, Madame, we applaud because we're glad to be back in our dear city."

I had never seen such warmth, such joie de vivre. I would come to learn that this was standard behavior for the gentle but spirited Lebanese.

. . .

A city as indulgent as its people, Beirut was a place where both the muezzin in his minaret and the peal of church bells summoned the faithful to prayer. When I first arrived I would often sit on a bench in Martyrs' Square³ in the heart of Beirut to take in all its sounds: the car radios blaring – sometimes French ballads, sometimes guttural, passionate Arabic songs – and all around me people speaking French, Arabic and accented English. When I closed my eyes I heard car horns honking, the roar of planes overhead, a gentle sea breeze rustling palm leaves, and the flutter of the doves' wings as they landed on the outstretched arm of the Martyrs' bronze statue. Cooks from inside a nearby cafe were yelling at each other, plates clattered as waiters rushed to clear tables, taxi drivers followed an age-old tradition and shouted out their destinations from their stands around Martyrs' Square.

Like an impatient child I could not wait for a free afternoon to go have a light meal at one of the outdoor cafes on Hamra Street. Afterwards I strolled the tightly-knit row of stores, stopping at The Last Word to buy the latest American bestsellers then continuing on to My Fair Lady, a block away. I entered this small store just to touch the Cacharel silk dresses, the cashmere sweaters, the stylish wool suits, and then leave, anticipating the day when I could actually afford to buy one of these readymade Parisian confections.

Nothing epitomized the social graces of the Lebanese better than their rituals involving coffee. It was offered at every occasion, even a condolence visit. After wishing the bereaved, 'Awat bi Salamtek,' (May God preserve your health), I would take a seat near the female relatives of the family. A neighbor, or a butler hired for the occasion, passed through the room serving the mourners coffee. Taking a demitasse of thick Turkish coffee from the silver tray, I would turn to the bereaved and say, 'Allah Yer Hamou,' (May he [or she] rest in Peace).

. . .

---

3   In 1916 a public garden in central Beirut was named 'Martyrs' Square' in memory of Lebanese nationalists executed by the Ottomans. A monument to the martyrs was erected in 1950.

I often stopped to visit a friend when I was running my morning errands. The excuse was coffee but the real reason was the pleasure of her company. People I hardly knew invited me into their homes and insisted I stay for lunch as casually as if I were a member of the family. When I politely refused, which was usually the case, I was served the de rigueur Turkish coffee. As with many Lebanese I had my clothes made by a dressmaker. In both autumn and early spring I would pay a visit to Kassatly Brothers, a fabric store in *Souk Tawili*. Invited to sit at a long table I was served coffee while the owner directed his assistant to roll out bolts of fine silks, wools and linens for my inspection.

My love of cooking drew me like a magnet to Beirut's open-air markets. Carrying two large plastic shopping bags and dressed in a modest summer frock and sturdy shoes, I zigzagged for three city blocks along two-thousand-year-old cobblestone alleyways, walking from stall to stall just as I had in Boston. There the similarities stopped. Unlike Boston, Beirut was about listening to how people talked to vendors, learning how to haggle in Arabic over the price of a kilo of tomatoes or fish. There were strange exotic fruits I had never seen before like red pomegranates, yellow quinces, burnt-orange persimmons, prickly pears, and yellow wrinkly-skinned pomelos the size of grapefruits. There were street vendors haggling with housewives and maids along the way as they pushed through the narrow city streets, their carts overflowing with eggplants, zucchini, baby green okra, tomatoes, lemons, and green beans.

Walking through the *souks* was an amazing olfactory experience. Alongside the mouth-watering smell of flat bread dusted with thyme and olive oil there might be the smell from the disinfectant the butcher had thrown on a leftover animal carcass. The rich aroma of Dunhill pipe tobacco, Cuban cigars and roasting coffee beans beckoned on one street. Turning the corner to follow your nose you might be hit in the face by the smell of a pile of donkey droppings and urine. In another alleyway your mouth began to water as you caught a whiff of spit-roasted chicken smothered in garlic mayonnaise. Or the pile of rotting fruits and withered greens on a nearby curb might almost dissuade you from eating at all.

Enchanted as I was with Beirut it still took me awhile to get around to reading its history. When I did I understood why I was in love with the place. It was at least five thousand years old. The ancient *souks* and the dark stone alleyways were the very same ones Cleopatra is thought to have strolled through in 48 BCE. I followed her steps as the warm sun played shadow games, light to dark and back, one minute hot, the next so cool goose bumps rose on my arms. In a place that in ancient times smelled of cedar and musk, of incense and myrrh, it was easy to conjure up images of women haggling over gold and bronze objects. Here Phoenicians traded their pottery and precious purple dyes to Persians, Babylonians and Greeks. At the far end of the *souk* there was a lovely flower shop in full sunlight, its splash of colors brazen: red gladioli, pink carnations, yellow daffodils, gardenias, roses, and orange tiger lilies. The owner spoke impeccable English. Curious, I asked how long his store had been there.

"Forever," he said. "As far back as a hundred years, my family has traded on this corner."

Ajami's, Beirut's culinary landmark, nestled along the back wall of *Souk Tawili*. To get a table at this popular restaurant we had to queue along the alleyway. No one minded. The anticipation of biting into a parsley, cinnamon and allspice meat kabob smothered in hummus, or into succulent, marinated slices of lamb folded into warm flat bread with a tahini, garlic and lemon sauce, made it worth the wait. Another Beirut hallmark on an early winter evening was a distinct smell coming from the skins of roasted chestnuts wrapped by the dozen in yesterday's newspaper; I only had to peel off the hot, loose shells as Michel and I strolled arm in arm along the *corniche*.

Beirut was home to the most prominent law school of the Roman Empire until the city – at that time called 'Berytus' – was partially destroyed by an earthquake in 551 CE. I was fascinated by this place with so many names. I used to sit on my balcony, look out over the city, and recite them: 'Beryte,' 'Berytus,' 'Beyrouth,' 'Beirut.' It was as though I had all the names of my new lover rolling around in my mouth.

As a foreigner bewitched by her lover-city, it was easy to be distracted at first by its more exotic side. In 1969, Beirut was at the height of its glory. 'You've come to the Paris of the Middle East,' I was told. And it was true, the sumptuous hotels and posh restaurants and nightclubs and beaches were as good as any on the French or Italian Riviera. But there was an uglier side to Beirut, the glimpse I caught on the day we arrived: corrugated tin-roofed hovels behind a barbed wire fence along the airport road. These were the Palestinian refugee camps of Sabra and Chatila, with piles of uncollected garbage in the gutters. In ever-increasing numbers Lebanon's Shiite Muslims were arriving from the south where the Israeli Army was systematically destroying their villages. They settled in Beirut's southern slums, a place I was told to avoid. Upper class Lebanese Sunni Muslims doing business with wealthy Christians in trendy Hamra cafes looked down on the poor Shiite Muslims sweeping up their cigarette butts and clearing off their tables. In private schools Lebanese children were taught Arabic, French and English; the literacy rate was an impressive eighty-eight percent. Refugee children from alleyways and back street slums, who lived in cement-block houses patched together with surplus building supplies, were taught only Arabic in UN-sponsored schools.

. . .

From 1969 to 1975 I lived peacefully with my family in a lovely rooftop apartment on Badaro Street with a terrace full of flowers and a breathtaking view of the city. I enjoyed the star-studded sky of the Mediterranean nights, the moon as it rose over the Metn Mountains, and the prevailing summer winds which blew the intoxicating scent of jasmine through the air.

One particular night in late March, 1975, I was seated alone on the balcony. The children were already asleep and Michel had just gone off to bed. I lingered a while longer sipping my glass of wine and enjoying a night of splendid calm. I found myself applauding the young woman who had accomplished a great many things in the six years since we left America. At the same time I felt great trepidation. Even if I wanted to believe that something would be done in time to stop it, I could no longer ignore the fact that my beloved city – and quite possibly my entire life – was slowly coming undone. The genesis of my anxiety was the news reports of civil unrest and mass demonstrations. Tens of thousands of refugees were pouring into the city and unemployment was on the rise. Israel routinely bombed Palestinian targets and Lebanese President Sleiman Frangie had just given a provocative address at the United Nations.

On the afternoon of April 13 my sister-in-law Andrée stopped by our apartment on her way from visiting Ghassan Tueni, owner of Lebanon's Arabic-language newspaper *An Nahar*. She wanted to warn us about a serious incident that had the potential to ignite a major catastrophe.

Earlier that day Pierre Gemayal, leader of the Christian *Kataeb* Party, was scheduled to participate in a ceremony consecrating a new church in Ain el Ramaneh, a neighborhood bordering ours. As he was about to enter the building gunmen from a passing car shot at him. Two of his bodyguards were killed but Pierre was unharmed. After the attack *Kataeb* militiamen were ordered to patrol the streets of the neighborhood to forestall another incident. Later that same afternoon a busload of Palestinians drove down the street where gunmen had fired on Gemayal. Normally Palestinians would not have traveled through this Christian neighborhood, but used the major boulevard two blocks away through the Muslim enclave of Chiah. *Kataeb* gunmen fired on the bus killing twenty-seven passengers and wounding nineteen others. The Palestinians accused the *Kataeb* of firing first while the Christians claimed the Palestinians opened fire. In an attempt to quell further unrest the *Kataeb* party handed the two men responsible for the massacre over to the Lebanese government. This gesture proved fruitless. By Sunday evening clashes between Christians and Muslims were spilling into neighboring streets. Young boys brandishing M-16's took up positions behind make-shift barricades and began firing at one-time friends who had suddenly become rival militiamen. Snipers hired by both sides took up rooftop positions and began picking off innocent men and women with the same indifference they would display shooting targets on a fence post. From that day onward bursts of machine gun fire at the end of our street broke into the former stillness of our nights.

My tranquil tree-lined street had become a deadly territorial divide – the infamous Green Line.

3

A Lesson in Civil War

Apparently I had not learned any lesson from my political awakening during the Arab-Israeli conflict in June, 1967, because I ignored a warning I had received some six weeks before the unprecedented Syrian attack that pierced my apron with a bullet.

Michel and I had been invited to a dinner party at Colonel Elie Hayek's home. The military attaché from the American embassy was also a guest that evening. During dinner we sat opposite him. It was not what he said during the meal that I remember so much as what he said over the coffee. The attaché got quite serious, leaned across the table toward Michel and me and said, "There's something you should know."

Puzzled and perhaps even a little amused by his suddenly somber expression I asked, "What is it?"

"In about a month and a half, the Syrians are going to attack Christian East Beirut."

I smiled nervously. "What are you talking about?" I said. "How could you know such a thing?"

The polite army officer, who had entertained us with stories of growing up in Greensboro, North Carolina, did not return my smile. "The Syrians feel the Christians are the stumbling block to a peaceful solution to this civil war," he said. "They need to be taught a lesson."

When he saw me smirk and raise my eyebrows in disbelief he got annoyed. "Everything I've told you is true," the attaché said. He urged me to take my family out of the country, or at least the city, for the summer. I was polite enough not to say anything to his face but I dismissed the prediction outright. Even if the Syrians were planning to attack how could the American government know about it and still do nothing?

. . .

Michel had a rare Saturday off the first weekend in July, 1978, three years into the civil war. He had gone to visit his mother a kilometer and a half away in Achrafieh but had promised to return in time to take us to the beach for lunch. It was a week to the day since I had given a large party for my daughter's tenth birthday. Michel telephoned shortly before noon to say that his mother insisted he have lunch with her, as she frequently did.

I was surprised to find that the children did not mind staying home from the beach that day. They were more interested in eating. They went into the kitchen, stood in front of the refrigerator and said, "We're hungry, Mommy. Come on, feed us." They began teasing me mercilessly because I was disappointed and moving slowly, but I had the food ready for our beach picnic. Naim and Nayla helped me carry the plates out onto the balcony. I unwrapped the asparagus quiche and liver pâté. I broke open freshly baked baguettes and we began eating. I soon got over my annoyance with Michel and his mother, and the afternoon was memorable for its stillness. The calm was so inviting, so relaxing, that I went back to the kitchen, removed my apron, hung it on its hook behind the door, poured a glass of red wine and carried it outside. It was as if the entire population of Beirut, all one and a half million, had done us the favor of leaving the city for the afternoon.

I recognized the sound instantly. My glass slipped from my fingers and shattered on the floor. Before the first rocket landed on our neighborhood half a minute later the children and I were already inside. After three years of war I knew exactly what to do. From my bedroom closet I grabbed the black leather briefcase in which I kept our passports, Michel's medical school diploma, his U.S. training certificates, our Lebanese ID cards, jewelry, and wads of cash. Then I boxed up the food from the refrigerator to take to Michel's office on the second floor where we took refuge when bombs fell. Naim and Nayla knew their routines and stuffed their bags with books and games.

As the children and I descended the stairs I heard Michel panting in the stairwell below. He had seen our building so shrouded in thick grey clouds from exploding rockets that he dashed out of his mother's apartment, down the stairs and into his car. I could tell from the rhythmic smack of his shoes against the stone that he was taking the steps two at a time. We met somewhere between the fifth and sixth floors. He took the children's hands, turned around and led them quickly down the stairs, their feet pounding as they rushed toward his office. I took the stairs more slowly. My chronic knee problems plagued me and under stress they became even more painful.

A shell exploded. I could not tell if it actually hit the building, but the handrail shook. I stumbled and banged my shoulder hard against the wall. I got so scared I forgot about my knees. Suddenly I was down the stairs behind Michel.

He looked at me, incredulous. "How did you do that? Don't your knees hurt?"

"They do now," I said, laughing.

When the war began I had stored four mattresses, blankets, pillows, and sheets in an empty closet in Michel's office. I added a small stove and refrigerator to a spare room which already had a sink and counter, and equipped the new kitchen with whatever else we might need for simple cooking.

We took at least two dozen French comic books with us to Michel's office; the hardback ones: *Tintin*, *Asterix*, *Chick Bill*, *Corto Maltese* – not as easily found in the United States as in Europe or the Middle East. We had some five hundred of them organized by series in a floor-to-ceiling bookshelf in the hall of our apartment. As soon as we set up our mattresses on the floor we piled the books where any one of us could reach to pick one up. It didn't matter which one we took, there was not a story we had not already read a thousand times.

On the morning of the fourth day, when the Syrians agreed to a cease-fire, we left Michel's office. As we climbed the stairs to our eighth-floor apartment I was heartened to see a new day filtering in through the broken window panes on each landing.

When I walked into the kitchen I discovered the bullet hole in my apron. On the table on the terrace I found a frenzied cloud of wasps and flies picking over the remains of our spoiled picnic. Michel found shrapnel and bits of shattered mortar scattered in the flower pots of my container garden, which measured some eighty feet in circumference.

We lost our next door neighbor to one of the bombs during that three-day battle. Most mornings when I opened the children's burnt-orange curtains I saw Mrs. Reyes sitting on the side of her bed in her apartment directly across from us. When she saw me she would smile and wave her hand in a certain way. We did this every morning for five years. I used to think she waited on her bed just so we could wave to one another when she saw me at the children's window. I prayed that she died instantly when the blast obliterated her apartment. After that day when I looked out all I could see was a torn piece of lace curtain blowing in the wind, reminding me of her waving hand.

During this same battle a bomb fell through the roof of a lovely old stone villa across the street from our apartment, gutting all three floors and sending most of the red tiles flying off the roof into Badaro Street. The building seemed uncertain whether to crumble or resist and stay standing. The green shutters hung askew and the balconies dangled like broken footbridges. As the weeks and months passed and the house still did not fall, I could have sworn its façade looked more and more like a face. The two round paneless windows on either side of the main staircase on the top floor were the eyes. But something extraordinary happened in the garden. After a few short weeks I noticed a stem or two with bright green leaves poking up from under large blocks of fallen stone that had crushed the plants around the building. Each day they grew a little more until a whole row of baby jasmine plants was intertwined along the black iron fence on Badaro Street and beginning to climb to the top.

. . .

During the Syrian shelling I forgot about the military attaché's warning to leave the city. Afterward, as I looked out over the neighborhood surveying the damage, his words came back to me. I turned to Michel. "When was that dinner with the attaché?"

He closed his eyes and thought for a minute. "About six weeks ago."

We looked at each other and nodded. We were merely pawns in the Middle Eastern game of chess, with many things still to learn about the history of the conflict, about the meaning of civil war, and about the important regional players.

. . .

In 1970, King Hussein had expelled Yasser Arafat and his Palestinian Liberation Organization from Jordan because they were attacking Israel from bases there. Hussein reasoned that if he did not restrain the PLO, Israel would destroy his country. Arafat transferred his headquarters to the Sabra-Chatila refugee camps in Beirut.

The city never recovered.

The Shiite Muslims of southern Lebanon, the most impoverished of all Lebanese, had begun to suffer from the PLO's presence in their villages as early as 1968. The Palestinians launched attacks into Israel from these villages. Israel responded with reprisal raids, destroying homes, crops and sometimes entire villages. The Israeli government maintained that if Lebanese villagers allowed the PLO to use their land to attack Israel they should be punished. Israel insisted that the only way to avoid retaliation was to expel the PLO. The Lebanese villagers were unable do this unaided and without weapons against the heavily-armed PLO guerillas.[4]

The Lebanese government could not help the villagers. The Army maintained a position of neutrality in all regional conflicts on the theory that a neutral Army could not be perceived as a threat by either Israel or Syria. However, the Palestinians saw the struggle against Israel as their sacred duty; Israel had taken away their land.

In 1971 President Frangie diminished the powers of the *Deuxième Bureau*, Lebanon's equivalent to the FBI. It was rumored that Frangie and the *Bureau* chief Johnnie Abdou disliked each other intensely. Frangie wanted Abdou out of power. This personal vendetta could not have happened at a worse time. A crippled intelligence-gathering apparatus did not have the resources to detect the ever-increasing Palestinian arms build-up in Beirut.

This would prove fatal to the country.

In April, 1973, Israeli commandos sneaked into a crowded residential neighborhood in Hamra, assassinated three prominent Palestinian leaders and escaped. I dismissed this as just another Palestinian-Israeli exchange but the other Arab governments could not. As fellow Sunni Muslims they denounced Israel's actions.

In May President Frangie ordered his six Army planes to strike

---

4   Fisk, Robert: *Pity the Nation The Abduction of Lebanon*. Atheneum, NY, 1990, p. 74.

the Sabra-Chatila Palestinian camps. Lebanon had suffered the Israeli incursions and Palestinian reprisals long enough. The Palestinian leadership had been treating Lebanon as though the camps were their own sovereign state, refusing to allow Lebanese police into the camps even to make arrests. They flaunted their own brand of 'law and order.' The Lebanese bombing was meant as a warning to Arafat and his PLO to behave. The city appeared to return to normal after this incident. We assumed the Palestinians had begun cooperating with Lebanese authorities.

When the children and I left home to attend a birthday party in West Beirut one Friday afternoon in early December, 1974, we found ourselves in the midst of an Israeli bombing raid. When Naim and Nayla climbed into my car they usually sat in the back. Even though VW Bugs had no seat belts in those days I felt the snug back seat and smallish windows made it relatively safe for the children. I never needed to worry they might fall out or get grabbed by armed men. The little rascals had an established ritual every time they climbed into the car: they knelt facing the back window and searched the compartment behind the seat where I threw my unpaid parking tickets. The game was to discover how many more I had accumulated since their last ride and then tease me about telling Poppy.

When we got to the end of Badaro Street we drove halfway around Teyouneh Circle and headed west toward the sea. I cannot remember the name of the boulevard. No one bothered with street names in Beirut except for the main arteries like Damascus, Badaro or *Corniche* Mazra. When I gave directions to our house I told friends to go two blocks past the National Museum on Damascus Street, turn right at the Buick dealership, look for the Colifichet and Lunettes boutiques on the left side of the street, then turn left, and park the car.

Beirut was calm that day so I thought nothing of taking my usual route around the Sabra-Chatila camp. The boulevard which ended in front of the camp had been paved through a stand of umbrella pines, an evergreen indigenous to the Mediterranean. A long scraggly row of trees, looking like the charred remnants of a nasty fire, lined the median strip.

As we approached the next intersection directly in front of the camp I heard a series of shrill noises followed by tremendous thumps. Leaning forward so my forehead almost touched the windshield, I could see three planes dropping bombs inside the camp. They were Israeli planes, clearly distinguishable from the Lebanese planes which had bombed the camp a year-and-a-half before.

I quickly reversed, drove over the median between two trees and returned home. Carelessly I stopped the car in front of our building and the children and I ran for Michel's office. As soon as I opened the door he practically pounced on me. "Did you see the planes?"

"What do you mean, 'Did we see the planes?'" I answered. "One of the bombs nearly hit us. That's why we're back here and not at the birthday party."

Michel appeared not to have heard me. He sounded like a young boy infatuated with watching warplanes flying low over his city. I, on the other hand, was a woman with two young children who had seen those same planes drop bombs practically on top of us. I threw up my hands. "Michel, we almost died!" He stopped in midsentence and sheepishly came toward us. He gathered us into his arms but I pulled away. "How can you be so insensitive?"

"I'm sorry," he said.

"What are the Palestinians doing in Beirut disrupting our lives?" I asked. "Sure, I feel sorry for them but Christ, does that mean the children and I should get rooted out too when the Israelis come to bomb them?"

Michel caught my attention in the middle of my fury by using that all encompassing Arabic word 'Wallouw,' which means, among other things, 'How can you say such things?'

"You exaggerate so."

"That is not true," I snapped. "The children and I almost died back there and I'm angry about it."

"Relax, Cathy. I'm sorry I upset you but you're really mad at Arafat and his PLO. I'm not Arafat."

There was a difference between Arafat and his PLO and the poor Palestinians, who are either Sunni Muslim or Christian. I sighed deeply and said, "You're right. I'm sorry."

. . .

In May, 1974, Lebanese President Frangie addressed the United Nations on behalf of the nineteen-member Arab League. His mission was to plead for the restoration of the rights of the Palestinian people. He then introduced Yasser Arafat to the General Assembly. I remember thinking it was clever of him to try to mend fences and improve the atmosphere of mistrust between the Lebanese government and the Palestinians. Or maybe he was just trying to appease the predominantly Sunni Muslim world which thought his Maronite Christian government had dealt too harshly with the Palestinians. After President Frangie's address, in which he admonished Israel for its treatment of the Palestinians, Arafat gave a conciliatory speech of his own. To this day, if I asked fifty people at random on any Beirut street, three-quarters of them would argue that Frangie's rebuke of Israel was one of the sparks that ignited the Lebanese civil war. Mac Godley, who was the American Ambassador at the time, visited Frangie in the Presidential palace before his departure for America and the United Nations. Rumor had it that he asked Frangie not to deliver that speech but the President refused. When Frangie's plane landed in New York narcotics agents used dogs three different times to check his entourage and their luggage for hashish.[5] Frangie refused President Ford's apology and made the American Ambassador's return to Beirut conditional on a formal, written apology. Relations with America never recovered during Frangie's presidency.

In January, 1975, serious unrest in Saida in the south resulted in the death of a popular local leader. His funeral turned into a massive

---

5   Randal, Jonathan C.: *Going All the Way: Christian Warlords, Israeli Adventurers and the War in Lebanon*. Vintage, 1984, p. 156.

anti-government demonstration. I presumed this was the South's problem but I learned otherwise on April 13, 1975, when my tranquil tree-lined Badaro neighborhood became a deadly territorial divide.

. . .

No one was prepared for civil war. We did not even know what it meant. When the first mortar fire rained down on our streets we knew enough to run frantically for cover, usually the nearest building or basement. But civil war was not about a single round of mortar fire. Initially, fighting between the Christians and Druze-Palestinian coalition was localized in the Ain-el-Ramaneh–Chiah area, a neighborhood bordering Badaro and the rest of Beirut was spared. But like an invasive cancer it slowly spread. Bombs began falling at random for days and sometimes weeks at a time on more and more areas. Eventually civil war invaded every neighborhood. Militias fought each other at intersections, across alleyways, between buildings. In the hotel sector they bombed one another's seized hotels until they destroyed Beirut's landmarks: the St. George Hotel, the Phoenicia, the Holiday Inn. In the city's center around Martyrs' Square they engaged in street-to-street combat, destroying Beirut's two-thousand-year-old *souks*. When the militias had finished hardly a single monument, building or site of any historical significance remained.

Imagine your own city: perhaps it is a large metropolis with tall buildings clustered together like New York. Mortar fire coming from Staten Island suddenly lands on your street in the Bronx and shatters all your windows. Rival factions volley 150 mm. mortar shells back and forth across the Potomac between your downtown Washington neighborhood and Arlington, Virginia. Warring gangs in Chicago settle their differences behind your building execution-style while masked gunmen roam Michigan Avenue terrorizing merchants and scaring away customers. Snipers on the roof of the Marshall Field's Building in downtown Minneapolis shoot at you as you walk up Nicollet Mall to your place of work.

. . .

Months pass; the senseless killings and kidnappings increase. Explosions become an integral part of each day. You try to ignore them. You must carry on, run your errands, send your husband off to work, put your children on their school bus. Young men from the neighborhood, whom you knew as children, become militiamen. They set up roadblocks and round up unsuspecting civilians. Fresh corpses turn up daily in every corner of the city. Your husband disappears on his way home from the office. Hours later he reappears miraculously to tell how he was robbed, beaten and left for dead. The grocer across the street whom you have known for years suddenly becomes the enemy because of religion. The taxi driver whom you have regularly used refuses you a ride because you are a Christian; he can no longer travel in your neighborhood for fear of having his throat slit.

Sooner or later your apartment takes a direct hit from one of those falling bombs. Many of your household possessions are destroyed in the blast. You now walk up and down the eight flights of stairs to your apartment because the bombing has caused a general power outage in the neighborhood. That means no hot water, if there is any water at all. Your car, parked on the street below and sprayed with shrapnel, looks like Swiss cheese but you do not get upset. You are grateful the bullets have not punctured your engine and you can still drive.

This war begins in the spring of the year. You are convinced that by winter the warring factions will have come to their senses and resolved their differences. Winter comes and they have not. When an opposing militia muscles its way into your neighborhood and tries to take control, you adopt a kind of psychological ownership of your streets, you think protectively about them. When your own militia takes up arms your husband joins them. Before you know it your neighborhood has erupted into a combat zone. You stay put, intent on fighting for as long as it takes to regain control of your streets. You are convinced your rights will prevail and that sooner or later you will win.

The war drags on through the winter. Your central heating no longer works. All the while you are trying to cope. You take care of yourself so you can take better care of your family. It is hard to find the guts to endure day after day. You no longer have the basic necessities and every task has become difficult.

Gasoline is in short supply. Every time you pass a parked car you fear a bomb. Your hair stands on end as you walk down the street. You are not sure on which roof the sniper is hiding. Your dog still needs her daily walk in spite of the bombs, if you want to avoid accidents under the bed. No matter how tired you are, your children need help with their homework. Despite constant fatigue you strive to capture and cherish fleeting moments of joy around your table, sharing good food and wine with family and friends. You seldom succeed. And at the end of a long day, when you crawl into bed with the husband you love, you are so tired from trying to stay alive that sex is the last thing on your mind.

You endure the bullets that fly through your windows, even three-inch ones that land in the kitchen sink from which you just stepped away. You ignore the bullet hole in the apron you took off and hung behind the kitchen door. Your sanity demands you pretend the bullets are wasps, nothing more than nuisance wasps that sting, not kill. You take precautions but sometimes they are not enough, and you die.

At times it was difficult to exhibit common sense while maintaining a routine when life could be snuffed out at any second. I am not proud of my irresponsible behavior in what was the most intense period in my life. I should never have kept our children in Beirut as long as I did. I should have listened to Michel when he repeatedly urged me to take them to the mountains. Instead I convinced myself that staying together as a family, even in Beirut, was more important than being separated and constantly worrying about my husband's safety.

. . .

Your love affair with Beirut affects your judgment in totally irrational ways and, as in any unhealthy relationship, you ask to be fooled.

However mad, the lover-city is clever enough to entice you back each time you think of straying. A credible rumor or a visit from some foreign dignitary lulls you into the false hope that the horrors will stop. When a truce is announced you are the first to cheer, 'See, I told you,' particularly when it lasts a long while and life seems to return to normal. It is only after you have become acclimated to the habit of war, when the daily skirmishes have stretched into week-long battles, that you are suddenly hooked. All logic deserts you and you abandon any notion of leaving.

My activities were restricted to East Beirut by machine gun-toting youths who manned roadblocks and insisted on seeing my ID card, asking menacingly if I were a foreigner. I developed an instinct for impending danger. Both unexpected sounds and sudden stillness took on new meaning. A shrill whistle-like sound that swelled in volume as it approached signaled an incoming rocket. I was told that if I actually heard the noise of the arriving shell I would have time to seek shelter and I would not die.

Both the PLO and Lebanese Muslim factions hired mercenaries as snipers. The *Kataeb* Christian militia used snipers too, but usually men from their own ranks. PLO mercenaries fired on our neighborhood, killing indiscriminately. We survived by darting between piles of sandbags or by ducking behind shipping containers – 17 foot by 8 foot rectangular metal boxes originally designed to transport goods by sea. Our militiamen discovered an ingenious way of adapting the usefulness of the containers for protection. Under cover of night they stole them from the docks, fork-lifted them onto trucks and delivered at least one to every neighborhood. Our container was dumped half way up Badaro Street across from *Pharmacie Alouf* two blocks from our apartment.

Despite the inventiveness of our neighborhood militia, snipers still found ways to kill innocent people like my neighbor Sonia. We usually met at the green grocery on the third right hand corner on Badaro. One morning I was almost there when I noticed a group of people huddled alongside a building on my side of the street opposite the store, staring at something. I followed their pointing fingers and saw a body in the middle of the street. I knew instantly it was Sonia, lying in the road face down in a pool of blood.

At first I could not understand where all the blood was coming from. I saw only the relatively clean hole in the back of Sonia's neck. When I moved a little and got a clearer view I saw that as the bullet exited it had literally blown off the front of her head. Oh Lord, I wish I had never seen it. She looked like a swollen, pulpy slab of slaughtered beef still oozing blood. How that elegant woman would have hated looking like that. She never left her apartment unless she had applied makeup and styled her hair. She had on a short black skirt that morning. When she fell the skirt rose up her thighs to reveal her panty line. Without thinking I took off my black cardigan, ran into the street and covered her legs so she would not look so naked. I heard people behind me screaming, but I was too stunned by her death to realize my foolishness or think of the sniper watching from somewhere. A man finally yelled loud enough to bring me to my senses. I rushed back to the side of the road where someone pulled me in toward the side of the building. I stood staring for some time. The contents of her grocery bag lay crushed under her body. There were oozing eggs, the whites running into the broken yolks. I watched Sonia's blood spill into the scrambled mix flowing slowly across the asphalt. I do not know how long I stood near my friend. I do not even remember walking back to my apartment. It was only when I opened my door and saw Michel that I reacted to Sonia's death.

I never met a sniper but our friends George and Marie Claire did. At a dinner party shortly after the war began Marie Claire was seated next to a Frenchman whom everyone, including the hostess, presumed to be a visiting businessman.

"What do you do for a living?" Marie Claire asked over coffee.

He responded, "Je suis franc-tireur, Madame." (I am a sniper, Madame.)

She told us later that his matter-of-fact boldness made her lose her composure. "You awful man," she cried, "how could you do such a hideous thing?"

"It's just a job," he replied, "and very well paid." With unabashed candor he explained that he was a professional mercenary. When he was hired as sniper his pay was directly related to the number of bodies he piled up by the end of each day.

. . .

I had lived in Beirut since 1969 and prior to the civil war never heard anyone say, 'He's Muslim' or 'he's Christian.' For this reason I assumed Beirut was a harmonious community of Christians and Muslims. One of the things I loved most about Beirut was to get up early, walk two blocks up an ordinarily busy street that was still asleep at 7:00 A.M. and attend daily Mass. I entered *Notre Dame des Anges* through huge oak doors, tiptoed down the left aisle toward the altar, nodding to my neighbors along the way, and sat in my usual pew. A whiff of cedar-scented incense filled the sanctuary as the priest celebrated Mass in a combination of Latin and Arabic verse which must have sounded very much like the Aramaic Jesus spoke – a language that is to this day still spoken in the region around Maaloula north of Damascus.

Several of Lebanon's seventeen different religious sects played major roles in the war. The Lebanese Christians are divided into three powerful minorities: the Maronites – who take their name from the fifth century hermit Maroun – the Greek Orthodox and the Greek Catholics. According to the French-inspired Constitution, the Maronites are the only legitimate heirs to the Presidency.

The Sunni Muslims – who consider themselves to be the true descendants of the Prophet Muhammad – are merchants, traders and businessmen. They acquired their commercial expertise from associating with the Ottoman Turks, an alliance based on shared Sunni faith.

Shiite Muslims have disputed the leadership of Islam with the Sunnis since the eighth-century murder of their leader Ali, the son-in-law of Muhammad. They believe that Ali's descendants, the Imams, are the lawful successors of the Prophet. Under the Ottoman Empire they were treated with contempt by the Sunni leadership and abandoned to the impoverished villages of southern Lebanon.

The Druze are a sect founded by the Fatimid Caliph of Egypt, al-Hakim, in 997 CE. Their faith was spread through a preacher named al-Darazi, from whom the sect took its name. Their theology combines elements of Islam, Christianity, and Greek and Hindu philosophy. They believe in reincarnation and the transmigration of the soul. They share a murderously antagonistic history with the Maronite Christians in the Chouf Mountains.

. . .

One quiet Sunday afternoon Michel and I noticed a van parked in front of our Muslim grocer's store across the street. At least a dozen armed men, members of the *Kataeb* Christian militia, were busy emptying the contents of his store into their truck. I watched as Michel crossed the street and asked what they were doing.

"None of your business," one of them said, pointing a gun to his chest. "I'll give you a minute to disappear."

When Michel did not move, the militiaman pushed the gun deeper into his chest. Michel backed away and retreated across the street.

. . .

Christians did not always cross the religious divide to commit murder. On June 13, 1978, Bachir Gemayal, the young *Kataeb* Christian militia Chief, ordered the assassination of his political rival, presidential hopeful Tony Frangie, son of former President Sleiman Frangie. The *Kataeb* massacred Tony, his wife Vera and his three-year-old daughter Jehane along with thirty-six others. Only his son, the young Sleiman – named for his grandfather – away at boarding school, escaped.

Muslims rarely fought each other. The exception was 1990 when the Druze-Sunni Palestinian coalition fought Amal, the Shiite militia, in a vicious battle when it tried to muscle its way into Beirut.

. . .

Our apartment building was a microcosm of Lebanon's different religious groups. Michel is Greek Catholic. The owner, Ali Acar, is a Shiite. His other renters were Sunni, Greek Orthodox, Syrian Catholic, and Maronite. During the war Michel assumed the role of guardian of our building in the absence of a concierge. The owner had temporarily moved his family to West Beirut and we were the only ones who lived in the building, in a small apartment on the eighth floor; Ali Acar had lived just below us. The rest rented office space and only came if the neighborhood was calm. Each night Michel locked the front door of the building and then walked up the eight flights of stairs, listening at each landing to make sure no one had left a toilet running, which would have emptied the water tanks. One evening when there was no water Michel noticed Ali Acar's car parked in front of the building. He wondered if the owner had turned off the water for some reason. He went down one flight of stairs to Ali Acar's apartment and rang the doorbell. After ringing twice Michel turned and walked back upstairs. Less than thirty minutes later I heard a commotion in the street. When I peered over the balcony I saw six cars from the Lebanese Internal Security Forces carelessly parked in the middle of the road. At that same moment our doorbell rang. It was our friend Kassab, the grocer, who wanted to know if we had heard anything about threats to Ali Acar and his family. Michel said, "I haven't seen Ali Acar. He wouldn't even open his door when I rang earlier."

Ali Acar was looking through the peephole when Michel turned and walked back to our apartment. He saw the gun Michel kept tucked inside his belt in the small of his back, and presumed that Michel had come to kill him, so he telephoned the Security Forces. Despite Michel's assurances that this was all a misunderstanding, Ali Acar insisted that he, his wife and eight children be escorted back to West Beirut. Later, when Michel wanted to talk with Ali Acar, he asked a Sunni Muslim friend to contact him on our behalf. Michel thought Ali Acar might listen to a fellow Muslim. Michel's friend refused. "You want me to talk to that Shiite dog of a landlord? Never!"

For some of our friends our home served as an indicator of the intensity of the war. I was besieged with early morning telephone calls from friends because we were just three blocks away from the site of the first battles at Ain el Rumaneh–Chiah. They wanted to know if the previous night had been a 'quiet one' and if they should send their children to school.

'Please,' I wanted to scream, 'how can you ask me that? How can I tell you what you should or should not do?' My own decision whether to send our children – who were at that time eight and seven – to school was difficult enough. I felt ill when I stood on the balcony and spotted their bright Bermuda-blue school bus making its way through the neighborhood, particularly if we had been forced to take refuge in Michel's office the previous night. I thought it was irresponsible to expect children to attend school after a night of fierce fighting. The Education Ministry insisted their bus drivers were perfectly capable of avoiding any 'hot spots.'

The novelty and excitement of war were not lost on Naim and Nayla. They were as delighted as I on those days when the schools were closed. When they reopened the children were morose, particularly Nayla. She was a brilliant student and loved to read, but she hated school. Reading suited her shy and retiring personality. From the age of five she would curl up on her bed and escape for hours into the worlds of her heroines.

Her eight-year-old brother could be overbearing from time to time. If Nayla made a comment at table Naim was quick to voice his opinion – which usually contradicted her – and drown her out. She backed off without a fight. In her world of books no one bothered her. Even during the battles Naim had an advantage over his sister: his friends lived in the neighborhood and invariably they ended up at our house playing Risk or Monopoly on the dining room table. Nayla's best friends Sylvia and Susie lived far away and Naim resented it when Nayla tried to join his group of friends.

"They are my friends, not hers."

On many occasions, when Nayla was close to tears, I took Naim aside. He was well acquainted with my modus operandi.

"What do you want this time to let your sister play with you and your friends?" I would ask.

"The Kit Kats she's hoarding in her dresser drawer."

Unlike Nayla, Naim was fascinated by talk of battles, militias and weapons. I had it on good authority that he and his friends talked of little else on the school bus. One night when he was going to bed he asked me what war was. I did not know how to explain to an eight-year-old how a peaceful city could suddenly become possessed by a peculiar appetite for violence. Lebanon's civil war was to a great extent a factional conflict: Palestinians and Muslims against Christians. What could I possibly say when the combatants tortured before they killed, maimed the dead by carving crosses into their chests, dragged their bodies behind Jeeps, and rarely took prisoners? If he did not already understand what was happening he would soon enough. What justification could I possibly give him when he had already seen *Kataeb* militiamen force motorists to drive over a dead body thrown across the road at the corner of Fourn ni Chebak and Sami Sohl?

. . .

During periods of heavy shelling I ran on adrenalin and so when things returned to normal I suffered a severe 'crash.' I had not yet learned to push a button in my mind that said, 'Okay, Cathy, carry on.' Gradually the familiarity of war crept up on me and I became more resolute. After a few months I began to feel more in control. My husband and children had long ago adopted me as the gauge of their well-being. Keen observers of my tiniest movements and expressions, they took comfort from my cool-headedness. I had grown accustomed to the sound of machine gun fire; I didn't jump anymore when a bomb exploded nearby; I hung my laundry out to dry in spite of knowing a sniper might have me in his sights; I shopped for non-perishable canned goods and large quantities of flour and sugar; I bought several canisters of cooking gas at a time, ignoring the possibility of a massive explosion should our apartment take a direct hit.

Little by little I acquired the coping skills necessary to resist and survive the absurd dysfunction of war. At the beginning I wanted to know everything; I read the French and English newspapers; I insisted Michel translate the Arabic news. Whenever I became discouraged by the missed opportunities for a peaceful settlement, the broken truces, the mounting death tolls, the kidnappings, the indiscriminate shelling, the insanely attractive lover would cleverly lure me back with promises of better behavior.

My world got smaller and smaller in reaction to the ever-increasing levels of violence. I desensitized myself to events around me. When bombing occurred elsewhere in the city my response was, 'Thank God it isn't us. Let it be someone else's turn for a change.'

In June, 1978, we escaped into West Beirut during a cease-fire and I was reminded of my words. We came to an intersection about a mile from our apartment along *Corniche* Mazra near Barbir Hospital and I thought we had by mistake driven into some other country where major traffic jams and congested sidewalks were the norm. People were going about their daily activities oblivious to what was happening just a few blocks away in our neighborhood. I was deeply offended by their apparent indifference until I realized they were just trying to cope in the same way I did each day. I promised myself that whenever I recited my 'Thank God it isn't us' prayer I would think of those people. We were all struggling to endure the same inferno, concentrating on things we could control while keeping our blinders tightly in place so we would not have to see the hideous world around us.

In a bizarre way the war had a beneficial effect on our marriage. Before the onset of hostilities I had taken care of the children and their activities by myself. I oversaw all things domestic, financial and social. This had less to do with my role as an Arab wife than with my role as a physician's wife. My husband's busy medical practice allowed time for little else. During the war this equation changed. Michel no longer carried a full workload. His Muslim patients did not feel safe crossing into Christian East Beirut to consult him and many of his Christian patients had fled to safer parts of the country.

Unless it was an emergency, people no longer went to the hospital for their bleeding ulcers, severe gastroenteritis or liver disorders. Even during periods of calm people chose carefully between seeing their doctor or spending their money on more urgent things. So while Michel devoted his mornings to the hospital it was primarily to be on hand if a patient needed a gastroenterologist.

Conversely, my household duties seemed to escalate. Despite the stress of falling bombs and sleepless nights I still had to grocery shop, keep the house tidy, cook two meals a day in an unheated kitchen, and deal with water shortages and power outages. Michel was now home for extended periods of time. When he saw how, with my bad knees, I carried the heavy groceries up eight flights of stairs during power outages, he hauled them up for me. When he saw how many hours I stood in the cold kitchen preparing meals for our family and for our frequent guests he began asking how he could help.

War had a humbling effect on Michel. As a physician he saw the critically wounded come into the hospital, he saw a morgue full of senseless deaths, and he was deeply moved. This awareness of man's helplessness in the face of such evil heightened Michel's own capacity for gentleness and patience, which he brought home to our marriage. He came to realize that the task of surviving as a family was not mine alone, it was a shared responsibility.

War turned a simple task like emptying the garbage into a major undertaking. Before the conflict began I only had to pull a lever in the hallway and throw my garbage down the chute. After the hostilities started, trash collection across the city stopped. Badaro had designated trash sites as did every other neighborhood. When neighbors began using the vacant lot next to our building as their private garbage dump, Michel had to take action. In an effort to keep the area clean and control the ever-increasing rat population he burned the trash every afternoon.

Water shortages were a daily occurrence. When we heard the water flowing into the large storage tanks on the roof just above our apartment – usually late at night – Michel would get up and fill the large buckets which we used for flushing toilets. If I boiled the water first I could also use it to wash dishes and cook. For drinking I purchased bottled water. If the water flowed long enough Michel watered the plants on the balcony while I washed a load or two of laundry.

The easier tasks fell to me. When mail delivery stopped I rented a post office box. Once a month I paid the telephone and electric bills at the appropriate offices. The water bill was due once a year, payable to a collector who showed up at our door.

We were able to find most things we needed. This was mainly a result of the entrepreneurial skills of the Lebanese merchants who still attribute their acumen to their Phoenician ancestors, the first and possibly finest traders in history. When their shops in the old *souks* were destroyed Lebanese businessmen, continuing a centuries' old tradition, relocated their stores to other parts of the city. In spite of daily obstacles, these traders supplied the city with vegetables, fruits, meats, and poultry. When the Beirut port closed they opened new ones elsewhere to import gasoline and cooking gas. They supplied bakeries with flour, pharmacies and hospitals with drugs and surgical supplies, and they kept the cinemas open and the video shops stocked with the latest films. Even the clothiers continued to import the latest fashions.

Beirut was a cash society. We paid outright for whatever we purchased, a refrigerator, a car, clothes. When we did not have money we did not buy. As a result Michel and I carried no debt. During the war many people were without work. Only a fortunate few received full pay checks at the end of the month. Michel, being self-employed, saw his income diminish significantly, so we had to make very wise decisions about how we spent our precious Lebanese pounds.

I kept my sanity during the war in large part because I loved to cook. Meals brought our family and friends together for moments of shared joy. I invited guests to my table almost daily. The more people we had, the better for everyone's morale, particularly the children's. I convinced myself that Naim and Nayla would be fine if they could feel securely embedded in our strong network of extended family and friends who were sharing the kinship of war and survival.

Any normal person living outside Lebanon would have found my behavior ludicrous. Somewhere inside my head I did still remember what 'normal' meant, but since there were no normal people around me, it hardly mattered. The surreal world of war which was forcing me and everyone around me to think and act differently gave new meaning to the word 'normal.' Now it was 'normal' when I hugged the side of a building so a sniper could not see me as I walked down a street. It was 'normal' when I asked Naim and Nayla to lie on the floor in the back of the VW Bug when we passed through an intersection so a sniper could not take aim at them. It was 'normal' to send the children to school after a night of bombing. It was 'normal' for Michel to get down on his knees on the balcony to water my plants out of range of the sniper's viewfinder.

I was not the only one to redefine 'normal' after the first three months of war. My husband and children developed a similar attitude. The terrible beauty of falling bombs was spellbinding. When Tel el Zaatar – a Palestinian camp in the mountains to the east – fired in our direction, the four of us stood huddled in the dark in our bathtub – which ran the length of the wall under the east-facing 3 foot by 3 foot square window which opened outward. We only had to push a lever out as far as we dared before it locked into one of the grooves. We gazed mesmerized at the approaching phosphorus bombs. In one immense thunderous explosion these graceful iridescent balls of fire fell into the darkness a hundred feet from our faces. Simultaneously the four of us dropped into the tub. With the last lingering vibration still ringing in our ears we stood up again like infatuated voyeurs in the false security of our darkened bathroom, watching, waiting, giddy with excitement. When word spread of our 'bathroom view' a steady stream of visitors begged to see too. They reacted just as we had. They ducked as the fire ball approached, yet longing to see more they slowly inched their heads back up toward the window.

. . .

When I see a demonstration or a hostile crowd I recall the day about three months into the war when we felt confident enough because of a prevailing calm to venture outside our neighborhood. The children and I decided to spend the day at our club, Coral Beach in West Beirut. Michel joined us there for lunch. When he left at two o'clock to begin his office hours the children and I lingered on, reluctant to end a perfect day by the sea. Instead of returning home through the congested *Corniche* Mazra, one of the city's busiest arteries, I decided to take my old quick route up Ouzai past the Kuwaiti Embassy and around the Sabra-Chatila Palestinian camps. A block from the camp I noticed scores of people running in the same direction we were driving. Within seconds they spilled onto the road alongside my VW Bug. Another time I might have been part of some triumphal procession, but this was not a joyous occasion. I saw these people as menacing giants surrounding us. My hands began to shake. I hurriedly rolled up my windows and inched my car forward, keeping pace with their onward thrust. I had no choice. The children sat motionless in the back seat, only their eyes darting from side to side, registering the frenzy around them. I tried to reassure them, at least I think I did. Moving with the crowd I continued toward the camp's entrance. Here the mood grew angrier and more unruly. I heard people chanting but paid no attention to what they said. Up ahead were columns of black smoke. When we got a little closer I was able to see through the crowd. As one group of boys threw tires across the road another ignited them. I had only one choice. I told Naim and Nayla to get on the floor and cover their heads. I put my hand on the horn and held it there. The crowd turned, startled that something as small as a VW Bug could make so much noise. I put my foot on the gas and advanced. I had no intention of stopping. People jumped out of my way as I drove onto the sidewalk, swerved around the burning tires and sped away.

. . .

Naim and Nayla studied at *Jamhour*, a Jesuit-run school their father and uncles had attended. Things rarely changed at this century-old institution; classes were conducted in French and Arabic; students were expected to complete several hours of homework a day; they wore navy blue and white uniforms. War brought about two exceptional changes. Since the militiamen began their two-hour lunch break at approximately one o'clock, the schools decided to end classes at the same time so that students could reach home before the battles resumed in the afternoon. In order to manage this without compromising actual class time the lunch hour was shortened by half and all non-scholastic classes were canceled. In addition, *Jamhour* – previously an all-boys school – agreed to open its doors to girls. The priests reasoned it would be less stressful for parents if brothers and sisters could attend the same school. If shelling began during school hours and the buses were unable to circulate, parents would only have to worry about getting to one school to rescue their children.

. . .

Six months into the war my mild-mannered husband joined the neighborhood militia called *Tanzeem*. Its primary goal was to stop or at least offer some resistance to a possible Palestinian incursion into the Badaro area. The Palestinian camps of Sabra and Chatila lay beyond Teyouneh Circle at the end of our street. Michel chose the nom de guerre 'Timur,' after a famous Mongolian warrior and favorite French cartoon character from the pages of *Spirou*. Despite being afraid of the potential risk to his life I was envious that Michel could participate directly in the war. I remember feeling a sense of relief when I learned he was assigned to work alongside Kassab the grocer, one of the nicest, gentlest men we knew, and also very strong. He could break open a door with one kick and lift a case of bottled beer with one finger. Armed with a pump action shotgun Michel stood guard behind a sandbag barricade in front of our building four evenings a week. While he was on duty I watched from our balcony. From my vantage point I could scan a wide horizon. With Palestinians controlling the end of Badaro Street, a Syrian barricade near the Museum a block away, and other Christian militia attempting to infiltrate our neighborhood in order to enhance their sphere of influence and rob empty apartments, the possibility of street-to-street combat was an ever-present threat.

One evening when Michel was on guard duty the children and I heard an explosion. I ordered them to stay inside while I crawled to the balcony and cautiously peered over. The noise had come from farther up Badaro Street. I saw several men shooting at something in that direction. Others were running back down Badaro toward their position in front of our building. From what I could observe it appeared the militiamen had staved off an incursion of some kind. I was wrong.

"When we reported for duty tonight we were told to start shooting toward the end of Badaro Street at precisely 9:30," Michel explained later. "Supposedly the *Kataeb* were expecting a Palestinian infiltration and they wanted back-up."

"And is that what happened?" I asked.

"No," Michel said, laughing. "When we started shooting the *Kataeb* blew up the Kentucky Fried Chicken shop. Our gunfire made it appear as though we were shooting at saboteurs who snuck in to do the job."

"Why would the *Kataeb* do such a thing?" I asked.

"They wanted to send a message to the Muslim owner not to do any more business on Badaro Street."

Another night Michel and his fellow guards were informed of a possible attempted robbery at the Buick dealership on the corner of Damascus and Badaro Streets. At midnight a car appeared in the intersection. Four men got out. Michel told me later that he was convinced they were the crooks. At that precise moment he was the only man standing behind the barricade. I watched as he fired his pump action in their direction. The men fell to the ground. I was too stunned to breathe; I thought my husband had killed them. When one of them finally moved and got to his feet I began to breathe again. He put his hands in the air and walked up the center of Badaro Street. The three others rose slowly to their feet. The man identified himself as he advanced; he was a *Kataeb* from Fourn ni Chebak. He and his men were there to participate in a prisoner exchange with the Lebanese Army. Minutes later an Army Jeep arrived. Michel watched as men were traded back and forth. He was certain that the person who had informed his group of the intended robbery was an *agent provocateur* who wanted to foment hostilities between the different Christian militias.

Despite this incident Michel continued his guard duties, at least until the night when he and Kassab were sent to the "hottest" spot in our neighborhood, Teyouneh Circle.

When he opened our front door at a little past midnight I saw the terror on his face, a look I have never forgotten. I threw myself into his arms and held him tightly. In a barely audible voice he said, "I almost died tonight."

He and Kassab had been assigned the top floor of one of the abandoned buildings at the end of the street. They were instructed to shoot at regular intervals into a known Palestinian position on the other side of the circle.

He paused then and leaned his head against the wall, closing his eyes; he was as near tears as I have ever seen him. He said he and Kassab kept firing over and over again from the same place, never stopping to think that in the dark the flash from their guns gave away their position. Within minutes he and Kassab came under heavy fire. The Palestinians shot RPG's into their building. One of the rockets whizzed all the way through the room they were in and out the other window and exploded on the opposite side of the building. I realized that if any part of the rocket had brushed against a wall or touched the floor Michel and Kassab would have died instantly.

After that night he did not return to his post. He knew that to die a Beirut death meant to die for no reason at all. Ultimately that was a lesson we all had to learn.

4

Had it Not Been for Family and Friends …

I inherited a mother-in-law named Wadia. Naturally I expected her to be the loving mother my husband Michel often described, one who doted on him as though he were her only child. I had hoped to fully integrate myself into Michel's family. Membership in his clan would mean that I had found a place where I could put down roots and grow. When Wadia greeted me at the airport in June, 1969, kissed me on both cheeks and pressed me to her ample bosom, I felt instantly secure in my dream of becoming her adored first daughter-in-law. I was surprised by Wadia's jet-black-dyed hair; I had expected it to be gray and tied back in a bun. Instead she wore it shoulder length like a young woman. In two inch heels she was the same height as I, five feet six inches. I can still remember the smell of Chanel in the fabric of her silk dress, the coolness of her amber necklace against my flushed neck, the hint of garlic on her breath as she pulled me to her and let loose a machine-gun chatter of completely incomprehensible guttural language.

My father-in-law Naim extended the traditional French welcome, "Tu es là bienvenue, ma chérie."

'This is going to be easy,' I thought, 'all I have to do is be an upstanding Lebanese wife and dutiful daughter-in-law.' I planned to call Michel's parents 'Maman' and 'Papa' in the manner of all the Sultan siblings even though most Lebanese women called their mothers-in-law 'Tante.' American women had a reputation in Lebanon of being brash and childishly independent; I was determined not to be seen to behave this way. Instead I strove to find the right balance, one which would incorporate the best of both cultures. Ironically I would very quickly discover that it was not only American women who could be brash and childish.

At first, when Michel and I decided to live with his parents until we could afford our own apartment, I did not think the living arrangements would be difficult. My in-laws lived in an eight-story building in Achrafieh, a cultivated hill in the center of Beirut where the wealthy used to spend the hot summer months. Their spacious fifth-floor apartment, situated in a tranquil neighborhood of narrow streets, offered a panoramic view of Beirut. Naim and Nayla shared a bedroom. Michel and I had a lovely room which opened onto a balcony lush with roses, gardenias, honeysuckle, hibiscus, geraniums, and jasmine.

I was able to throw myself into the study of French and Arabic because Maman's maid Nademe helped look after my children for part of the day. It also helped that I was living in a household where no one but my children and husband spoke English. I found myself soaking up the languages at a rapid pace, particularly the more familiar French, although it took its toll. I often fell into bed at night with my head throbbing and dreamed in French and Arabic mixed with English. Michel's *Tintin* and *Spirou* comic books were useful for light entertainment. To see the words in print helped reinforce some of the basic French I had only heard.

Even though I was trying to learn the easier colloquial Lebanese Arabic I still found it difficult. The task was made even more challenging due to the fact that while every Arab country has its own dialect, diplomats and broadcast journalists speak the more complex, incomprehensible classical Arabic.

It was several months before I had the gratifying experience of bargaining down a Beirut taxi driver in Arabic. I wanted to go across town to visit a new friend. Michel had taken the car for an afternoon appointment so I hailed the first taxi I could find in Place Sassine in Achrafieh. When the taxi stopped I found myself asking in Arabic how much it would cost to go to Hamra. The first thing he said when I asked, "Adesh bit reed min hon la Hamra?" was a ridiculous amount. I raised my eyebrows and clicked my tongue the way Lebanese do when they want to say no. "Homstash," I responded, which was half of what he asked. He looked at me with a slight grin at the side of his mouth and then with an inclination of his head motioned for me to climb in. It had begun to rain and while I was negotiating with the taxi driver I stepped in a puddle. I hardly noticed my wet feet as I sat in the back seat beaming triumphantly. As we drove away I watched with enormous pleasure as the deluge came down, flooding the streets.

I actually thought I was getting quite proficient with my French until Wadia began commenting on my mistakes. The first time we were seated together in my children's bedroom and I responded with the wrong verb tense she laughed and said, "Oh Cathy, you'll never learn French." I laughed, too, thinking her remark was a joke.

"But Maman," I said, "I've only just begun."

On another occasion, when she corrected my "il manque moi" with "il me manqué" and yelled, like some furious teacher, "Tu es incapable d'apprendre le Français," I was so deeply offended I got up and walked onto the balcony. As I looked out over the city trying to recover my pride and understand why Wadia was so unkind I innocently concluded that she must be testing my resolve. I thought it was natural that she harbored some resentment toward me. Michel could easily have married into wealthy Beirut society.

In the early 1960s there was a scandal in Beirut involving American women. Several of them had married Lebanese doctors who were studying in the States, and when they finished their training the young physicians returned to Beirut with their wives. Eventually all of these women could not adjust to life in Beirut and returned to America, taking their children with them. Michel and I had discussed this possibility in great detail before our marriage but it did not deter me. My resilience had gotten me through my first twenty-two years and surely it would help me adjust to Beirut and stay in my marriage. Ironically it also kept me in a relationship with a very destructive place.

At the first dinner party Michel and I attended for the hospital staff, I met a physician who was unusually cold toward me. I asked Michel why.

"His first wife was one of those Americans who left."

I never knew the exact number who abandoned their husbands; some said four and others six, but the stories about these women grew to almost mythic proportions. At first I thought Wadia's irrational behavior toward me was directly related to these Americans. Being liberal I even sympathized with her misgivings. My father, on the other hand, had assumed the only reason a Lebanese would want to marry me was to obtain his American citizenship. Wadia's reaction to our marriage was chillingly reminiscent of my mother, who had lived vicariously through my love interests and on occasion acted like an envious rival.

Wadia seemed to perceive me as a threat to her influence over Michel's life. She displayed a kind of jealousy that went far beyond suspecting I might abandon Michel. She behaved like a jilted lover.

It took me a long time to realize what I had believed was the antithesis of life with my parents was in fact a much more immature kind of behavior. Although I felt trapped in my parents' home, now it was worse because I could not afford to antagonize the woman whose apartment we shared. Her propensity for sarcasm was legendary and she scrutinized my every action critically. I could not complain to my husband, watching not unsympathetically to see how I dealt with his mother, so I had little choice except to act like a lady. At times Wadia made that very hard.

Shortly after we settled into Michel's parents' apartment I received a telephone call from an American woman who had gotten my name from the Embassy. She invited me to a luncheon with other American women who lived in Beirut because their husbands either taught at the American University or worked for American companies. When I returned home Wadia was exceptionally friendly. She wanted all the details: the lunch menu, the women, what their husbands did.

"I didn't particularly care for any of them," I said. "All they did was talk about their bridge games and complain about their maids. They don't speak Arabic or French and their children go to the American Community School."

"Et alors?" She said. "What did you expect?"

"I don't know," I replied. "I thought they'd be taking advantage of being in a foreign country. They may as well be living back in the States."

"Don't kid yourself, Cathy," Wadia said, "you will end up just like them. Sooner or later, you'll get tired of making an effort and leave."

"No, Maman, that will never happen. I am much too stubborn."

. . .

One afternoon Wadia invited me to sit with her on the balcony. A little bird inside my chest quivered at the thought of being alone with her but I did not dare refuse. I wanted to be amenable to doing whatever she asked. She motioned for me to pull my chair next to her. She insisted on close proximity when she spoke to you, not because she wanted to reach out and touch you affectionately, but because she liked to take jabs at your arm, to punch it when she wanted to make a point. As annoying as I found this constant poking at my arm I did not dare pull away. She wanted to tell me the story of her youth.

"I was the most beautiful woman in Lattakia, Syria," she said. "I was the toast of every social event." She went on to mention her many suitors – several French officers, a prominent businessman

– all vying for the privilege of escorting her and dancing with her at the balls.

"Many of them proposed marriage," she said. "I teased them and hinted that I might accept but, in the end, I refused them all." She claimed that when she encounters former suitors some still touch their hearts and sigh, 'Oh Wadia, you were so beautiful.' Wadia looks them in the eye and asks playfully, 'Am I not *still* beautiful?'

The oldest of six children, five girls and one boy, Wadia was born in 1912 in Tarsus, Turkey, to a Greek mother, Ramza, who grew up in Alexandria, Egypt. Her father Feurjallah Chalfoun was a Turkish-born Maronite Christian whose Lebanese parents had moved to Turkey from Mount Lebanon. Wadia's father was a dressmaker who ultimately became a modest land owner while his brothers became exceedingly wealthy ones.

When the Ottoman Empire collapsed in 1918, France already occupied Cilicia, the area in Turkey along the eastern Mediterranean south of the Taurus Mountains which included Tarsus, Mersine and Adena. Christian families in Tarsus, and in particular the Chalfoun family, openly celebrated the demise of the Ottoman Turks. One of Wadia's paternal cousins Hend made a public speech in support of France which angered the Turks, who believed the Christians had been well treated under Ottoman rule.

Wadia's uncle Amine, Hend's father, held the title of *Bey*, an honor for a Christian. *'Bey,'* the French for the Turkish word *'Beg,'* was a title given officers in the Ottoman Army and high dignitaries in the Turkish administration. A *Bey* is just below a *Pasha* as a duke is to a prince. When the Turks began to slaughter Armenians in 1915, on the pretext they were Russian partisans, Amine saved hundreds of them. Like refugees granted sanctuary inside a church any Armenian who sought asylum inside a *Bey's* house was safe for as long as he remained under his roof.

In 1921, before the French withdrew their troops from Tarsus because they could no longer afford to keep them there, they quietly informed the Christians of their imminent departure. By this time the Turks had begun to condemn to death those Christians who supported the French occupation of southern Turkey. When France withdrew its eighty thousand troops from Tarsus, the Chalfoun family fled right along with them. With large quantities of gold coins sewn into saddles and belts Fourjallah and his family left under cover of night for Lattakia, Syria. His brothers went to Tripoli in northern Lebanon – not to be confused with the more famous Tripoli in Libya.

Wadia's wonderful story about the different countries and crossing borders, about invasions and spheres of influence, inspired me to study the history of France's role in Turkey, Lebanon and Syria.

. . .

In 1916 France and Britain signed the secret Sykes-Picot Agreement which essentially divided up the Middle East into nominally independent states. France, historically the protector of Lebanese Christians, gained control over Lebanon and Syria. Britain, which already occupied Egypt, acquired Basra and Baghdad. They argued over control of Palestine. In the end Britain got the port of Haifa while France got the bay of Alexandretta north of Syria which included Tarsus, Mersine and Adena.

Tarsus, under Roman rule one of the most important cities in Asia Minor, was the birthplace of Saint Paul. Alexander the Great almost died there when he caught a cold bathing in the Tarsus River, and Frederick Barbarossa drowned in it during the Third Crusade. The Byzantines and Persians fought there, as did Genghis Khan and Tamerlane, the Mongolian conqueror who led his nomadic hordes from Samarkand in Central Asia to overrun areas of Persia, Syria and Turkey.

On May 23, 1926, while still a French Protectorate, Lebanon was given permission to write its own constitution. It elected Charles Debbas as its first president. When his term ended in 1932 a dispute between Émile Edde and Bechara el-Khoury, both of whom wanted to be the next president, threatened to divide the country. A Sunni Muslim, Muhammad el-Jisr, president of the Chamber of Deputies under Debbas, took advantage of the division and declared himself

❦

a candidate. France did not want a Muslim elected president so it suspended the constitution. In 1936 France reinstated the constitution and allowed new elections. The same two candidates ran, Edde, who wanted to remain aligned with France, and el-Khoury, who was pro-British and wanted an independent Lebanon, one which would be more open to the Arab world. Émile Edde won.

When the Second World War began in 1939 France once more suspended Lebanon's constitution. The Lebanese took to the streets with angry protests. The cost of living had risen dramatically and there were food shortages.

Under pressure, Émile Edde resigned and Marshall Pétain, who was governing occupied France, immediately appointed a new President.

On June 8, 1941, the British Army – with the help of a battalion of De Gaulle's Free French headquartered in London – invaded Lebanon from Palestine and threw out Pétain's men. Free French planes dropped thousands of pamphlets declaring Lebanon free and independent. The declaration was signed by General Catroux in the name of General de Gaulle. Lebanon gained its formal independence in 1943 and the last French troops finally withdrew in 1946.

. . .

My father-in-law Naim Michel Sultan came from a family that can be traced back to the Tajiks of Central Asia and Persia. Part of the Sultan clan settled in Aleppo, Syria, while the rest went to Turkey. Papa was a Greek Catholic born in Adena in 1910, the fourth of seven children. His father Michel was Director of the *Poste de Téléphone et Télégraphe*. Papa's older brothers studied law and engineering in Europe. When Papa's turn came to enter the university to study his life-long ambition, pharmacy, his father announced he no longer had the money to educate him. Papa would have to begin working. He was named Director of a French factory in Syria that manufactured *grignon*, a by-product of compressed olive pits used for fuel. In 1946 he purchased a car repair garage in Beirut and moved his family there. When that failed Papa started a gypsum and trucking business in Lattakia. He supplied gypsum, an essential ingredient in making cement, to a Swiss-owned cement company in Chekka, near Tripoli, Lebanon. He was an astute businessman who lost and rebuilt fortunes over the course of his lifetime.

The naming of the first son alternately 'Naim' and 'Michel' was a family tradition already several generations old. My father-in-law was named Naim because the oldest son had died. In Middle Eastern societies a male first child is of the utmost importance. He will carry on the family name and he will be responsible for life for the female members of his family.

. . .

Whenever Wadia lost her temper neither Michel nor his father dared suggest she was overreacting; they were too busy running for cover. One morning I was washing the children's clothes in cold water. She walked into the washroom, saw what I was doing and chided, "You American women don't know how to do anything. You must wash those clothes in hot water."

"No, Maman," I responded. "They'll shrink if I do."

"How dare you talk to me in that tone!" she snapped, and walked away. It was ironic that she was deaf in one ear because she behaved like someone unwilling to hear anything. She certainly would not hear anything critical of herself or her way of doing things.

I accepted her harsh remarks and did not answer. Shortly after I arrived in Beirut I had the good fortune to meet a very wise woman named Eva Hayek. She told me never to come between my husband and his mother. Of course she was right. I gained far more respect from Michel and the rest of the family by appeasing his mother.

My in-laws, who often entertained after their siesta, were grateful whenever the children and I disappeared for a few hours. I usually took them down to the entrance of the building where there was an area spacious enough to ride tricycles and play with toys. One afternoon a car drove up and parked near the entrance. A couple got out speaking English. It appeared they lived in the building because they were unloading groceries. My heart fluttered at the thought of English-speaking people as neighbors, so I introduced myself.

Edith and Fouad lived two floors above us. Edith was Dutch and had lived in Beirut for five years. Like many Dutch she spoke perfect English. She also spoke French, Arabic and German. Her husband Fouad, a Greek Orthodox Lebanese, was a banker. Their children, MaryAnn and Rami, two and a half and one, the same ages as my children, had the same facility with languages. We arranged to see each other as much as possible. Edith worked mornings for Ericsson, the Swedish telephone company. Our children became inseparable, either playing in Naim and Nayla's bedroom or upstairs under the supervision of Edith's maid. As soon as Edith had returned from work and eaten her lunch I joined her for tea while our children played together. The freedom to walk out of my in-laws' apartment any afternoon I chose, climb two flights of stairs and be warmly greeted in my mother tongue by a woman as kind-hearted as Edith, made my daily frustrations more tolerable. She gave me permission to talk about my problems. She understood that this was how to deal with an attention-seeker. After listening to me not only did she acknowledge how I felt, but she could respond to me in a way that satisfied me even though she had not experienced similar problems. Once I had poured out my troubles she expected me to put them aside and be strong enough to move on. This quality of Edith's made her a valuable friend.

I asked Wadia one day if she and her maid Nademe would watch the children while I attended the annual tea at the home of the American Ambassador.

"Why should I do you a favor?" she snapped. "You live in my house and hardly ever smile."

I was surprised by her sudden outburst but after some very private soul searching I had to admit that her complaint had merit. The constant clashes between us had as much to do with me as they did with her. It was hard to smile around my mother-in-law. Since her behavior reminded me so much of my mother, I was probably starting to act the same way around her by trying to push Wadia out of my life.

Had I known Wadia would turn this seemingly minor incident into high drama I would have apologized immediately. After her retort she got up from her chair, walked to her closet, put on her coat, grabbed her purse, and stormed out of the house, declaring she was going to live with her daughter Andrée because, "I refuse to share the same house with someone who does not smile."

If I had not been so frantic at the prospect of having to tell Michel I drove his mother from her own home, I might have been tempted to call a Lebanese film director and suggest he hire Wadia to play melodramatic parts. Silliness aside, when the door slammed behind her I thought my world had fallen apart. I was so distraught I altogether abandoned the idea of attending the tea. I could have asked Edith to watch the children but I did not want to appear to be ignoring the crisis I helped create.

If I hoped that Michel would intercede on my behalf, I was wrong.

"You've already apologized to her at least a dozen times. What's one more?"

Easy for him to say! He did not believe in apologies, preferring to let any storm blow itself out.

My head and heart were pounding as Michel accompanied me to his sister's apartment the following afternoon. Wadia sat regally in a tall, cushioned armchair in the living room, waiting to receive her insubordinate subject. With my heart in my stomach I walked in, stopped in front of her and said, "Maman, I'm so sorry I have not been smiling enough. I promise I'll try harder." My knees wobbling, I turned and walked back toward Michel. He rushed to kiss my flushed cheeks, followed by Papa and Andrée.

To me Papa was the attentive, loving father I never had. Because of my frequent tangles with Wadia, and Michel's unwillingness to confront his mother on my behalf, sometimes I felt Papa was my only friend. He was tremendously handsome, in part due to his great face and full nose and the grandeur of his lovely, tanned, bald head. He had twinkling brown eyes which danced behind black-rimmed glasses. He brushed his impeccably clipped remaining gray hair around the sides. The way he carried himself, the way he stood up straight and walked with the confidence of age and accomplishment, allowed his gentlemanly demeanor to shine through. Papa wore three-piece suits with a gold watch chain hanging from his vest pocket. His shoes were so well-shined he could see his face in the tops, and his nails were always well-manicured. He had a hat collection, one for every occasion; I could smell them when he went to his closet and opened it. He knew when he tipped his hat to a lady to say, 'Mes hommages, Madame,' instead of the irreverent 'Enchanté.' Papa also had a lovely voice. He often sang, particularly if he was working alone in his room, and he sounded like the Corsican tenor Tino Rossi. My children loved it when their *Jeddo* Naim gathered them into his arms and two-stepped them around the room, singing one of Rossi's songs as he twirled.

. . .

Once Michel began his practice he was seldom home. On rare occasions the four of us would join Fouad and Edith and their family for a Sunday picnic on a deserted beach north of Byblos, or hike trails, with the children on our backs, alongside gushing waterfalls of melting snow in the Metn Mountains. Papa generously supplied the wine for these occasions, donating a bottle or two of *Chambole-Musigny* from his cellar. Because of Michel's busy schedule it was Papa who taught me how to become a savvy Beirut insider.

Foreigners living in Beirut needed some form of identification. Samir, an employee at the American Embassy, suggested that because we planned to reside permanently in Lebanon the children and I apply for Lebanese citizenship. Papa knew whom to bribe (*wasta*) and how much was necessary (*baksheesh*) to get the job done in the most efficient possible manner. As foreigners we were also required to carry permanent resident cards which had to be renewed annually. No *wasta* could do this for us, we had to go in person. But our *wasta* could put my children and me at the head of the line when we arrived at the Ministry, and arrange for us to see the Minister as soon as he sat down at his desk.

Our cars required an annual inspection. The Department of Motor Vehicles did not care who brought in the cars so, for a small fee, Papa found someone to do it for us. He was also able to negotiate down the fine I owed on my unpaid parking tickets.

When, for the third time, I failed to get my Lebanese driver's permit because I could not maneuver the stick-shift Jeep up and down a required dirt hill, Papa got permission for me to take the road test in my VW Bug, and hired two policemen to accompany me. Their presence was meant to intimidate the testing officer. It worked.

A *Service*, an old Mercedes-Benz used as a five-passenger taxi, was a Beirut institution. When he took me on my first ride Papa insisted that a lady purchased the two front seats and sat at the window so the chauffeur could not accidentally touch her. Otherwise, when necessary, she paid for the whole back seat and sat alone.

Papa thought he was doing me a favor when he hired a maid to help me with the children. I did not realize that my mother-in-law's maid Nademe had taken a dislike to her. One morning after Michel had left for the hospital, Maman and Nademe came into my room. According to them I had complained to my maid about having to live with my in-laws. I had indeed begun to question the wisdom of staying there, but I was certainly not so foolish as to utter my thoughts to anyone, least of all my maid. I denied having said anything to her, but I was the outsider and so it was my word against theirs.

. . .

Papa suffered a mild heart attack in October, 1970, while we were still living with my in-laws. Wadia insisted that the children and I leave the apartment. Papa needed complete quiet. She said our presence and whatever little noise the children made disturbed his rest. I disagreed, thinking a visit from his grandchildren every morning, sitting on the edge of his bed and holding his hand, was just the right prescription for a speedy recovery. If something worse happened, if he lay dying, it would have been a wonderful thing to have his grandchildren whispering in his ear that they loved him. I was afraid of leaving him too, afraid I might never again see my friend and ally. Wadia was not swayed. The children and I were packed up and moved to my sister-in-law's summer house, already closed up for the winter. We stayed two weeks.

. . .

In December, 1970, on the day Michel and I finally moved to our own apartment, Papa called me into his room.

"I know it has not been easy for you this past year and a half. I want you to know how much I appreciate how courteous you've been toward my wife. She is not an easy person to live with." He had one more favor to ask of me.

"Sure, Papa," I replied. "What can I do?"

"Please say something nice to her. She is crying in her bedroom."

When I entered her room I saw a pathetic figure hunched over in her chair. I felt enormous pity for this woman who had spent most of her life at war with other people. She looked up and sobbed. "Ah, ma chérie, je ne vais plus tu voir." (Oh, my dear, I am not going to see you again.)

"Don't cry, Maman," I said, giving her a hug. "You'll see us so much you'll swear we never moved out."

I smiled as I left her room. In some part of my heart there was a small surge of triumph. I felt I had connected with Wadia, even if it was only for a moment. In many respects this conflict was very much like a war. Even if no one declares total victory there is at least a semblance of peace when it ends. I was mistaken to think I had won the war when it was only a cease-fire.

In the first two months of the real war, we saw some twenty cease-fires.

. . .

In late June, 1975, when the Department of Education declared the school year officially ended, our friend Lucien Cassia offered us his house in Faraya. Michel and I agreed this was a unique opportunity to get Naim and Nayla out of Beirut and so we accepted the invitation. During normal winter months I usually took the children to Faraya to ski on Saturday mornings. Its peak, Sannine, six thousand feet above sea level, and only one and a half hours from Beirut, enjoys an abundant snowfall from November to April. Summers are equally splendid when Faraya and the surrounding villages trade in their white blankets of snow for a carpet of purple iris, red poppies and white daisies. When I found that several friends and their children were in Faraya for the same reason, I joined in their peaceful daily routine. We met around the pool Monday through Friday mornings. While our children amused themselves we would chat or have a game or two of tennis on a nearby court. I enjoyed playing despite my bad knees.

Michel joined us on weekends. Often on Sunday mornings just before sunrise we would set out for a hike in the mountains. Twice we reached Uyan Al-Siman at the top of Sannine and picnicked. From there I could see the soft green Bekaa Valley and Mount Herman in the distance. I remember how serene it looked basking in the heat of the afternoon sun and how sharply it contrasted with events on our side of the mountain range.

In mid-September we returned to Beirut to prepare for the school year, which normally ran October through June. On October 5, with the school year just started, the Department of Education announced it was ending then because of renewed fighting and lack of security. Naim and Nayla were elated by the closure. We were still novices at coping with war, but I refused to let this new round of fighting deprive the children of their education. Being idle for any length of time would have been detrimental to their young minds. I found the perfect solution in Michel's cousin Samir, who was studying to become a pharmacist at the American University of Beirut. Since his classes had also been canceled, I asked him to move in with us and tutor the children.

On Saturday, December 6, 1975, we left Samir in charge of our apartment for the weekend. Michel, the children and I packed our overnight necessities into duffle bags and left Beirut to visit Fouad and Edith in Cornet Chehouan, forty minutes north of Beirut.

On our way out of town we stopped at St. George Hospital so Michel could make rounds on his patients. When we drove into the parking lot dozens of gunmen were crowded around the entrance. Several of the hospital employees who were now *Kataeb* militiamen recognized Michel and walked over to our car.

"Marhaba (Hello), Hakeme (Doctor), did you hear what happened?"

Michel shook his head. Someone had hacked four Christians to death. The bodies, discovered earlier that morning, had just been brought to the morgue.

Nabil, who worked in the cafeteria, stepped forward. "Hakeme, the chebab (boys) inside have gone berserk. They are running around the hospital shouting, 'Death to all Muslims.' Take your family and get out of here while you still can."

I remember the look that passed between us as we listened to this gruesome story. The words 'death to all Muslims,' spoken with such fury and fanaticism by young Christian men, made the back of my head feel numb. Some distant intuition in me signaled that a dark, unspeakable horror lay in wait as if we were trapped in a nightmare.

Michel sat thinking for a few minutes and then he started the engine. Without a word he drove out of the parking lot, which alarmed me even more. Michel skipping rounds on his patients meant he thought there was imminent danger. My hands got cold and I began to shake.

"Are we going to be okay?" I whispered, not wanting the children sitting in back to hear. Michel glanced at me but did not speak.

As we descended the hills of Achrafieh, taking a curve rapidly and then slowing down just enough to round the next, the tightly-knit Christian neighborhood with its high-rise apartment buildings, its cinemas, churches, and stores – their metal shutters already bolted to the ground – faded into a blur. It was only later I remembered seeing groups of militiamen armed with pistols, rifles and knives congregating on street corners.

It took no more than five minutes to reach the coastal highway where we turned right and headed north along the sea. A hundred yards up the road we were stopped at a Lebanese Army checkpoint.

An officer approached our car. "You can't get through," he said.

"Why not?" Michel asked.

"The Kurds are shooting at people crossing the bridge." He was referring to the people of Karantina, a shanty town housing thousands of impoverished Kurds sympathetic to the Muslim-Palestinian coalition fighting the Christians. Their presence was a potentially deadly obstacle for anyone wishing to cross the bridge, the only route north out of the city.

"You'll have to turn back," the soldier said.

"That's impossible. All Hell has broken loose. The fighting has started again between the Christians and Muslims."

"We heard something was going on," said the soldier. "How bad is it?"

"The whole place is closing up. There are four bodies in the morgue at St. George's. Young kids are going around screaming, 'Death to Muslims.'"

"Shit," said the soldier. "That's all we need. Look, if you have to chance it you'd better be going at least 90 miles an hour across that bridge. It's the only way you're going to get through alive."

"Okay, we'll do it," said Michel.

I glanced at my husband. "Are you crazy? We won't make it. Turn back."

"No way," he replied. "We're not staying in Beirut for this explosion. This is our only chance to get out."

"Naim, Nayla," I said, turning in my seat to face them, "you know the routine, darlings. Get down on the floor. Cover your heads with your hands and don't look up until I say you can."

Even at that speed, with the engine roaring and the windows

open to the rush of wind, in my imagination I saw a bullet pass through the car and hit Michel in the left arm. He gasped and let go of the steering wheel. The car swerved and smashed into the guard rail along the edge of the bridge. I heard screams as the car rolled, turning in slow motion to fall crashing on the rocks below.

I was still immersed in my dream when Michel reached over and touched my arm. "You can open your eyes now, Cathy. We're safe."

When we arrived in Cornet Chehouan, Edith told us Fouad had gone to his bank in West Beirut that morning and she expected him home by mid-afternoon. It was obvious from the cheerful way she welcomed us that she had not heard the news. She was delighted we were in time for lunch. I caught Michel's eye and an unspoken agreement not to say anything passed between us.

Finally in the late afternoon we saw Fouad's gray car round the bend. The road ended half a mile away. We left our cars in a small clearing and walked up a steep dirt path to the house. We walked down to Fouad in time to see him stagger from his car and fall to the ground. His sobbing, at first barely audible, grew so loud it sent shivers up my arms. He kissed the ground repeatedly. He must have inhaled some dirt, because suddenly he began to cough. Spitting, his chest heaving, he rose to his knees gasping for air.

He looked up, shut his eyes, and mumbled, "Oh God, I have seen such awful things today."

Michel rushed to Fouad and helped him to stand. We walked him up the path toward the house, Michel on one side, Edith on the other, me a short distance behind carrying his briefcase, as he began to tell us the story.

He had left the bank at around 1:15 with his friend Ali, a co-worker whom we all knew. Ali had taken the *Service* to work that morning so he asked Fouad to give him a lift home. Since Fouad practically went right past Ali's house in Dora on his way to Cornet Chehouan he was happy to oblige. They had no idea anything was wrong until they crossed into East Beirut.

As a Greek Orthodox Fouad could pass on either side of town in relative safety because the Greek Orthodox community maintained good relations with the sixteen other religious denominations. On the other hand any Muslim, especially one named Ali, had a problem in East Beirut.

Fouad used an overpass called the 'Ring' to cross from Hamra into East Beirut. When he came off the ramp at the base of Achrafieh he was surprised to be stopped at a barricade by hooded gunmen. One of them was holding a knife behind his back and Ali noticed blood dripping on the ground. He glanced nervously at Fouad who said, "Don't say a word. Let me do the talking."

Fouad handed over their ID cards. "What's going on here?"

"None of your goddamned business," the gunman replied, scanning the papers. He returned Fouad's ID and peered inside at Ali. "You, get out of the car."

One gunman tore open the passenger door while another, shouting profanities, grabbed Ali by his shoulders, pulled him out and threw him against the side of the car.

"Da Heelkum" (I beg of you), Fouad implored, jumping out of the car. "This man is my friend. Spare his life! Ali lives peacefully alongside his Christian neighbors in Dora," he said. "A sniper shot a young boy there just last week. He lay bleeding to death. Ali dashed into the street, picked up the child and drove him to St. George Hospital. He saved the boy's life. Why would you want to kill such an honorable man?"

Without a word the gunman let go of Ali and motioned to him to get back in the car. Fouad could not remember if he thanked the gunmen for sparing Ali's life. He had such a throbbing pain in his head it was all he could do to put the car in gear and drive away. He felt as if he was going to have diarrhea and he did not know what he would do if he did. Then there was the incredible guilt he felt for being so lucky. Just because he was not Muslim he would not be killed like an animal. But for that same arbitrary reason the gunmen had wanted to cut Ali's throat.

"Madness, sheer madness!" he shouted, beating the steering wheel while Ali sat staring ahead like a man who had already lost his soul.

♥

At the next checkpoint they watched a well-dressed man being pulled out of the car ahead of them in front of his wife and children. He was thrown onto the hood of his car. One gunman held his beard back while another slashed his throat, splattering blood across the windshield. His body went limp, slid off the hood and on to the road. Militiamen grabbed his feet and dragged him away trailing a stream of bright crimson. Taking an arm and a leg each they heaved his body onto a pile of corpses alongside the road.

Then one gunman leaned his head inside the car and ordered the woman to drive it away.

"I don't know how to drive," she cried. The militiamen screamed insults and threats at her until she climbed into the driver's seat. When she finally found first gear, the car suddenly jerked forward, then stopped abruptly before it chugged away like a tired old engine about to give out.

When Ali saw this he turned to Fouad. Trying to suppress his own horror Fouad repeated as calmly as he could what he had already said. "Don't say a word. Let me do the talking."

When they finally reached Dora, Ali tried to find words. Instead he grabbed Fouad's hands and kissed them before getting out of the car.

By the end of Black Saturday, as this day came to be called, each side had murdered some three hundred innocent men.

. . .

When Edith and Fouad bought their weekend house in Cornet Chehouan in 1971 the children and I were their first visitors. At the time it seemed inhospitable, perched on the edge of a precipice at the farthest end of the village, with the balcony dangling and the terraces crumbling. Over the next few years Fouad installed wiring and plumbing, and gradually transformed the abandoned stone structure into a welcome refuge from the chaos of Beirut.

After Black Saturday the fighting intensified, forcing us to remain in Cornet Chehouan for three weeks. Out of fairness Michel and I reached an agreement with Edith and Fouad. Any time we took refuge in their home we would pay half the expenses and help with household chores. For an hour each morning Michel gave the children math and reading assignments. Then he chopped enough firewood to feed the wood-burning stove for the day. Nayla and MaryAnn finger painted, played house and dressed up in Edith's clothes after their homework was finished. When they got bored they joined their brothers in their tree fort. Under strict supervision Naim and Rami, who was six months younger than Nayla, got to try Fouad's machine gun.

Edith and I tidied up, did laundry, cooked, and carried water from the well. When our work was finally done we warmed some *glögg* – a Swedish brew of vodka, red wine and spices – and relaxed with our feet up on a stool in front of the wood burning stove.

. . .

The warring factions did some very strange things. Aside from the neighborhood militias like the *Tanzeem*, regular militiamen were salaried. At the end of the month the fighting stopped so the *chebab* could collect their paychecks. In a neighborhood like Ain el Ramaneh–Chiah, where Muslim and Christian families had previously lived in peaceful co-existence, the children all knew each other and often attended the same school. War placed some of them on opposite sides, but when one of the mothers arrived at the barricade bearing coffee and cakes they thought nothing of inviting their former friends to partake. The militias typically proposed truces for each others' religious holidays. When they agreed to stop fighting for Christmas we were able to come home from Cornet Chehouan; by December 25 the militias had forgotten the agreed upon cease-fire and our neighborhood came under heavy shelling.

In a psychological act of resistance I closed the Venetian blinds and spread my table with a red and gold tablecloth from Damascus, laid out my best china and silver, lit candles, and invited my family to feast on a kilo of *Beluga* caviar and a bottle of *Dom Perignon*, both courtesy of one of Michel's patients.

The Lebanese traditionally ushered in the New Year by firing both small and large caliber guns from their balconies. On the eve of 1976 militias from both the Christian and Muslim factions agreed that instead of firing on each other they would collectively put on a light show for the benefit of all Beirutis.

The four of us sat just outside the kitchen door on the balcony floor under the overhang, where we had a clear view of the sky. At midnight hundreds of streaming red phosphorescent lines lit up the night sky. The militiamen were such experts at firing their tracer bullets that they could actually 'draw' stars, balls, diamonds, and the like across the sky. Before we even heard the deafening sounds the images exploded like thousands of simultaneous flash bulbs. Then the tiny flares, remnants of their 'drawings,' fell in graceful slow motion before dissolving into nothingness. With only brief respites to recharge their guns the militiamen performed for forty-five riveting minutes.

. . .

On January 2, 1976, I learned from a friend of Michel's that the Voice of Lebanon radio station, owned and operated by Bachir Gemayal's Christian *Kataeb* militia, was looking for an English news translator and broadcaster. Eventually every major militia would have its own radio station reporting its own version of events. However in late 1975 the Voice of Lebanon was the only Christian station on the air. English-speaking journalists and foreign embassy staff tuned into the Voice of Lebanon for the *Kataeb*'s slant on the day's news. Since I had always sought attention, I liked the idea of being the person who delivered that point of view.

"Hi, Cathy," Bachir said, as I sat down for the interview. "I've seen you before at my cousin André's dinner party last month."

I smiled and nodded, a little embarrassed but nonetheless pleased that at such a large gathering he had noticed me. His memory for people was part of Bachir's charm. Within a few minutes he had made me so totally comfortable that I dared ask him if he had heard the latest joke about the Syrians. He leaned forward to hear the punch line and burst into such contagious laughter that I began to giggle too. When he finally got around to describing the job and the hours he asked, "Have you ever spoken over radio?"

"Never," I replied nervously.

He looked surprised but when he burst out laughing his big brown eyes, dancing mischievously, so much as said, 'Baseeta.' (Never mind)

After answering a few of my questions he stood up. "Well, are you ready to start work, Cathy?"

I do not remember agreeing but evidently I must have because he shook my hand. Moments later there I was, walking along the pavement of the vibrant city that I loved, feeling as if I had just seen God.

"I'm going to be on the radio," I said to myself. "I can't wait to tell Wadia. She will actually be quite proud." I knew that her greatest thrill would come from telling her sisters, cousins, and anyone who would listen that her daughter-in-law was now someone important. I wanted to share the news with Grandma Catherine too. Given the opportunity she also would have accepted the challenge.

During the interview Bachir had shared with me his vision for the future. Lebanon was the only safe haven for Christians in the Middle East and he wanted to keep it that way. In 1943, when Lebanon gained its independence from France, the constitution stipulated that the President would always be Christian, which assured Christian dominance. Bachir felt very strongly that if the status quo changed in light of the rising Muslim population, the Lebanese Christians' special status would also change. In 1975, he transformed his father's *Kataeb* political party into a militia capable of defending itself against a Palestinian-Druze-Muslim coalition. This was imperative because the Lebanese Army had declared neutrality in the conflict.

Nonetheless on an individual basis Army personnel did participate in the war. They warned Muslims and Christians respectively whenever there was trouble. One day Michel and I were passing through the Army barricade near the Museum on the Green Line not far from our apartment. As he waved us through the soldier said, "The Muslims are kidnapping Christians at Barbir. Take an alternate route."

My work schedule, 3:00 to 6:00 P.M., fit nicely into Michel's day. Since his workload had dropped off significantly, he saw his patients during the morning.

On my first day at the radio station I was handed the news already translated from Arabic into French. I had two hours to translate everything into English. I barely had time to reread and proof the news and repeat aloud some of the more difficult Arabic words before I went into a small soundproof broadcast booth that smelled of cigarette butts and stale coffee. I sat at a long table with the microphone in front of me and faced a wall.

The words 'This is the Voice of Lebanon,' were the only ones I spoke with any degree of confidence. My hands shook so uncontrollably I could hardly read the rest of the page.

At night the foul-smelling broadcast booth followed me into my dreams: my voice cracked, I mispronounced words, my live audience jeered angrily, and my boss – who bore a strong resemblance to Wadia in my dreams – threw up her hands shouting, 'Hopeless!'

At home I practiced aloud certain names and places that I routinely mispronounced, with Michel correcting me until I got them right. Only as my nervousness disappeared some weeks later did I begin to pay attention to what I was saying.

Over the next three months I spouted propaganda, told half-truths, and in some cases outright lies. The disinformation was discreetly edited in. When, in late January, the radio station lied shamelessly about how badly the Christian militias were losing the battle for the hotel section, I almost handed in my resignation. It was Michel who urged me to stay on the job. By the end of February I could hardly stand myself when I was not allowed to report not only that our boys lost a particularly savage battle in the Chouf Mountains, but scores of them had died. That night as I was leaving the studio I heard a man crying in the hallway. He was talking to Alex, the *Kataeb* in charge. He wanted to know if his son had been assigned to the Chouf, as he had not heard from him in days. Alex assured the father that his son was safe. I stepped back into the dark hall and watched the man thank Alex. With drooping shoulders he walked as though he already knew his son was dead. When he disappeared through the door I heard Alex say, obviously in response to someone else, "Yeah, I know his son's dead, but what did you want me to do, tell him the truth?"

Things got worse when Syria's Foreign Minister Abdul Halim Khaddam began visiting Beirut to broker a cease-fire. He carefully monitored what was being said, and by whom. Before the war Lebanon had prided itself on a multilingual free press and the open discussion of political ideas. During the crisis this form of liberal expression vanished. After the body of Riad Taha, President of the Lebanese Union of Editors, washed up along the shoreline every broadcaster understood what was expected of him or her. In 1975, my program was the only English news broadcast. My name was known, even if I never said it on the air. I may have even been on someone's hit list – although at the time the thought never occurred to me.

I quit at the end of March.

Salim al-Lawze, who was later killed, was certainly the most tragic example of what happened to journalists in Lebanon. He was editor-in-chief of the Arabic magazine *al Hawadess*, published in London. He wanted to return to Beirut for his mother's funeral. He hesitated because he had written critically of Syria's regime. He asked his friend King Faisel to obtain assurances from Syria's President Assad that he could return unharmed. In spite of these guarantees he was abducted when he arrived at the Beirut airport. He was tortured for eight days before his body was dumped on a public road for all to see. When I saw the first black and white photos of his body, I could not tell that his fingers had been burnt to the stumps by acid, that his eyes had been gouged from their sockets, or that his tongue had been yanked out, but that was all described in the newspaper article. There was another photo of him taken in London shortly before he traveled to Beirut. Something about him, maybe his elegant baldness, reminded me of Papa. I was upset by the thought of the grief his wife and children must have felt when they learned what had happened to him.

In 1978, Bachir Gemayal started another radio station run by his own newly-formed militia, the Lebanese Forces. When he asked me to be his English news broadcaster I refused.

"Oh, but you can't do that to me!" he said.

When I finally persuaded him to look for someone else it was Wadia who got terribly offended. "What am I going to tell my friends? That my daughter-in-law gave up a great opportunity?"

Perhaps she expected me to go on to become some glittering television news personality so she would have something else to boast about. On the other hand my grandmother would have been proud of my decision.

5

Will I Ever Dance Again?

*T*oward the end of January, 1976, the Syrian government pressured both the Christians and the Palestinian-Muslim coalition into a cease-fire, at least in Beirut. The Department of Education responded by ordering the schools to reopen. We were also enthusiastic about the truce even though it was our thirtieth in nine months.

Michel and I loved to dance. Our first thought was to spend an evening at the Caves du Roi in the Excelsior Hotel on the corner of Phoenicia Street but that had been reduced to a pile of rubble. In fact the entire neighborhood – the Holiday Inn, the Phoenicia, the St. George Hotel, the restaurants like The Bucharest, which belonged to our friends Fay and George Chidiac, and the glitzy night clubs – was now no more than collapsed roofs, sheared-off walls and blackened hollow shells of buildings. Dogs and cats eked out a meager existence amid broken water mains and open sewers.

Some Lebanese visionary had already thought to open a new club, The Retro, in Achrafieh a block west of the Sursock Museum in the Accaoui neighborhood. The entrance was on a narrow side street and almost hidden from view by tall shrubs and trees. Parking anywhere near the club was impossible; Achrafieh was one enormous maze of crowded streets. The steps leading from the restaurant to the disco in the basement were so narrow I had to go down sideways, which strained my knees, but I forgot all about them as soon as I got inside and heard the music. As I danced in Michel's arms I could feel the city of Beirut all around me, almost as though my husband disappeared and my lover, the city itself, took his place. I knew on some level that the city was a terrible lover, a dangerous character to hook up with; nevertheless I danced with joy and complete abandonment. Michel and I, already quite good at swing, foxtrot and samba, had only recently taken up disco-dancing. Sometimes in the privacy of my bedroom, when my imaginary Beirut-lover was the only one present, I would open the closet with the full-length mirror on the door, play the sensuous music of Farouz, and have a try at belly dancing. Of course Michel was my real lover; but I was also in love with the city and the people. It was my sense of my liberated and confident self which let me be able to swirl my hips like a belly dancer in front of my husband as he lounged in bed laughing, hands behind his back.

At home, Michel and I often played our LPs and danced, to the delight of our children, who leaped onto the couch to watch. They cheered when Michel swirled me round and round to the beat of a Chuck Berry tune. They booed just as enthusiastically if I missed my cue and forgot to turn. And when they least expected it, when they thought we were completely lost in the dance, Michel and I would separate, grab hold of their arms and pull them to their feet. Carefree, Nayla squealed with delight in her father's embrace as he led her around the room. Naim, self-conscious about unfamiliar moves, stiffened up like a wooden soldier when I tried to move him. At nine he was already a funny little man-child.

On March 11, 1976, the music stopped.

. . .

When Michel and I switched on the French language TV station we expected to see the regular newscaster, an attractive woman in her mid-thirties. Instead the camera zoomed in on an unoccupied anchor desk and lingered in complete silence. The most striking detail of this bizarre scene was the absence of sound. We sat quietly staring at the picture of the empty room. After what seemed like several long minutes, with the camera still fixed on the desk, we heard footsteps across the hardwood floor. A dark haired man in military uniform came into view, a full array of medals across his chest indicating his senior rank. I did not recognize him. He stood behind the chair for a moment before he sat down, unfolded a piece of paper, and despite the black-rimmed glasses he placed on his broad nose, held his speech at arms-length. I was surprised that while this was the French news hour he chose to speak in classical Arabic, which I did not understand. I glanced at Michel, who was frowning. When the speech was over, I gave my hand and wrist a little twist to ask what happened, "Shoo?"

"There's been a coup d'état," Michel replied. "His name is Brigadier Ahdab and he has just declared himself Military Governor of Lebanon."

"So that's why the camera was staring at the empty chair!"

"He has demanded that President Frangie and his cabinet resign within forty-eight hours and he has already asked Parliament to elect a new head of state."

. . .

Frangie refused to resign and vowed to fight the Brigadier. When, several days later, the presidential palace was shelled and heavily damaged, he fled to the north of the country.

Because renewed hostilities on the Green Line were inevitable Michel decided we should take refuge in his parents' apartment in Achrafieh. We did not go there because it was safer, since both the living and dining rooms and two of the bedrooms faced West Beirut. We left our apartment because Badaro Street was technically on the West Beirut side of the Green Line and Michel was worried

A BEIRUT HEART: ONE WOMAN'S WAR

there might be some sort of formal closure of the two sectors which would restrict our activities and prevent Michel from getting to the hospital in Achrafieh.

The original Green Line was designed by a Frenchman named Écochard. Under his supervision bougainvillea and eucalyptus trees were planted the entire length of Damascus Street from the city center all the way to the end of Fourn ni Chebak. The warring factions had transformed the Green Line into a deadly territorial divide between East and West Beirut, a virtual no-man's land where identity papers and Fate determined life and death.

From the onset of the war I had never had the leisure to pack away my valuables in their proper places. We usually threw a few things into a suitcase and scampered to get out the door as shells fell around us.

This time was different.

In the Sultan family certain possessions like carpets and antiques were highly prized. Michel and I had two Persian carpets, wedding gifts from one of Papa's business associates. Each was approximately twenty-five feet long; they were nearly seventy-five years old and had to be rolled up very carefully. Once I finished tediously lifting chairs and moving tables and sofas, I rolled up the carpets and tied a plastic bag on each end to prevent moths and mites from crawling inside, and stored the carpets one on top of the other behind the couch. I pulled up the Venetian blinds and tied the living and dining room curtains in knots and wound them over the rods.

Our most important treasures were a dozen three-thousand-year-old vases, some only three inches tall. They came from my father-in-law's collection, which included some five hundred amazingly intact artifacts: vases, Roman busts, oil lamps, and coins, which he kept in a *vitrine* in the Achrafieh apartment.

I loved to touch these precious objects and run my fingers along their smooth surfaces. Their transparency made them seem so fragile, yet they were as solid as if they had just been made. Their colors varied from pale blue to turquoise. Several of the taller foot-high vases had frosted exteriors which gave an added visual dimension. Their uses varied too. The tallest ones held spices. Body oils were stored in the medium sizes: musk and cedar-wood for the men, lavender and jasmine for the women. Perhaps the smaller wide brimmed ones, used as receptacles for tear drops, held the sorrow of another war or some abandoned lover.

I laid the vases on the ground next to a heavy metal box which I had taken from the floor of the closet, got a towel from the bathroom, folded it in three to cushion my knees, and knelt.

This time as I put them away it struck me, as it never had, that many another woman before me had cared for these vases. How arrogant of me not to have thought of that! I was only a curator honored by being entrusted with these precious artifacts of ancient civilizations. Since at least the Babylonian, Roman and Greek invasions women had made it their job to preserve these particular vases while their men were away fighting. Here I was, another housewife in the midst of war, carrying out the same ritual thousands of years later.

I was still on my knees wrapping the last vase inside a remnant of cotton fabric when Michel came and stood beside me. He saw that I was upset and he knew how much I hated putting away our precious things.

"Have you finished?" he asked.

"Yes," I sighed.

"Then let me help you to your feet," he said, grinning.

"Why are you smiling like the Cheshire cat?" I asked as he gave me a kiss.

"Because it's your birthday, silly. Have you forgotten?"

I smiled and nodded.

Naim and Nayla leapt in, laughing. "Mommy forgot her birthday, Mommy forgot her birthday!"

We reached my mother-in-law's shortly before noon. I was surprised to find no one there. One of the reasons I disliked going to Wadia's was the way in which she cared for her precious objects. I liked to touch mine and use them when I entertained, particularly the silver and crystal. I accepted that a break now and then was inevitable. Wadia did not allow any of us to handle her things. Because she had something on every shelf and table in her living room it was difficult to respect her rules. Wadia's chandeliers were an exception; she loved these family heirlooms and liked it when people reached up admiringly and gently touched them. They hung low from the ceiling on heavy metal chains, one in the living room, the other in the dining room. Their unusual deep orange and dark blue cut glass glistened when lit by the sun and they chimed ever so softly in the gentle sea breeze.

"Where's your mother? Didn't she know we were coming?" I asked.

"Didn't I tell you? She and Nademe left yesterday morning for Lattakia. Papa called and asked them to come."

"No," I replied, turning my head to conceal my enormous smile.

The previous day Michel had ordered chocolate cake with raspberry filling. On some pretext or other he and Nayla rushed to the bakery around the corner to pick it up. When they got back they hid it inside the buffet until after lunch. I honestly could not say if it was the faces of these three people I loved most in the world beaming with pride because they had succeeded in surprising me with the cake, or if it was the absence of Wadia that made this my best-ever birthday.

The first few days alone in Achrafieh were delightful, almost as if we were there under false pretenses. We expected something to happen between Ahdab's forces and Frangie's at any minute, particularly after the bombing of the Presidential palace, but nothing did. However only a week later Achrafieh came under heavy shelling from a more formidable, long-standing foe, the Palestinian-Muslim positions in West Beirut.

In a vacant lot next door to my in-laws' building the *Kataeb* militia some months earlier had installed a mortar emplacement with six 150 mm. cannons. The twelve militiamen who manned the guns were in their late teens and early twenties. We could hear them talking when the neighborhood quieted down after lunch and we tried to sleep. They worked with their shirts off, tanning; their torsos and the gold chains around their necks glistened in the heat. Now and again they fired off a round. Much to our relief no one ever answered back. As at so many other times during the war we got careless like everyone else and forgot they were even there. I decided we should invite our friends Myrna and Tony Esta for lunch, and Michel agreed.

It was a Wednesday, a perfect day in late March after the long rainy cool months of January and February, the kind of day when you feel lucky to be alive. We had all the windows open and the wind was blowing in from the sea.

As I was putting the finishing touches on the hors d'oeuvres I heard a neighbor playing a Coleman Hawkins tune. When that man played his jazz saxophone I could hardly keep my feet still. I was swaying to the beat when Michel walked into the kitchen, took hold of my outstretched arms and we began to dance a slow swing. When Myrna heard us laughing she came and stood by the door. As Michel dipped me toward the floor she shouted over her right shoulder, "Tony, come here. Children, come and see your parents. They are dancing. I think it's …"

In the middle of her sentence everything shook. The chandeliers started to tinkle. A rocket exploded. We were not sure whether it had landed or taken off. We looked at each other for a moment and I distinctly remember everyone silently deciding to ignore the explosion.

"Come on, then," I said. "Let's go and eat this wonderful food."

I put the hors d'oeuvres, an assortment of duck and rabbit pâté and smoked salmon, on the table alongside a platter of grilled shrimp with aioli and a large bowl of green salad. Everyone served themselves while Michel opened a bottle of white wine.

There was another muffled noise and I glanced up at the chandelier, which did not move. This time, instead of looking at each, other we kept eating.

"To your health," I said, raising my glass.

"Sahah," (To your health) Michel echoed as we drank and smiled at each other over our wine glasses.

A huge explosion shook the building. Myrna dropped her fork on the plate. "Oh my God," she said. "What's going on?"

"Nothing," said Tony, rolling his eyes. "Nothing but these wonderful shrimp."

"They're from ..."

This time the whiz from the shells was shriller; they were getting closer.

I caught my son looking at me. I knew I should react, but in that brief second or two I resolved not to let the war bully me, enough time for Tony to stuff more shrimp into his mouth before I did react. When I stood up so did Myrna, overturning her chair.

The mortars next door began firing.

This time Tony jumped to his feet.

"Shit, we can't even eat in peace," he said, stuffing the last shrimp into his mouth.

"Come on, Myrna," Tony said, "we'd better go."

"I'll see you to your car," said Michel.

I could tell when the rockets were approaching, so I took the children into the corridor and we squatted down in the corner near the front door. For a second I thought of taking them into the stairwell, but when I opened the door and saw the neighbors rushing down the stairs in panic, trying to get to lower ground, I decided against it.

Michel came back and said, "We're better off here."

The first rocket landed nearby and the second one was closer. Michel laid his body over the children just as the third rocket hit the building. Somewhere glass shattered. We did not dare lift our heads to see where it was but I felt something sharp like a needle prick the back of my right leg. I put my hand to my calf and when I brought it back my fingertips were bloody. I thought it was probably just a small piece of glass.

Everything went quiet.

There was something very welcome in the unexpected abrupt

stillness after so much noise. I sat up and realized I had barely taken a breath for the last three minutes. When I did my ribs hurt and my chest ached. I looked at the back of my leg. The blood had dried. The children stirred and sat up and I pulled them into my arms and held them until their bodies relaxed. Michel stood up and helped me to my feet. My swollen knees hurt as if they were on fire. Dust was everywhere. I shook it off my skirt and out of my hair. My first instinct was to get a broom and start sweeping up the hallway. Several minutes must have passed before any of us ventured into the living room.

The rocket had torn an opening about ten feet in diameter between our fifth floor apartment and our neighbor below. The metal window frame was twisted into an odd shape which might have passed in some other context for modern art. The wall air conditioner had been blown out of its brackets and flung across the living room. Shrapnel and crushed mortar from the front wall cluttered the floor. Wadia's velvet couch and matching chairs were no longer navy blue but white with dust, and shattered glass was everywhere, in the bedding, inside my slippers. But none of Papa's ancient vases had broken, the *vitrine* was not even cracked. The glass we had heard shattering was Wadia's antique chandeliers. The one in the living room lay in a heap of colored ice, the other lay shattered over the dining room table, burying the remnants of lunch.

Michel called me to the edge of the balcony and pointed to the street below. I leaned over with my elbows pushing into the metal railing. A dozen people stood around three dead bodies. A man was lying face down, his legs completely unspoiled down to the crease in his trousers, his head a mangled mess. Next to him was a woman, and for a second I thought of Myrna and Tony. The man was wearing the same color trousers as Tony and the woman ...

'Of course, it's not them,' I told myself.

Naim and Nayla wanted to see what we were looking at and before I could prevent them from peering over the rail their eyes were riveted on the street. I tried to turn Nayla around and take her back inside so she would not have nightmares but she pushed my hand off her shoulder. She was staring at the dead little boy. A man in his mid-thirties pushed through the crowd as he walked toward the child and fell to his knees beside the body. The child, about seven or eight years old, looked as if he were asleep. The young man lifted the boy into his arms. Two men standing nearby helped him to his feet. He pressed the child to his chest and tenderly kissed his forehead. As the man moved away carrying the small body the boy's head bobbed and his thin arms dangled. The man took a few steps and stopped. He looked up, lifting the boy's body and asked, "Ya Allah?" (Oh God, why?). The crowd parted and we all watched in silence as he walked away.

Someone was tugging at my arm. I looked down. It was Naim.

"Mommy," he said. "Mommy, why can't you hear me?"

"What did you say, darling?" I asked.

"I said, 'This is going to give me nightmares.'"

I looked at him and wrapping my arms around his shoulders said, "We all have nightmares, darling, but I know you're quite capable of dealing with yours. All you need to do is come and get me or Poppy."

"Yes, that's true," he said.

I kept my hand on his shoulder. I looked for Nayla. I was worried about her. Things like this hit her very hard whereas I seemed to shift into automatic pilot. I was not sure how much Nayla could suppress. She turned and looked at me, her face flat and white.

"It's Myrna," she said. "I know that's Myrna on the ground. She was wearing a sweater just like that."

I stared at the woman and back at my daughter. Could she be right? Was that Myrna? Did Michel actually see them drive off or did he just assume they did?

"It's them," she cried, "I know it's them." She started to shake.

"No it's not," said Naim.

"Prove it," she said, so furious it looked as if she might strike him.

"Look at her hair, dummy. It is not the same color as Myrna's."

"Darling," I said, "it's just someone we don't know." As I heard myself I realized how callous I sounded and I wondered how long it would take for the rest of my civilized veneer to disintegrate.

The morning after the explosion I woke up exhausted, but glad to be alive. Before I went to bed I cleaned up as much of the mess in the living and dining rooms as I could. I covered the hole with a large piece of clear plastic and Michel secured it with hammer and nails. Our beds were covered with glass and I swept them off and changed the sheets. I could not get rid of the taste of dust in my mouth.

I wondered how the children would be when they awoke. Neither of them had wanted more than a bowl of soup before bed. During the night Naim got up to go to the toilet but he didn't come into our room, so I assumed he did not have a nightmare. And as far as I knew Nayla had slept peacefully. I slept fitfully on and off. I dreamed about my family. Everyone was dead. They all lay on the ground with wide open eyes. The sun was bright and the whites of their eyes looked like marbles. My children, my husband, Wadia, Papa, even my own parents – all were dead. My mother's eyes were ripped out and I could see inside her head.

I turned over on my pillow and saw Michel staring at the ceiling. His face was drawn and unusually pale. His lips had lost their color.

"Have you been awake all night?" I asked. When he did not answer, I knew to ignore him.

I got out of bed. My knees still hurt as if a fire were raging inside but I wanted to call the glazier before he got too busy. Glass factories worked overtime during the war to keep up with the demand for new windows. Although they charged exorbitant prices the service was excellent and I knew the glazier would be at our apartment within the hour. He would take measurements, leave to cut the right size glass and return a short time later to install the new windows.

When I went back to the bedroom Michel was staring out over the city. "We've got to get out of here," he said, "let's go to Cornet Chehouan."

"I've already called the glazier. We can leave just as soon as he's finished."

Robbery was becoming more of a problem in Beirut, so with all the valuables in Wadia's apartment, I did not want the glazier to know we were leaving. I packed a few suitcases and hid them in the bedroom closet while I waited for him. Meantime Naim and Nayla had awakened but were still dazed. They came to life when they heard we were going to Cornet Chehouan.

The windshield of my VW Bug was shattered. We cleaned the glass off the seats as well as we could and Michel drove it into an underpass a block away and parked it. Michel's Fiat was pock-marked from shrapnel and the windshield was badly cracked, but the engine worked. As the children climbed into the car I glanced over at the vacant lot. The mortar emplacement was still there without a single sign of disruption. The boys dressed in their battle fatigues were there too. It was odd that I had not noticed their hair before, particularly since Michel now wore his thick, black curly hair the same way below his ears and had grown a beard and moustache. The boys were lying about on the ground smoking what smelled like hashish. It was rumored that the fighters smoked it to help them do their dirty work. With the thriving drug trade in the Bekaa Valley hashish was easily accessible. Between puffs one of them was eating pumpkin seeds from a plastic bag and passing them around to the other *chebab*.

. . .

Cornet Chehouan in spring is a magical place. It is a small village of some fifty families about nine hundred feet above the sea. The homes are built on stone terraces that from a distance look like giant steps. It took only about fifteen minutes to reach Cornet Chehouan once we left the coastal highway to Jounieh, a half hour from Beirut. It was a lovely day and we drove with the windows open. Naim and Nayla sat in the back seat with luggage piled between them. I was behind the wheel while Michel, as usual lost in thought, stared out the window. As we neared the last bend in the road I said, "We're almost there." That was the cue for everyone to look up to the right and catch the first glimpse of Fouad and Edith's house, perched on the edge of a mountain ridge atop a canopy of green. It was the roof we saw first, the bright red of the tiles lit by the brilliant sunlight. Great clusters of red poppies ran wild along the terraces below the house. After we parked the car and began walking up the path a multitude of speckled butterflies danced around our legs. Our feet brushed against the new crop of wild thyme bordering the path, releasing a delicate perfume. Trees full of white apple blossoms with soft red-rose interiors dotted Edith's green terraces, and pink flowering succulents overran the cobblestone pathway leading to the house. As we neared the front door, Naim gently pulled one of Edith's trumpet vine flowers to his lips and pretended to play it, announcing our arrival.

"We're here!" he shouted.

Within a few days the children appeared to have recovered from the bombing. Nayla and MaryAnn fell into their usual routine of playing with dolls and collecting wild flowers while Naim and Rami ran down into the valley doing whatever young boys do when they are looking for adventure.

It was amazing after all the death and destruction of Beirut how a simple thing like a wounded bird could galvanize everyone's attention. It was the Monday before Easter, a week after we arrived, when Naim and Rami on one of their treks heard someone shooting. They fell to the ground and waited for the noise to stop. When the guns fell silent they discovered an injured stork on one of the terraces. They rushed back with the news.

Watching from the window I saw the two boys emerge from the woods about fifteen minutes later followed by Fouad, who carried a large white bird in his arms. Edith had already covered the table on the terrace with newspaper and Fouad placed the bird carefully there so that Michel could examine it.

"It's been shot," he said, "and probably broke its leg when it fell."

The bird trembled and we could see its tiny heart pounding in its breast. Michel held it firmly but gently as he looked for other injuries. Working by his side Fouad prepared a little splint while Michel set the leg as the rest of us looked on fascinated.

The children made a straw bed in the storeroom in the front of the house. Hoping it would recover, Fouad gently placed the wounded stork there. We left water and bread soaked in milk and the children took turns sitting quietly beside it.

"It needs peace and quiet if it is to get well," Nayla said in a strange tone of voice. I stared at my daughter. I wondered from the urgency in her voice whether she was referring to the stork or herself.

The following day, while Edith and I baked cakes for the holiday Nayla, MaryAnn and her four-year-old sister Katia decorated Easter eggs. Painstakingly they dipped the eggs into a variety of colors from deep purple to bright yellow and hung them on a rack in the sun to dry. They spent a joyous afternoon at a white square table in the living room near the tall windows. The sun beamed down on their heads. When I peeked in on them they appeared to glow in the light and even their giggles sounded angelic. Judging by the smile on her face Nayla appeared to have forgotten her plea for peace and quiet, whether for her or for the stork. I was greatly relieved. I thought what a wonderful thing peace was. All I had to do was look at their faces to see it. In that moment in time in Cornet Chehouan everything was right with us. Edith and I enjoyed each other's company, Michel found camaraderie with Fouad, Naim and Rami went off exploring each day, and in the storeroom we had a wounded stork who appeared to be recovering.

On Thursday morning when Nayla and MaryAnn went in to check on the stork they found it dead.

"Why did it have to die?" cried Nayla.

"I don't know, darling. We did everything we could," I said. "It wasn't what we wanted, but it's what happened. The stork knew it would never fly again so it gave up living."

On Good Friday we buried the stork. Nayla and MaryAnn organized the funeral. Naim and Rami were put in charge of digging the grave while Michel and Fouad fashioned a cross for a marker. We adults stood on the balcony and watched while the girls, singing 'Ave Maria' and holding lit candles, led the procession. Naim and Rami walked close behind them carrying the bird in a cardboard box to its final resting place alongside the barn where Shaater the donkey lived.

As our two families celebrated Christ's Resurrection at Mass on Easter Sunday in a hot, crowded, incense-filled village church, I must have drifted off. I imagined I saw the stork behind the altar, its white feathers glistening in the brilliant light as it prepared to take flight. It was the word 'lamb' that brought me back to the Mass. I heard the priest say, 'Lamb of God,' and I was reminded of my son. Just the day before a shepherd accompanied Naim and Rami home from their walk. Naim carried one of the baby lambs draped across the top of his shoulders. After the priest's third and final, 'Lamb of God' I responded for the stork in all of us, "Grant us the courage not to give up."

. . .

One morning I looked in the mirror and saw a line of white along my scalp. I did not know what it was. I pulled my hair back off my forehead, certain it was just poor lighting. I leaned closer to the mirror and looked again. My hair had gone white at the roots. I used my fingers to part other sections and the white was everywhere. It was as if someone had injected me with a potion that turned me into an old woman overnight. I pulled down the toilet cover and sat. When my tears dried and my chest stopped pounding I stood up again and stared at the woman in the mirror. I had been too busy hiding from bombs and hardly sleeping at night to pay attention to how I looked. I washed my face and brushed my teeth each day, and may or may not have applied lipstick, but the last thing I had time to do was study myself in the mirror. Nor did I wonder, when I ran a comb through my hair, what my roots were doing because it was not important. But now I was quite distraught. I had lost weight, too, and the first place it showed was in my face. My cheeks had shrunk into hollow pits and I no longer looked thirty-three. I looked forty, maybe older.

How cruelly war tramples your self esteem.

I was reluctant to leave Cornet Chehouan and return to Beirut. Despite the bombings, Parliament had managed to convene to elect a new President, but people were openly pessimistic about the chances for a long-term truce. This scared me. For the first time I considered the possibility of leaving. I can still remember the shame I felt. Michel had called me 'the woman with the nerves of steel.' Foolishly I thought it would disappoint him if I admitted I could no longer tolerate the war. Or was that just a convenient excuse? Deep down did I really think I would be failing myself if I abandoned my destructive lover, Beirut?

The city I loved, the place I called home was vastly altered. The discos and night clubs were shut. My favorite landmarks, historic mansions and ancient *souks*, had crumbled under heavy shelling. Gardens of hibiscus, bougainvillea and cypress with their old thick stubby trunks, lay abandoned. Open spaces had become garbage dumps. Miles of white sandy beaches had been turned into shanty towns for the city's new homeless. Balconies which had once been dressed in layers of pink geraniums were transformed into distorted metal forms protruding from gaping holes. In my dreams they recurred as the shrieking mouths of blinded captives nailed into concrete to die from starvation and neglect.

On our street the buildings were pockmarked from shrapnel and bullets; the awnings on the shops were torn and tattered; broken windows lay in disrepair; there was a severe shortage of water and electricity; noisy generators hummed across the city in place of the shelling; black electric wires were strung haphazardly across streets and alleyways.

When I saw all this I wondered if I would ever dance again with my tantalizing lover, Beirut.

6

Departure

onvincing Michel we should leave Lebanon for a while was not a problem, particularly since he agreed that Beirut's music might never play again. The problem was finding the safest way out. The Christians were suffering major defeats on every front. We could not cross the Green Line into West Beirut or travel the airport road manned by the Muslim militia, for fear of kidnapping. By late May, 1976, forty thousand Syrian troops were massed at the Lebanese border preparing for a full-scale invasion, purportedly to restore calm and save the Christians. Walid Jumblatt, Arafat's Druze counterpart in the Muslim-Palestinian coalition against the Christians, went to Damascus to plead with Syrian President Hafez el-Assad not to send in his troops. Jumblatt assured Assad that he and Arafat were close to restoring calm; they needed only a few more days to complete the task. Assad despised Arafat. Apparently Jumblatt was unaware of this. Assad would never allow Arafat to win a victory of any kind in Lebanon if he could prevent it. By invading Lebanon Assad would accomplish two goals. On the one hand he would appear to be the savior of the Christians; on the other he was making sure that Arafat could never declare victory.

By the first of June, twelve thousand Syrian troops had entered Lebanon. Eyewitness reports described Syrian tanks lined up for miles along the Mediterranean coastline, waiting for orders to take the Arida border crossing into Lebanon. When they came through the Bekaa Valley, over the mountains and down through the villages of Alley and Bhamdoun, villagers watched for hours in the hot sun as some three hundred tanks filed past. When Papa announced the news, I was elated. I no longer had to worry about the family members and friends I left behind.[6]

The Lebanese Christian leadership also embraced the Syrian intervention. Otherwise they faced military defeat on every front. According to an article in *Al-Nahar* on June 6, 1976, Pierre Gemayal declared: "Once security was achieved, Lebanon would reach an agreement with Syria limiting the duration of the Syrian military presence, subject to renewal at the request of the Lebanese authorities and parties to the Lebanese conflict."[7] Apparently, it was not just I who never gave a thought to what the ramifications of a protracted Syrian presence would mean for Lebanon.

We all should have.

. . .

In October, 1976, Syria's intervention was officially sanctioned at an Arab summit convened in Saudi Arabia. The Arab Deterrent Force, as it was called, a thirty thousand strong peacekeeping force composed primarily of Syrian troops and firmly under Syrian command, was created to 'bring security to Lebanon.'

At about the same time President Ford ordered all Americans to evacuate Beirut. When the Embassy called with instructions to go to an area along the sea in Ain Mreisse in West Beirut I told them we

---

6   Quoted at www.Cedarland.org (The Lebanese War).
7   *Loc. cit.*

could not make the perilous journey across town. When they suggested I travel to Damascus I explained that a taxi across the mountains through the Syrian controlled Bekaa Valley was even more dangerous. In fact for Christians there was only one way out of the country. A small passenger boat left twice a week for Cyprus from Jounieh, a seaport north of Beirut. Tickets were impossible to come by unless we were willing to pay outrageous black market prices.

Imagine my surprise when, the day after we decided we had to leave, the one woman who disrespected me as much as Wadia appeared at our front door to help us out of Beirut.

Nademe had been my in-laws' maid for some forty-two years. In poor Syrian villages where there were too many mouths to feed, it was common practice to sell female children, and she was only eight when her father sold her as a maid to Michel's maternal grandmother. Often these child-maids were still so physically small that they needed a stool to stand on in order to reach the sink to do the dishes. When Michel's grandmother died Nademe moved to my mother-in-law's house. She was born an Alawite, a minority Muslim sect found almost exclusively along the coast of Syria and southern Turkey. Hafez el-Assad was an Alawite who ruled over the majority Sunni Muslim population for close to thirty years. At my mother-in-law's urging Nademe had converted from Islam to Christianity when still a young girl.

Since I showed Nademe the respect due her years of service I expected the same in recognition of my status as the wife of Wadia's oldest child. But because of my tumultuous relationship with Wadia, Nademe presumed to treat me in the same manner as did her mistress. Nor was I the only one to suffer from her disdain.

Nademe also exerted a kind of blackmail over my in-laws. As long as they turned a blind eye to her occasional lie, to an occasional missing object, or to a stash of cash which mysteriously disappeared from the household fund, she faithfully carried out Wadia's every dictum and desire. On those occasions when she surpassed her usual arrogance and was reprimanded by my in-laws, she would feign terrible headaches or painful back spasms and put herself to bed for days.

So when Nademe appeared at our front door and explained that my father-in-law had sent her to help us get to Lattakia I was so glad to see her I planted a kiss on each of her cheeks.

She had arrived on a small freighter which was due to depart in two days with a cargo hold full of Lebanese apples. The captain was a friend of Papa's and offered to let us use his cabin for the sixteen-hour journey up the Eastern Mediterranean to Lattakia in exchange for what I presumed was a handsome fee.

Papa knew we were running low on certain provisions and sent four five-gallon plastic containers of gasoline with Nademe. Gasoline was extremely difficult to procure in Beirut even for physicians, who were given top priority. Papa asked only that we leave what we did not use with Michel's sister Andrée. Nademe was the right person to bring things like gasoline. She was well-organized and good at getting people to help her, so she never had to lift a heavy container herself. After a crewman had set the gasoline on the dock a dozen taxi drivers approached Nademe and offered to take her anywhere she wanted to go. Obviously they regarded a woman with many gallons of gasoline as easy prey. Those poor men had no idea with whom they were dealing. After she chose a taxi driver and he loaded her baggage, she demanded he turn over his car keys. She still had to retrieve her papers from Immigration and was not about to run the risk of finding the taxi with its precious cargo gone when she returned.

Nademe also brought a large cooler full of small meat balls, called *kibbeh*, and half-moon-shaped flaky pastries called *sambusak*, smelling of cinnamon and allspice and filled with fried meat and pine nuts. Papa knew I loved *lambajeans*, paper thin garlicky meat pizzas that only needed to be heated in the oven and squirted with fresh lemon, so he sent two dozen of those as well.

We were given the opportunity to bring a car on board, so Michel and I decided to take his Fiat 134 which had gotten us safely over the Karantina bridge on Black Saturday. We stored my VW Bug in a friend's underground garage. On the day of departure we said our good-byes to Andrée and her family and left early for Jounieh. Michel and I wanted to see a number of friends before we left. One of them was then-Colonel Elie Hayek, who arranged to have one of his soldiers handle the loading of our car on the boat.

We arrived at the port an hour before the 9:00 P.M. departure time. I took one look at the large, boisterous crowd already gathered at the gangplank and panicked. Salim, a friend who accompanied us had the same reaction.

"You couldn't pay me enough money to get on that boat with all those anxious people," he said.

One man said most of the other passengers had been waiting in line all day hoping to secure a place on the boat.

"West Beirut's been bombing us, too," he said. "It's as if those bastards knew we were trying to leave."

A dozen armed *Kataeb* militiamen posted near the gangplank added to the tense situation. They stood with their M-16s cradled under their right arms pointing the guns toward the crowd. Like brazen street thugs they demanded a so-called 'departure tax' in dollars before allowing their fellow Christians onto the boat. The ultimate insult was knowing they were collecting the money for personal use.

It was almost dark when a rocket plunged into the sea and exploded, rocking the 150 foot-long boat furiously against the rubber tires along the pier and splashing water onto the crowd.

Nademe had wandered off to look for the crewman she knew and returned not a moment too soon with the sailor, who led us to the back of the boat away from the crowd and the militiamen, where one of his mates waited to help us aboard. Nademe and Michel lifted Naim and Nayla into the sailor's outstretched arms. Then they jumped into the boat and gave me a hand getting aboard. We stood quietly for a moment to give our eyes time to adjust to the darkness and then cautiously felt our way across the deck. A number of cars had already been loaded onto the flat deck, but I couldn't tell if one of them was ours.

The sailor led us down a narrow staircase to a clean room sparsely furnished with one bed, two chairs, a table, and a secure lock on the door. Before she left Achrafieh Nademe had prepared a picnic basket and by this time we were all hungry. We spread some *Vache Qui Rit* cheese on Arab bread, munched on small cucumbers and sipped bottled water. We kept the grapes, bananas and pound cake for breakfast.

I shared the bed with Naim and Nayla while Michel and Nademe sat on chairs and rested their heads on the table. Naim and Nayla fell asleep almost immediately, but I stayed awake to make sure we were on our way before I fell asleep. I had no desire to peer out the window for one last fleeting glance at the city I had once called 'Lover.' I, once so willingly seduced by Beirut, was now completely disenchanted.

I fell asleep only when I finally felt the gentle sway of the boat heading for the open sea.

. . .

I dream I am sitting with Wadia in her living room. Her arms are folded across her ample chest and her smile is actually a smirk.

"See, I was right," she announces triumphantly.

"What do you mean?" I ask.

"I said you would leave and go back to America like all the others."

I sit up with a jolt.

"Oh my God, Wadia is going to think she won when she really didn't."

My heart is racing and my gut churns as I think how Wadia might reinterpret the conversation we had in 1969.

I will protest if she does, I will insist I am leaving because of the war, not because I could not adjust to life in Beirut.

. . .

Several hours later I awoke again needing to go to the toilet. Michel unlocked the door. The corridor was lit. I lifted my foot to leave the room but I stopped in mid-air. The narrow corridor, about twenty feet long, was clogged with people. Some were sitting upright with their backs against the wall while others were curled up on the floor. They all were trying to sleep. I stepped around each body as deftly as I could. When I reached the toilet the door was open and a woman was asleep inside. I awakened her and asked her to step outside so I could close the door.

We must have slept late the next morning, because by the time we opened the door the corridor was empty and we even had the toilet to ourselves. When I wondered why it had not backed up with so many people using it, Michel reminded me that it probably emptied directly into the sea.

After we ate breakfast we decided to spend the rest of the morning on deck. By our calculations it was only another hour before we reached Lattakia. Climbing the stairs we found ourselves on the observation deck next to the captain.

"Did you sleep well, Hakeme?" he asked.

"Yes, thank you," replied Michel.

People turned around when they heard the captain talking.

"Who's that?" I heard someone ask.

"She's a foreigner, I know that much," a woman replied. "She made me get out of the toilet last night because she wanted to use it."

The first voice spoke again, "Is she someone important? Is that why she and her family got such preferential treatment?"

I pretended not to hear them. The last thing I wanted was a confrontation with any of the passengers. We walked to the far end of the deck where there was a space big enough for the five of us to sit. Meantime Nademe had asked the captain how many passengers he had on board.

"There are one hundred twenty people on this boat."

She guessed there were normally ten, including the captain and his crew.

I asked, "How much money do you think the captain made on this trip?"

Nademe rolled her eyes. "Kteer," (a lot) she said. "Kteer."

As we approached Lattakia I saw huge metal cranes standing up like dozens of oddly-shaped legs. I did not notice the huge cargo ships anchored offshore until Naim said, "There are thirty-eight ships out there, Mommy."

I turned and saw the cluttered horizon. I thought this was an unusually high number, even with Beirut's port closed, until Michel reminded me that Lattakia was one of the oldest operating commercial seaports in the world. Goods destined for Lebanon, Jordan, even merchandise sent from Marseilles for Saudi Arabia and beyond came through Lattakia. Shipping companies often found it more economical to ship directly from Europe to Lattakia rather than through the Suez Canal, where they often faced delays and high passage fees.

Syria exports large quantities of agricultural goods through Lattakia's port including cotton, tobacco and a variety of fruits. Wheat and barley from Aleppo, northeast of Lattakia, are used to manufacture European beer. In one of his earlier business ventures Papa exported snails to France where they were miraculously transformed into *escargot de Bourgogne* and sold as a French product.

. . .

I had visited Syria before when my parents came to Lebanon in 1974 and we took a bus tour. I remembered Lattakia as one enormous ugly port with row after row of rusted shipping containers. That part had not changed. But I had forgotten how beautiful the clear turquoise color of the Mediterranean water was, so different from the port of Beirut. Time had forgotten the rest of the city, the quiet residential neighborhoods where my in-laws lived and the seaside cafes where we ate grilled fish and shrimp.

The most interesting sights lay just outside the city limits of Lattakia in Ras Shamra at Ugarit, where I planned to take Naim and Nayla. In an overgrowth of aniseed clumps and red poppies are the ruins of a highly sophisticated kingdom that flourished when Tyre, and Byblos in Lebanon, were only in their infancy. Here man's first complete alphabet was written on clay cylinders. Only the consonants were written, the missing vowels had to be supplied by the reader.[8]

. . .

In 1974 my parents and I had also visited Palmyra. I remember approaching the town, an oasis in the middle of the Syrian desert, just as the sun was about to sink into the horizon. We stopped to watch a herd of camels cross the road ahead of us with their deliberate, graceful swaying gait. Palmyra was the capital of Syria in the time of Christ and it served as an important political and commercial center on the Silk Road between Europe and the Orient. It is still famous for its impressive Roman temples and colonnades which cover some six square kilometers.

As we were leaving Palmyra a van passed us on the road. It looked like a square tin box with tiny windows and bars sitting atop an open truck in the middle of the Syrian desert. Disturbed by this, I asked our tour guide what it was.

"Oh, that's just the van transporting prisoners to the underground prison in Palmyra," she said.

"How can they breathe in such heat?" I asked.

"It doesn't really matter whether they breathe or not," she said, shrugging. "They all end up dying in that jail anyway. No one ever leaves Palmyra."

That image and those words summed up all I disliked about Syria and why I did not want to be coming back. Everyone knew that Syria's streets were full of *Mohabarat*, the all-powerful secret police, and you had to watch every word you spoke. In Lebanon we used to say, 'It doesn't matter how bad things get in Beirut. It is still

---

8   Fox, Robert: *The Inner Sea: The Mediterranean and its People*. Knopf, NY, 1993, p. 445–446.

a thousand times better than being in Syria.' Of course, Michel's family was in Lattakia and that did make it a little safer.

I was distracted from these upsetting thoughts by Nayla. Pulling at my arm she said, "Mommy, why aren't you listening to me?"

"Sorry, darling," I responded. "My mind was off thinking."

"What were you thinking about?"

"How I really don't want to be landing here," I replied.

"Aren't we going to be able to visit places and go the beach?" Nayla asked.

"Yes, of course, darling. It just isn't a good place for grown-ups," I said.

Our visit to Lattakia would not have been an option if President Assad had not changed the rules because the Syrian government had run out of money recently. Therefore it was decreed that any man who had not done his military service could pay a fine of one thousand dollars in lieu of serving and be absolved from any further military obligation. My father-in-law promptly paid the fine for Michel and his two brothers, both of whom had recently returned to Lattakia to help Papa run his gypsum and trucking business. While Michel carried no official document stating that he had paid the fine and was therefore exempt from military service, he was confident the matter had been taken care of, and arriving in Lattakia on an apple boat would pose no problems.

Our passage from Jounieh to Lattakia was uneventful, which turned out not to be the case once we disembarked.

By the time we walked into the sunlit immigration hall the staff had already left for lunch. Nademe suggested we sit down while she hurried off to see how long we would be kept waiting. Aside from her square face and short brown hair, cut in an almost mannish style, Nademe was a woman with no remarkable physical traits. She was about five feet four inches tall and almost always wore a cotton T-shirt, a knee-length skirt and zip-up tennis shoes without socks. Only on rare occasions did she wear a dress. Because her boss, my father-in-law, was a well-known and well-respected local businessman, Nademe knew everyone important in Lattakia and was held in high esteem. She carried out complicated tasks with ease, was a skillful interlocutor and knew whom to trust. Papa often asked her to carry large sums of cash between Beirut and Lattakia strapped inside her underwear.

While Michel and I waited, the children explored the large room, running up and down the rows of straight backed wooden benches, occasionally climbing onto one to locate our whereabouts and shout hello.

The Immigration officer was walking into his office just as Nademe returned. He stopped and greeted her: "Marhaba, Nademe, what are you doing here?"

"I've just brought the doctor and his family from Beirut," she replied.

"Ma Bi Sir," (How could I have done such a thing) he answered. "How inconsiderate of me to have kept him waiting."

He then walked into his office, sat down behind his desk, shuffled a few papers, then shouted, "Doctor Sultan, Ta Faddel (come in), please come in."

While Michel went into his office I came and sat beside Nademe. Almost immediately I saw Michel's facial expression change. I turned to Nademe who was already on her feet. I stood and followed her to the door.

"You are under arrest, Hakeme," the Immigration officer said in a voice that betrayed no emotion, "for desertion from the Syrian army."

I started to join Michel but Nademe put out her hand.

"Don't go in there, Sitt (Madame) Cathy," she said. "It might make matters worse. Go and sit with the children, while I call Hawaja (the master) Naim."

Nademe marched into one of the empty offices as though she owned it, picked up a telephone and called Papa. After a brief conversation she went and reassured Michel that his father was on his way.

"It shouldn't take him more than ten minutes to get here," she said.

I watched Michel slump forward in his chair, cradling his head in his hands. I saw the muscles in his face twitching and I knew he was cursing himself for ever coming to Lattakia. Probably in his head he was running through a quick list of all the horror stories he had ever heard about Syrian jails. Syria's judicial system was identical to Lebanon's, which was modeled on the Napoleonic code: the presumption of guilt until proven innocent. In Syria when an unfortunate soul was arrested he was rarely found innocent.

It took Papa less than five minutes to arrive. When he pulled Michel's exemption papers out of his pocket and placed them on the desk the Immigration officer apologized.

"I was only doing my job," he said.

Michel's name was listed on all border crossings as a deserter from the Syrian army. The officer urged Michel to get the matter cleared up before he left Syria. Otherwise he would have the same problem anytime he entered the country. The next morning Michel visited all the necessary government offices where he was given every assurance that his name would be erased from all the lists.

. . .

In June, 1976, we visited the United States and stayed with my grandmother Catherine in Washington. Michel contacted his former bosses, Drs. Bob Barreras and John Morrissey at the University Hospitals in Madison where he had done his Gastroenterology Fellowship in 1968. He told them he was looking for a job and they offered him a Visiting Assistant Professorship for a year, which would give him time to study for his state medical boards. In order to practice medicine in the United States Michel had to pass the Flex – an examination equivalent to the boards – for foreign medical school graduates.

Within three weeks of arriving in America we had rented a townhouse, furnished it modestly from secondhand stores and thrift sales, bought a car, and enrolled the children in a parochial school. Madison was an ideal respite from the stress of Beirut. The pace was slow enough that we could catch our breath and relearn normal living skills. Our townhouse was one block from a small sandy beach on Lake Mendota. For the first time in their lives the children could ride their bicycles without fear of falling bombs or busy city traffic.

. . .

Jacques' best friend Joe Soussou called us in September with some tragic news. I was in the kitchen when the telephone rang. Naim answered and I watched the color drain from his face.

"Just a minute, Joe," he said in a strange voice. He put the receiver down on the table, walked to the bottom of the stairs and called his father, who was upstairs resting. When he heard his father's voice on the line he hung up, turned to me and said, "Mommy, Jeddo is dead."

"Did Joe tell you that?"

"He didn't have to," Naim said, "I just know."

Papa had apparently returned home not feeling well after his afternoon walk. He called the doctor, got undressed and climbed into bed. By the time the doctor arrived five minutes later Papa was dead. Wadia made the decision not to tell Michel of his father's death right away because the funeral had to be held the very next day. In the Middle East, where bodies are not embalmed, the dead are buried within twenty-four hours. When we learned of the tragedy Papa had already been dead a week.

Michel took his father's death very hard because they had argued just before we left Lattakia. Michel's brothers told him that Papa was interfering with the day-to-day operations of the business. When Michel confronted Papa with these accusations Papa told Michel that he was actually trying to save the business since he did not agree with what Jacques and Raymond were doing. They had just fired a man who had worked for Papa for twenty-five years and Papa was furious. It was only after Michel left Lattakia that he realized his father was right, so he wrote to him apologizing for ever doubting his business judgment. Michel also told him how much he loved him and how fortunate he was to have such a generous father. Papa had made sure Michel received a fine education and paid all the bills. When we arrived in Beirut penniless in 1969 after Michel finished his medical training in the United States, Papa made sure we had everything we needed. Michel's sister Andrée said Papa received the letter a few days before he died.

I would miss Papa too. He showered me with the same love and attention he gave his own daughter. Papa was generous; as a wedding gift he gave me a diamond and ruby ring. He was the consummate shopper, always bringing home the latest gadget. When Michel and I moved into our apartment in December, 1970, and I needed to buy furniture, Papa was only too happy to help. He suggested we look for furniture in Basta, a neighborhood full of antique and second-hand furniture stores. It was there I fell in love with a unique square walnut table with a Chippendale base which could seat twelve if you added two leaves. An Englishwoman and her husband were admiring the same piece of furniture. I whispered this to Papa and he said, "Don't worry," and wandered off.

A short time later he returned and asked, "Would you like eight or twelve chairs with that table, ma chérie?"

Papa also knew where to get the best bargains on appliances and when he ordered a new two-door Westinghouse refrigerator for me he could not resist buying one for himself.

Before we left Lattakia in early June Papa had entrusted me with an exquisite diamond necklace.

"It's Turkish and it's over a hundred years old," he said. "It may even have been made for one of the wives of the Sultan. You can wear it now but you must promise to give it to Nayla. I want her to wear it on her wedding day."

. . .

In February, 1977, Michel passed the Flex and immediately applied for a Wisconsin state license. Grandma Catherine was the first to hear the good news.

"I knew all along he would pass," she said. "He's the smartest person I know."

Dr. Morrissey encouraged Michel to send out his résumé in the hope of finding a gastroenterologist who was looking for a partner, and he received an interesting offer from a physician in Harrisburg, Pennsylvania. Michel interviewed there and was giving the offer some consideration when he received a letter from his brother Raymond. He insisted Michel come to Beirut to see how things had improved before making a decision. He said the Lebanese were openly optimistic about the future and once again spending money entertaining. Banks and schools had reopened, stores were full of new merchandise, developers – mostly from the Arab countries – were pouring money into beach resorts and new building projects, obviously hoping to entice tourists back. There were plans for new road construction, for a more sophisticated telecommunications system, and for improved water and electricity services. Raymond reminded Michel of the three hundred fifty days of sun. Beirut's sun and temperate climate sounded very appealing after a particularly cold winter in Madison.

If we had been living in Beirut at the time and following the news more closely, we would not have been so surprised to learn of the assassination of Kamal Jumblatt, father of Walid, on March 16, 1977, by pro-Syrian forces. The incident took place a few meters from a Syrian checkpoint in the Chouf Mountains. Apparently the Druze leader was already a doomed man before he pleaded with President Assad in April, 1976, not to intervene in Lebanon's civil war. In November, 1975, Assad had drawn up a Constitutional Document calling for a more balanced religious representation in the Lebanese government. It addressed some of the grievances of the Muslims without undermining the foundations of Lebanon's political system. Jumblatt did not think the document went far enough and refused to endorse it. His murder was a reminder that one does not publicly defy Syrian President Hafaz el-Assad.[9]

"You're just going through the motions with this Harrisburg

---

9   *Ibid.*

offer," I said. "Your heart's so full of missing Beirut it's about ready to burst. Raymond sent you a round trip ticket. Go and see if we can really go back."

To me the choice was clear. For a whole year no one had invited us to dinner. I realized that people in America had little time for or interest in, entertaining, but I had been spoiled by Beirut's social life. I missed stimulating conversations with people who kept abreast of the news, who came from diverse cultural backgrounds and spoke multiple languages. I missed the place that nurtured friendships as though they were precious commodities, never taking them for granted. After Mass in Beirut I left *Notre Dame des Anges* feeling blessed, whereas my Madison church with its guitar and folk songs did little to satisfy my spiritual needs.

I was accustomed to throwing my arms around people and kissing them on both cheeks, but I understood this was cultural. I realized these were not things most Americans held dear, and that was perfectly all right. But I could not live in a place where people shook my hand at arm's length, where they did not bother to call or offer to run my errands when they knew I was confined to bed. I did not like being alone when I was sick, I loved a room full of friends. I knew Americans were not devoid of emotions, they simply were not comfortable displaying them. The problem was not them, it was me. I needed to live in a more demonstrative environment where people showed their feelings openly. And finally, I missed not having my feet firmly planted on the concrete pavement of the lover-city with which I was infatuated, the one that had so graciously granted me insider-foreigner status.

In April the children and I waited in Madison while Michel traveled to Beirut to see for himself if the situation had improved. He almost did not return.

After two calm weeks in the company of family and friends Michel was preparing to return to Madison. On his way to Lebanon he flew Chicago–New York–Frankfort–Beirut. When he reconfirmed his return flight the travel agent suggested he change his ticket to take a faster, easier route via Damascus–Frankfort–

Chicago, and Michel agreed. The idea of a better connection and saving time overrode the commonsense decision to stay out of Syria. His brother Raymond volunteered to accompany him to Damascus the next afternoon, a three hour drive from Beirut.

When Michel and his brother arrived at Mesnaa on the border between Lebanon and Syria they were turned back because they did not have an entry permit. After obtaining the right documents in Chtaura in the Bekaa Valley they returned to Mesnaa at around 8:00 P.M. on April 16, 1977. Raymond told Michel to wait in the car while he presented their permits to the border guard. Moments later the office door swung open smacking furiously into the mortar siding. Raymond stood in the doorway alongside a man who was taller than Raymond's 6'1". It was obvious by the way Raymond was leaning that the thick-chested soldier had his arm in a solid grip. According to Michel it looked as if the soldier could have used Raymond's arm to lift him bodily off the ground and throw him like a discus. The officer pushed Raymond, which caused him to lose his balance and stumble. Michel watched but did not know what to do. Before he could react, the soldier flung open the car door and pulled him out by his shoulders.

"Your Syrian papers," he yelled, "hand them over!"

Michel was so scared he could barely remember where he had packed the documents. When he finally found them the soldier took a minute to examine the paper before ordering him inside.

"You're under arrest as a deserter from the Syrian Army," he shouted. Michel tried to explain there had been a mistake, he had papers to prove his innocence. A simple telephone call to Lattakia would clear up everything.

Raymond said he would drive to Lattakia to get the documents but when the soldier heard this he snatched Raymond's car registration papers out of his hand. Without those Raymond could not legally drive in Syria. Then the soldier grabbed Michel by the arm and led him to a cell.

"I'll get to Lattakia somehow," Raymond whispered in English. "Don't worry, I'll get you out."

Raymond was willing to risk arrest by the *Mohabaret* for driving without his papers in order to get his brother out of jail. A mile past the border crossing he saw a soldier hitchhiking. He picked him up, reasoning that with a soldier in his car he would have less chance of being stopped at one of the multiple security checks along his route. At about four in the morning Raymond ran out of gas miles from anywhere. Then a miracle occurred. A taxi driver saw the soldier in Raymond's car and stopped. He siphoned gasoline from his car to Raymond's. Six hours later, with the soldier still at his side, he arrived in Lattakia.

Raymond went directly to his office to retrieve the papers. When he discovered that the file cabinet was locked he called in a local thug and paid him to break it open. With papers in hand he went to see a General he knew in Lattakia who in turn called the Commandant of the Military Prison in Damascus. Over the telephone the General assured him that Michel's papers were indeed in order. The General in Lattakia knew that Michel would automatically be transferred to Damascus from the border jail, routine procedure for anyone detained at a border crossing. He requested that the Commandant keep Michel in Damascus until his brother could return there with the documents, to which he agreed. Before Raymond left Lattakia he called his cousin Gisèle who was visiting her parents in Damascus, gave her the numbers of the official documents, and asked her to go to the Commandant's office with the information while he was en route.

Meanwhile back in Mesnaa Michel had spent a long night on a narrow wooden bench in a windowless cell. A hole in the ground served as a toilet; he was given neither food nor water. The next morning a guard approached his cell, introduced himself and said he also was from Lattakia. He warned Michel that he was going to be transferred to Damascus and on to Palmyra. Then glancing to either side to make sure no one was looking he pressed his face between the bars and whispered, "I'm not supposed to do this but is there anyone I can call for you? Once you leave here no one will ever know where you are."

Michel gave the guard Gisèle's name and her parents' telephone number in Damascus. Because the arresting officer had not taken his personal belongings Michel still had money in his pocket, so he gave the soldier the equivalent of twenty-five dollars for his kindness.

During the three-hour transfer from Masnaa to Damascus Michel was able to close his eyes and rest in the back of the van.

Looking out a small window in the detention room where he was being held in Damascus pending transfer to Palmyra, he caught a glimpse of Gisèle as she walked past. His relief was enormous. Minutes later he was ushered into the Commandant's office where she was sitting. She reassured him that Raymond was on his way with the papers. The Commandant spoke up.

"So, you're a physician."

Michel explained that he was a gastroenterologist, and the Commandant took that as a license to recount his personal medical history, wanting to know if there was a treatment cheaper than Tagamet® for his ulcers. When he was satisfied Michel had answered all his questions he sent him back to the detention room.

Word got out that Michel was a physician living in America, and six guards crowded into his room, each with his own chair, forming a semi-circle around Michel's bench in the corner. They sat backwards with their feet curled around the chairs' back legs, arms resting across the chest-high backs. Michel thought their questions would be medical but the guards were more interested in life outside Syria. They wanted to know how blacks were treated in America, could they find jobs easily and were they allowed to live anywhere they wished? Their questions were asked out of curiosity and admiration, not envy nor hate. One man wanted to know about Israeli technology, whether it was true that America supplied Israel with all its weapons or if the Israelis manufactured their own. Did Israel really tell the United States what to do? He said that was what they heard all the time on the news. "We even heard that they bought off the entire U.S. government"

"Only Congress," laughed Michel.

Since Gisèle had assured him that Raymond was on his way with his papers Michel had a question of his own to ask.

"What would have happened to me if I hadn't been able to prove my exemption?"

The guards exchanged nervous glances; they were forbidden to speak of such things and no one said a word. Then one began to laugh and shake his head, as if to say 'Surely you've already figured that out' and they all joined in. Finally one of them was brave enough to speak.

"Hakeme, you would have been loaded into a windowless van and taken to the underground prison in Palmyra," he said. "No one would have ever known where you were. You would have died there because no one leaves Palmyra."

. . .

Once the children and I knew Michel was on a plane headed for Madison we were too excited about the possibility of returning to Beirut to waste any more energy worrying about Syrian jails. However unfortunate the incident it had a happy ending. Before he boarded the plane, Michel had spoken on the phone with Naim and Nayla.

"Have a think about whether or not you'd like to come home. We'll discuss it when I get there."

After talking with her father Nayla wanted to know if we could leave before school finished. "What would be the point in staying for exams?"

"I want to buy Camille Hayek (son of Colonel Elie Hayek) a gift," said Naim. "Maybe I'll get him a piece of Lego or a game of Risk."

"Can I bring all my Barbie stuff with me?"

"Are we going to stop in Paris? We could stay with Gisèle and take a *bateau mouche* along the Seine. Could we, please?"

"Hey, guys," I said, "sounds to me like you've already made up your minds. Are we going home?"

"Yessss!" they shouted gleefully.

. . .

Shortly after Michel's return I related his adventures to Jean, a woman whom I had known since 1968.

"You're actually going back?"

"Yes. I'm so excited, I can't wait to get home."

"Cathy, you just finished telling me that Michel was thrown into a Syrian jail. Then you tell me you're going back. Are you crazy?"

I resisted the temptation to roll my eyes like my mother. "You don't understand," I said, "Syria and Lebanon are two different countries."

"But the Syrians have forty thousand troops in Lebanon."

"True, but they're mostly in West Beirut, and if you avoid their roadblocks you don't usually have to tangle with them."

"That's a pretty simplistic way of seeing things," said Jean.

"Not if you understand Middle East politics," I said. "Look, even during the war Syrians risked their lives trying to get to Beirut to buy luxury goods. Syria has nothing. Their locally-made toilet paper is as rough as sandpaper, their supermarket shelves are bare and their pharmacies have little or no medications. On the other hand the Lebanese are great merchants. Did you know they're descended from the Phoenicians?"

"Of course I've heard that," said Jean. "Who cares about history or the Syrians? What about your children? Don't you care about their safety?"

"Jean, don't forget that we only brought the children out of Lebanon because of the fighting, and according to Michel the war is over. He's just been there for two weeks checking it out and he says it's safe to go back. I understand where you're coming from and I appreciate your concern. But you've lived happily in Madison most of your adult life and it's become home so it wouldn't occur to you to want to live anywhere else. In the same way I call Beirut home and it's the only place I want to live."

7

Homecomings

As we flew toward the eastern shore of the Mediterranean I pressed my face to the window of the plane. I watched with the eagerness of a woman about to embrace her lover again. When Beirut finally appeared the bluffs along the *corniche* shimmered in the afterglow of the setting sun. I thought I saw gentle sea waves caressing deserted shores but alas, I was mistaken.

To the right of the runway parallel to the sea an ugly slum community stretched down the once pristine sandy beaches. Hordes of people occupied the small white cabañas of what was, until the previous year, the St. Simon and St. Michel beach clubs. The rest had set up tents or constructed tin hovels. Laundry dangled from make-shift clotheslines and sheets covered windows and doors for privacy.

At least nothing had changed at the airport. I was relieved to still see the familiar Lebanese institution of money being exchanged for services rendered: the *wasta* and *baksheesh*, the porter and the customs officer in collusion. It was apparent from the state of downright grunginess that no one had taken water or soap to the terminal in a very long time. People waiting for arriving passengers were now cordoned off a hundred yards from the terminal for security reasons. I walked toward the crowd, loving the feeling of living in a foreign place like Beirut where I was a foreigner all the time, where the city constantly astonished me. Nothing had ever surprised me in Madison. In Beirut it was the noises and smells; the signs in Arabic, French and English; the discordant sounds of all those languages spoken at once; the gentle way people greeted one another, their hands gesturing in the air. And there they were in the crowd, the faces of our family. The first one I saw was Andrée waving her hands over her head, her mouth open as if in song, shouting "Michel, Cathy." Wadia was beside her, trying to smile when she wanted to frown, which made me laugh. Poor Wadia, the arrival was not about her, it was about us. The person I missed most was Papa. I wanted to see his shining bald head and have him grab my hand and kiss it like a chivalrous, elderly knight.

I was dismayed by the dramatic change in the landscape between the terminal and our apartment, some eight kilometers north and slightly east of the airport. Beautiful villas had fallen prey to families of squatters. The surrounding fields were crowded with makeshift dwellings. People were living in bombed-out buildings.

"Who are all these people?" I asked.

"Shiite refugees from the South," said Andrée. "They've been run out of their homes and villages by the Israelis. They had nowhere else to go."

As we approached Teyouneh Circle the familiar landmarks were gone. I was trying to remember where the parasol pine park had been when Nayla tugged at my sleeve. "Mommy, look at that building. It doesn't have any walls."

She was right. What was left resembled the Roman Coliseum with pillars supporting the floors stretching back into darkness in a haunting symmetry. In spite of the violence and ruination it possessed a strange beauty, which spoke of the power to resist the kind of battering that knocked down walls while leaving the rest intact. And it spoke volumes about how solidly Beirut buildings were constructed.

We fell silent when we reached Teyouneh, where some of the fiercest battles had been fought. The building Michel and Kassab defended had fared better than most, looking as though it had been inhabited in the recent past. Through a gaping hole on the third floor I saw a dining room with the tablecloth still on the table. I wondered why it had not blown away. Perhaps it had been set with lots of dishes and platters for a large family gathering or a birthday when the explosion occurred. It was odd that whoever came to inspect the damage or to carry away the injured or dead had not bothered to clear the table.

It was Nayla, usually a silent observer, who spoke up again. "Mommy, it's horrible here now."

She was right. In that moment I gained a newfound appreciation for the orderly way things worked in Madison. Just a smidgen of that orderliness and cleanliness would have worked wonders in Beirut.

Despite evidence of widespread neighborhood clean-up and renovation, no one had repaired the huge hole on the second floor of the building across from our apartment. Perhaps the owners had died there and had no living family members to clean up the mess. It was the bedroom I saw, the large double bed obviously not made-up for some time, the sheets and blankets lying half on and half off the bed. I felt like a voyeur peering into a private life, wondering if someone had been in the bed when the bomb fell.

Our building had a large hole on the seventh floor below our balcony on the kitchen side. Mrs. Eid, a refugee who now occupied the owner's abandoned seventh floor apartment, had covered it with layers of clear plastic rather than repair it. Renovations were under way at Lunettes and Colifichet, the two boutiques on the ground floor. The damage looked no more serious than at other places: shattered windows, tattered awnings and fractured plastic display cases. Considering the battles and the repeated rocket attacks Badaro had suffered, it was amazing to see how little the neighborhood had been altered.

On Badaro Street restoration was underway. I was surprised to see municipal workers paving streets, repairing sidewalks and replacing dead or dying trees. I would not have thought the Lebanese government could afford to spend money on such seemingly frivolous things after three years of war.

"On the contrary," Andrée said, "the President thinks it's important to restore the city's aesthetic beauty. It's a smart move on his part and it will help restore people's confidence."

Azzam, the delicatessen two buildings away, was already open for business. The dry cleaner, the barber, even the bookstore had painted, repaired, and replaced façades and looked like new stores. Alfonso, an old established neighborhood restaurant, was advertising its dinner menu. More enterprising were two new restaurants, both serving Lebanese food, which had opened within a block of Teyouneh Circle. The traffic snarls, the usual headache of finding a parking space, things I had formerly found frustrating, now appeared healthy signs of normality. Badaro was recovering, and people were out walking the streets, going about their business, obviously optimistic about the future.

. . .

The ceiling-to-floor bookshelf in our living room had collapsed. Two crystal decanters I had forgotten to store had shattered into tiny pieces. The large elk horn fern I had left hanging from the ceiling had fallen, breaking the clay pot and strewing dirt everywhere. The sheer beige curtains were shredded and the furniture had faded. On the terrace many of the flower pots had been knocked over and their dried-up roots were on the ground. The mess in the apartment and my neglected container garden were an overwhelming disappointment. I had known it was going to be like that, yet part of me had hoped otherwise. I could not stop sobbing but not wanting anyone to see me I went into the toilet and locked the door.

I did not care that Wadia probably thought my behavior was petulant and childish. Michel knocked on the door immediately.

"Just leave me alone for a minute," I remember shouting. Then my mother-in-law, the ultimate authority on mature and rational behavior, approached the door.

"Don't worry, ma chérie," she said. "You and your family can come live with me."

Wadia and Nademe were powerful motivators; I channeled all my energy into renovating our apartment.

. . .

Leila had been my cleaning lady for five years. She lived in West Beirut, and had no telephone, so I could not contact her that way. Instead I used what we housewives called 'the Arabic telephone line.' I contacted my English friend Fay, who employed Leila's cousin Lena; she in turn contacted Leila to tell her I had returned and needed her help. Before she could start the windows and the glass balcony doors had to be replaced. Two glaziers from the glass factory showed up on the first morning and spent most of the day cutting glass, fitting and caulking it into window and door frames. As part of their job they swept the balcony and apartment clear of any shattered glass. When that was done I was ready for Leila.

Devoted and energetic, she was the only person I wanted by my side as I began the seventh clean-up of the war. At the age of twenty-eight, Leila's small frame was lean and well-toned. As soon as she arrived she removed her shoes and as she was wearing pants, rolled them up to her knees.

She washed the balcony first, swirling a short stemmed broom with a full head of feathery bristles and plenty of water mixed with detergent, around the pots and furniture. In some places she would go after the dirt on her knees, her jaw firmly closed, her hair wobbling, the muscles on her arms rippling, the curve in her back perfectly arched, her eyes searching for any speck she might have missed. I lovingly called her my 'Ray-O-Vac battery'; according to Lebanese television commercials of the time, they never quit working.

When Leila cleaned windows they sparkled. She hosed down the glass on the outside, then wiped it clean with newspaper, which does not leave smudges. She found an old toothbrush worked best for cleaning between the radiator panels and in and around the bathroom and kitchen fixtures. The marble floors were next-to-impossible to clean. Unlike those in expensive and elegant homes ours did not have a finely polished, high quality surface, but were more porous, trapping dirt and shattered glass. Leila and I got on our knees and worked on one small section at a time. Progress was painfully slow and tedious. I do not remember which hurt more at the end of the day, my knees or my arms.

Leila's lovely voice singing Arabic songs made the work seem less tedious. I often heard her humming while I was in the kitchen preparing our lunch and she was getting ready to say her prayers to Mecca. I would put lunch on the kitchen table and go rest on my bed while she prayed on her mat. When she was finished we would sit down and eat together.

Leila taught me how to cook Lebanese food. She had worked in several prominent Lebanese homes and learned from some of the city's finest cooks. In addition to the more traditional dishes like tabouli, stuffed grape leaves and hummus, she taught me how to prepare fresh quince with veal shank flavored with garlic and fresh mint. She added chopped cilantro and grenadine syrup to okra stew, cumin and red pepper sauce – a combination of roasted red peppers and hot spices – to her *kibbeh*, and generously doused grilled white fish with a blend of chopped walnuts, garlic, cilantro, and lemon juice. The most valuable lesson was to clean up as I cooked so that by the time I finished preparing the meal there was no mess left in the sink.

Luckily the kitchen was very minimalist by American standards and easy for Leila to clean. It was bare except for a marble sink with a relatively spacious work top on either side. For the most part she only had to clear out a cabinet, remove the contents, scrub the cabinet and return things to their proper places. My four-burner stove was hardly a challenge since all stoves in Lebanon worked on gas canisters which were in a closed compartment that hid the ugly canister from view next to the oven. I only had to attach the hose through a hole in the back of the unit. We used matches to light the burners. During the war we had no heat in our apartment since the owner refused to pay for fuel. Though the temperature rarely dropped below forty degrees Fahrenheit during the winter months, Beirut was extremely humid. We used gas heaters to warm the other rooms but I relied on my stove to heat the kitchen.

This time the clean-up in the kitchen was the hardest so far. Thick clumps of black mildew grew like hungry weeds across the ceiling and down the walls. The more we tried to scrub it off the more the smudge spread, so finally we conceded defeat. A primer and two coats of oil-base paint would have to do what we could not.

After Leila had scrubbed the walls throughout the apartment it was my job to paint them. Swedish blue paint in the kitchen helped to hide the cracks and grime. Naim and Nayla liked the color so much they wanted me to use it in their bedroom too. Apricot on the living and dining walls accentuated the same hue in the Persian carpets.

One day I was up on the ladder painting the ceiling. From my vantage point I was able to look out over the city. I could see a window washer, a team of men beating carpets, one housewife hanging her laundry and another painting like me. I saw a woman pacing her balcony with an infant in her arms. I heard a city alive, traffic bustling, horns honking, music blaring from passing car radios. It was a perfect cloudless day and the sky was that blue only the Mediterranean can produce. I heard street vendors shouting and mistresses haggling, bargaining a final price. Arabic music poured forth from the taxi stand across the street, and I could hear Leila's lovely voice on the other side of the balcony, singing the words to the music which she knew by heart. I could tell from the energy and rhythm in her voice that she was scrubbing a floor.

. . .

Two weeks later we moved back into our apartment on July 1, 1977. Before we left for the States in May, 1976, Wednesday had been the one day of the week I tried to see my friends. With the clean-up and moving I had forgotten all about it. One day I was sitting resting with my legs up on the couch, thoroughly enjoying a sat-isfying moment of leisure in my newly cleaned and painted liv-ing room. Leila had made me a cup of tea before leaving at noon. Michel had taken Naim and Nayla to his mother's for lunch because he wanted me to have the afternoon off. The elevator, which was working again, came up to the eighth floor. I could tell by the shuf-fle of feet that several people had gotten out and I heard English being spoken. Fay's British accent echoed in the hall followed by Edith's precise, clipped Germanic-sounding English. There was raucous laughter as they began banging on the door. I jumped up from the couch, remembering it was Wednesday. How marvelous of my friends to have remembered! I opened the door and in they came with tremendous hugs. They both carried lovely bouquets of flowers and Fay pulled a bottle of champagne out of her bag. We settled ourselves on the balcony and sipped wine, giggling through a year's worth of news.

. . .

In many ways our return was easiest for Michel, who had no expectations. To him Beirut had never been a clean city. As for the bombed-out buildings, they were a shocking but unfortunate con-sequence of war. As for the disheartening state of our apartment, it was not something to which Michel gave much thought but left up to me. His primary concern was his medical practice.

Because of the division between East and West Beirut, Michel changed the way he saw patients. He rented office space at St. George Hospital in Achrafieh where he saw his Christian patients five mornings a week. Since he was concerned his Muslim patients might be reluctant to travel into East Beirut, he repaired his office on the second floor in our building, which was only a block from the Green Line and convenient for anyone coming from West Beirut. He rehired his former secretary Freyha to answer the phone and scheduled his Muslim patients in the afternoons in Badaro.

When Michel first returned to Beirut in June, 1969, it was as an internist with a subspecialty in gastroenterology, and he brought the first gastroscope to Lebanon. He had trained under Dr. John Morrissey, the foremost authority on the scope and its use. The Japanese firm Olympus manufactured the delicate fiber-optic scopes and Dr. Morrissey tested them. At the end of his training Michel purchased a used gastroscope.

Michel's patients paid him in cash. There were no insurance companies in Beirut in the late sixties and seventies, so every time a patient saw his doctor he settled his bill. Fees were negotiable. If a patient was poor Michel did not accept money. Even the poorest patient felt a sense of pride, so he or she returned the favor with a gift of some kind, a freshly caught fish, a farm-raised chicken, home-made jam.

When admitted to the hospital, patients had a choice of five classes of service, and doctors charged according to the patient's class: most expensive was Luxury, which included a private salon; First Class cost less; and Second and Third Class rooms with three or more patients cost the least. At the end of his hospital stay the patient paid both the hospital and doctor bills in cash. Poor patients in *weezara* (large wards) were treated for free by both the hospital and physician.

Our return was hardest on Naim and Nayla, which surprised me. Their school, the Jesuit-run *Jamhour*, did not recognize their studies in America, so if they wanted to move up to the next grade they had to pass two exams, one in Arabic, the other in French. As soon as we moved back into our apartment I hired private tutors. Every morning Naim studied at home with Mr. Aoun while I drove Nayla to Mlle. Yvette's house for an hour and a half of Arabic. Three days a week Samir, who had been their tutor during the first year of war, helped them with French and Mathematics. On their free days I rewarded them by taking them to Coral Beach. Sometimes they brought their homework and sat under umbrellas in a quiet corner until they finished, while I sat nearby making a feeble attempt to read. The fat men in speedos trying to catch the attention of bejeweled, bikini-clad women who were more intent on sun worshiping were far more interesting than any book I ever brought along.

In mid-September the children sat for their exams. Two days later we returned to *Jamhour* to read the results posted in the school lobby. Nayla passed all her tests but Naim failed his Arabic exam. He was dismayed at the result and the pain in his face nearly broke my heart. My first impulse was to comfort him, the last thing he wanted his mother to do in public. I noticed a priest standing nearby; he came forward and introduced himself. Père Bruno Pin was the new French teacher for Naim's class. When he heard the whole story he said, "But Madame, he is so young. It will be much better for him if he does not move up a grade."

As a matter of fact Naim had begun first grade at four years and nine months, quite young even in the French system. Père Pin reassured me that he would ask the school principal to assign Naim to his class. "And," he said, "I'll take very good care of him, Madame Sultan."

I hoped Nayla would have as caring a teacher. I had been watching her behavior closely ever since the bombing at Wadia's the previous year. It was obvious from her performance on her exams that she was in no trouble academically. When she was called upon to tackle a challenge she did it brilliantly. I did not know enough at the time to wonder how her psyche was adjusting to all the upheaval in her life.

. . .

The 1977–1978 school year began in October. Egyptian President Anwar Sadat's visit to Israel in November, 1977, sent shock waves around the Arab world. It also marked a turning point in the Syrian-Lebanese relationship because Syria suddenly found itself isolated and facing Israel alone. Syria then reversed its support for the Christians and began rearming and strengthening the Leftist-PLO forces. In the Syrian view Lebanon could never be allowed to separate itself from the conflict with Israel, nor could any unified Lebanese force be allowed to emerge. Syria assumed the role of an occupying force and spread its army over all areas of Lebanon, including the Christian sectors. The Christians turned to Israel for support, which vexed the Syrians even more.[10]

Although calm prevailed in Beirut for the next seven months, that was not the case elsewhere. In March, 1978, some twenty-five thousand Israeli soldiers invaded southern Lebanon in 'Operation Litani.' Prime Minister Menachem Begin claimed his intended goal was to annihilate the Palestinians and their infrastructure in the south. There were actually only a small number of Palestinian bases in the south, and he was hardly concerned about a few thousand innocent Lebanese civilians who were forced to flee their homes.

Begin's real objectives were two-fold. The first was to create a permanent foothold in southern Lebanon, for obvious reasons. The second, not so obvious, was the Litani River water source. Water is a major issue in the Middle East, almost as precious as oil. Begin wanted to divert the Litani for settlements in northern Israel. When Israel appeared to give in to international pressure a month later and withdraw its forces, the South Lebanon Army was created to take their place.[11]

The peculiar thing about southern Lebanon was that there were any number of men willing to fight as mercenaries: former *Kataeb* fighters, soldiers from the Lebanese Army – both Christian and Muslim – and local thugs, all ready to work together so long as their paychecks came regularly at the end of the month. The Israelis named a renegade major from the Lebanese Army, Saad Haddad, to head the South Lebanon Army in what Israel claimed was a 'self-declared security zone.'[12]

Two weeks later UNIFIL, the United Nations' peacekeeping force, was ordered into southern Lebanon to oversee the Israeli

---

10 Fisk, Robert, *op. cit*, pp. 142–143.
11 *Op. cit*, p. 148.
12 *Op. cit.*, p. 136.

withdrawal and assist the Lebanese government in effecting the return of its authority over the area. UNIFIL was unable to carry out its mission and was eventually ordered out of the area.[13]

From that point forward the dynamics of the Lebanese civil war changed rapidly. The two nations which would decide the future of Lebanon, Syria – with a force of some forty thousand men already on the ground – and Israel with its proxy army – had entered onto the battlefield.

The twenty-two year occupation of southern Lebanon by Israel did not finally end until May, 2000, and even then, although the Israeli troops were for the most part withdrawn, they continued to occupy the Shabba Farms near the Golan.

. . .

These days when Michel and I visit Lebanon every summer I leave him with his family and go off to spend a few days with my friend Edith. Last year instead of staying in Cornet Chehouan we traveled through the mountain villages above Tripoli in the North. When we came to Ehden, Edith drove me past the house where Tony Frangie and his family had been massacred by Bachir Gemayal's men. The idea of walking around that house where such awful things had happened made my flesh creep. I found myself imagining the bloody walls and the bodies on the floor. Tony Frangie, the son of President Sleiman Frangie, had harbored the same political ambitions as Bachir – to be President of the Republic.

Critics of the corrupt Frangie dynasty, which was renowned for its widespread racketeering – most notably in the cement business near Chekka in the North – claim that Tony's *Marada* militia began killing Bachir's men in order to keep *Kataeb* influence out of his fiefdom. Bachir decided to strike when the *Marada* killed the *Kataeb* leader in Zhorta and refused him burial in a local church. Bachir's

---

13 *Op. cit.*, p. 137.

father Pierre denounced his son's actions, calling them a violation of *Kataeb* principles. For many Christians it was worse than a crime. According to Robert Fisk in his book, *Pity the Nation*, "... it was a monumental error that complicated the plight of all the country's Christians and only played into the hands of the Israelis and Syrians who were interested in keeping Lebanon in turmoil for their own purposes."[14]

After Tony Frangie's assassination, Bachir Gemayal formed his own militia, The Lebanese Forces. When I met Bachir for the first time in 1975 he appeared the farthest thing from a warlord. Had my initial perception of him been pure illusion? Yes and no. Looking back now it is obvious that I chose to see only his chivalrous side then because I wanted a leader who was prepared to preserve Christian dominance in Lebanon at whatever cost. Even the Muslims who cared nothing about his defense of Christians felt at the time he was the only valid leader. He was part of a myth that insisted Lebanon needed fresh young leadership. I bought into that myth as people do in difficult times. I believed this charismatic young man was probably the only one who could restore stability and unify the country.[15]

. . .

On June 20, 1978, seven months of peace had come to an end with the bombing of the Christian enclaves by the Syrians. This was the attack Michel and I had been warned about by the American military attaché at Colonel Hayek's dinner party.

After the cease-fire we inspected the damage to our apartment and found the bullet hole in my apron. Michel and I decided it was wise to move across town to the Coral Beach Hotel. We were due to depart on a vacation to Greece in less than a week, and the hotel was a short distance from the airport.

---

14 *Op. cit.*, p. 76.
15 *Loc. cit.*

The problem was to find a safe way out of our neighborhood. I packed two suitcases and grabbed the black leather bag with our important documents while Michel called Kassab, who would know the best way out. In reality there were few options. We could not cross through the 'no-man's land' between the Museum and Barbir Hospital on the *Corniche* Mazra because the road was full of Syrian-manned roadblocks and we were not sure if Michel's name had finally been taken off their list.

Kassab suggested we leave by a back road parallel to Teyouneh. "If you're lucky," he said, "the Syrians won't be there."

"We'll just have to take our chances," I said, trying to sound brave and upbeat. "We must get to West Beirut if we're going to Greece."

A lone Syrian soldier was at the barricade. We slowed down and our hearts nearly jumped out of our chests as we approached him. His face passive, he waved us through with an arm and wrist movement almost like a girl's.

We stayed at the Coral Beach Hotel for a week. It was luxurious, set in a garden of pink laurel and bougainvillea not far from the sea. On most days a group of four French diplomats, in suits and ties despite the heat and humidity, sat by the pool sipping whiskey and munching pistachios. They formed a sharp contrast to the flashy arms dealers with their slicked-back hair, who entertained the movers and shakers of the city. So different from the French, these people sat there with open shirts, jewelry nestling on their hairy chests, laughing loudly and drinking copious amounts of wine. They pulled wads of notes out of their pockets with rough-looking hands, distributing them as though indifferent to whether they were French francs, Lebanese pounds or American dollars. One man had a scar down his right cheek and one black eye that focused somewhere else when he looked at you, so you were never quite sure whether he was actually staring at you or not. He liked to take the money for the waiter out of his pocket and peel it off with one of his very large hands.

One afternoon Nayla went running up to his table. She was trying to catch the ball her brother had thrown to her, and it slipped through her hands and rolled next to his chair. He picked it up with his large fingers and gave it back to her with a smile that revealed he was a parent too.

One evening Walid Jumblatt, the Druze leader, walked in and sat two tables away. One of the men with him said hello to Michel.

"Who is that?" I asked.

"He's one of my patients," replied Michel. "He is also Jumblatt's right-hand man. I saw him earlier today and he invited us to lunch tomorrow."

"Good idea," I said. "You never know, we might need his help getting to the airport."

We did have lunch with him and afterward he offered to park our car in his underground garage and escort us to the airport.

The day before our departure for Greece, Michel took a taxi to Hamra Street to pick up our airline tickets. At noon the children and I took our places at a pool-side table, expecting him to return any minute. I had just ordered a cold beer when several Israeli F-16 bombers flew in low, breaking the sound barrier. The air around us shook and blast waves rippled across the pool. People stampeded for the nearest door. So intent was one woman on saving herself that she left her small child on the beach. When the four French diplomats jumped up in unison and ran for the hotel lobby the arms dealers burst into raucous laughter. The children and I did too, particularly since the Israeli planes had in all likelihood already returned to their base.

. . .

In Greece we rented a villa on the island of Skiathos in the Aegean with our friends Gino and Nancy and their three sons. From the spacious terrace we could look out over the lush green cliffs to our own private beach. We had to wear sunglasses outdoors because of the reflection from all the whitewashed walls. The red, peach and fuchsia bougainvillea were stunning against the backdrop of white walls and deep blue sky. For two weeks it was like paradise and we forgot Beirut and the war. We sunbathed, we played tennis, we drank good wine, we ate feta and olive salad, we ate succulent barbequed pork, we laughed, we went on long walks on the beaches and in the hills. Then one night I was sitting on the balcony watching the sun go down and I heard that BBC voice somewhere in a distant room.

"This is Derek Shambles speaking to you from Beirut, where the situation has once again deteriorated."

I saw Michel get up and walk into the back room to listen more closely, and something in me sank. I tried to listen to the broadcast but it was too far off, and I stayed where I was, a sick feeling inside me. I knew what would happen next. Michel went to the phone and dialed and I heard him speaking Arabic to his mother or Nademe. He came back to the balcony and announced, "Cathy, I'm going back to Beirut."

The rest of my vacation turned into a bad dream the morning Michel left Skiathos. According to the BBC, the airport was closed due to intense fighting. I had no way of knowing if Michel had arrived before it closed or, if he had, whether or not he was able to cross safely into East Beirut. I kept my haunting images to myself so as not to worry the children.

Most days I awoke before the others and took the portable radio out onto the veranda to listen to the BBC for news from Beirut. One morning Gino walked out as I was listening.

"Beirut had another horrific day of battles," I said.

Gino did not respond. Instead he picked up his newspaper and began reading.

"Gino, didn't you hear me?" I asked.

"Oh, I heard you," he said. "But spare me."

"But you're from Beirut. Your parents live there," I said. "How can you not be interested in what's going on?"

He turned to me and put the paper down, his eyes gone dead. I could tell he was very tired of me. "I've worked hard to be able to take this vacation and I don't want to have to worry about a thing. Got that, Cathy?"

"Well I'm sorry, but I can't stop thinking about it. I've got loved ones back there. I'm worried about Michel getting killed."

"Never mind that. For the next two weeks do me a favor. Keep the bad news to yourself. Unless we get a call from somebody saying Michel has been hurt, it's highly unlikely that he is. Okay? So relax."

Gino had organized the whole vacation so I had no choice even though it was like keeping a volcano inside me. For the children's sake I wore a smile, I played volleyball on the beach, I went snorkeling and fishing, I dressed for dinner, and I put on make-up. And all the while inside my head a tempest raged. I was offended by Gino's refusal to understand my emotional needs. What I did not realize at the time was the precarious state of my mental health, although it was probably very obvious to Gino. I babbled on about Beirut, not even conscious of how emotional I was, and certainly never intending to offend anyone, but I did. I was demanding more than our friendship could bear.

After we returned to Athens Michel called. I remember picking up the receiver and saying 'hello.'

His voice said very quietly, "It's started again. They're shelling Achrafieh. You have to stay there. It isn't safe to come home."

"But what am I to do? I'm all alone with the children. Everyone here is upset with me."

His voice was calm. "You need to relax, Cathy. It'll be okay."

Two weeks later Michel finally called to say we could come home, which was a tremendous relief. I was going crazy in Athens. Nancy had already told me the children and I would have to move to a hotel. She said a friend was coming to visit and she needed my room, but I did not know if her explanation was true.

When Michel met our plane he immediately took us off toward Jounieh, where his brothers had recently purchased an old house.

"Why aren't we going home?" I asked

"We can't, it's too dangerous in Beirut. And besides, our apartment was robbed. It's a mess."

When I recovered from that shock he explained that the culprit had probably been our concierge, Karim, the only one who knew we were away. He had left the Persian carpets because they were too heavy to carry down eight flights of stairs, and he underestimated the value of our artifacts, completely overlooking the silverware and china. I was thankful for that. I did not care that he took all the electric appliances, we could replace a radio or an electric typewriter or a television. I was upset about the amber worry beads which had been a special souvenir from Papa. They cost very little but had great sentimental value. The stereo was a big loss because we played music all the time, but at least he didn't steal our LPs. We could not go right out and buy a new stereo, we had to wait until we could afford a nice one, because they were expensive. He had taken my perfumes, my scarves, and Michel's silk ties. And it was very annoying that he had taken the guns. Without them we felt even more vulnerable.

War transformed Jounieh, a once-tranquil seaport some fifteen miles north of Beirut, into the Christian capitol. When Beirut divided into East and West and its ancient *souks* succumbed to the ravages of war, many Christian businessmen had reopened their stores in Jounieh. The war also produced a windfall for area residents who preyed on fleeing refugees. Shopkeepers hiked up prices on vegetables, fruits, meats, and bread, and real estate agents made millions, demanding and getting exorbitant rental rates.

Jacques' and Raymond's house was far enough from the commercial center to be peaceful and secluded. In the front of the house was a small courtyard with palm trees and low, dusty green shrubs, which opened onto the old Jounieh road. The green front door stayed locked at all times for security. Mercifully, a major highway some miles away diverted much of Jounieh's traffic from this narrow, coastal byway. We entered the one-story stone house by opening a gate to the left of the courtyard and walking down a sidewalk which stretched the length of the house. At the end we turned right and entered a large, low-walled private terrace directly over the sea. From this lovely spot we had a breathtakingly beautiful view of the Mediterranean sunset. Turning the opposite direction we could marvel at the spectacular green mountain range jutting abruptly toward the sky. This would have been a perfectly peaceful sanctuary if we had not had to share it with twelve other people: Wadia and her maid, Andrée with her family and maid, and Jacques and his family, who had come from Lattakia for a brief visit before leaving for Boston.

The large room just off the terrace served as both living and dining rooms. We used the straight back chairs and long Formica table for both socializing and eating. The bathroom and small kitchen, neither of which had hot water, were located to the left. There were two enormous rooms beyond that as you walked toward the front of the house. One was used as a bedroom for Andrée and her family, and Jacques and his family used the other one. Nademe and Andrée's maid Hasna slept on the living room floor on mattresses. There were three more bedrooms along the side of the house opposite these enormous rooms. The four of us shared the one at the front of the house closest to the road, Wadia took the one at the opposite end just off the living room and Michel used the middle bedroom as his office, where he saw patients three afternoons a week.

Michel went to the hospital in Achrafieh most mornings. Since he did not return until noon I volunteered to go out and buy the daily provisions for twelve people, which gave me a necessary break from the stress of living with so many family members. I began to wonder why I had ever wanted to come home. Even a hotel in Athens would have been better than this. At least Naim and Nayla were happy. If I was out of the house running errands either Nademe or Hasna fixed them breakfast before they left for the beach with their cousin Philippe, Andrée's youngest son, two years older than Naim.

The major activities of the day started shortly after siesta. An ideal day was one in which at least two or three visitors dropped by to play cards with Wadia. She was happiest when so engaged, and so were we. That freed us to play wild and raucous ping-pong matches with our friends at the front of the house just outside our bedroom. Some die-hard players brought their own paddles, but to no avail. Nobody ever beat the reigning champ, Michel.

In August, 1978, we joined Kaslik Beach Club, a fifteen acre paradise of manicured lawns, pink laurel and red bougainvillea. It had a choice of either an Olympic-sized pool or a sandy beach, and was located on the bay of Jounieh not far from our house. Several of our friends and our children's friends already belonged. It was important to have a common place to meet, to relax and discuss the ever-changing events unfolding around us, particularly that summer when everyone we knew had taken refuge out of Beirut.

Bachir's Lebanese Forces were openly courting Israel, and received arms shipments at a beach not far from us. Rumors abounded about what might happen next. While we were powerless to change the course of events, it was essential to our collective mental stability at least to try and figure out what was happening. In reality we were nothing more than a bunch of addicts who needed our daily fix of rumors.

After August 15 I no longer had to worry for Michel's safety. The Syrians cut the road from Jounieh to Beirut and he could not get to the hospital. It was the only time in my life I was grateful to the Syrians. What remained of the summer passed as uneventfully as possible, given the turmoil surrounding us.

In mid-November a cease-fire was announced. As part of the deal the Syrians agreed to reopen the road to Beirut and pull their forces out of Achrafieh. Wadia and Nademe went back to Beirut, Andrée and her family packed and left and Jacques and his family flew to Boston. Our family was not as fortunate. Our neighborhood was far from calm, and prospects for an early return appeared bleak. If the schools decided to open, Naim and Nayla would have to commute from Jounieh. Selfishly I wished the schools would remain closed until we could go back to our own apartment.

When their school did open it lasted all of two days. As part of the cease-fire agreement the Syrians had retreated from Achrafieh and set up camp in the fields surrounding *Jamhour*, so the Jesuits decided to close the school since they could not guarantee the safety of the students.

It was the end of November, 1978, when four miraculous things happened.

Andrée invited us to stay with her in Beirut until we found a place to live.

Shortly after we settled into her apartment Jacques called from Boston. He suggested we move into an apartment he continued to rent a few blocks away from Andrée in Achrafieh.

A school in the same neighborhood, *Dame de Nazareth*, agreed to take all of *Jamhour*'s students. School would begin December 1. The classes were crowded and the teachers were overworked, but no one seemed to mind. That was the Lebanese way of handling a crisis, everyone helped and everyone participated. All of us knew how important it was to keep our children's minds busy, even if it meant doubling up on students. Both teachers and parents were willing to work together to do whatever was necessary to give the children a proper school year.

And fourth, my brothers-in-law guaranteed Michel three thousand Lebanese pounds a month – approximately one thousand dollars at that time – until his work picked up again. The Lebanese pound stayed at this three-to-one ratio until the mid-eighties when it fell to six pounds to the dollar. By the early nineties it had collapsed to three thousand pounds to the dollar. Today it is the equivalent of one thousand five hundred pounds to the dollar.

As we prepared to move into Jacques' house I made several trips to Badaro to retrieve kitchenware, cookbooks, games, our winter clothes – anything that would help us feel at home in his apartment. I found Badaro a battle-scarred neighborhood with a few intrepid souls who had stayed behind only because they had nowhere else to go. The buildings, including ours, looked desolate and haunted, pockmarked and blackened by bullets and explosions. Brown and leafless poplars rose from the pavement like upturned broomsticks. Once again the windows had been blown out of our apartment. I resisted the urge to repair the shredded curtains, to brush off the broken glass strewn over my couch, to salvage whatever might be gone before my next visit. I stored my apartment and my belongings in some recess in the back of my mind. I had done this every time we fled, learning to think only in present-time. If we were safer elsewhere, in this case Jacques' apartment, then I needed to concentrate all my energy on that alone.

While we were still in Jacques' apartment and before any of us could exercise an ounce of common sense, Foxy Lady, a German Shepherd, joined our family. Edith and Fouad's dog Tina had a litter of ten puppies. I do not recall actually planning to get a dog, it just happened. And we were all smitten with this one in particular.

"Look how fast she runs," said Nayla. "And she is much foxier than her litter-mates." The name stuck.

. . .

We moved back to our own apartment in June, 1979, after an entire year away. This time our return was different, it was more purposefully organized. The children and I were scheduled to leave for the States just as soon as they finished their school year at the end of the month. I generally went back to the States every two years. I could have rushed and had us moved back as early as May and been better organized before our trip, but I did not want to disrupt the school routine. They could walk to school from Jacques' house and many of their friends lived in the neighborhood, so the least I could do was wait until the end of the school year to take them to the States.

Leila and I worked several hours each day, nothing exhausting, just a slow easy pace. We still faced the same gruesome cleanup, particularly after a year-long absence. The windows had to be replaced. Rain and wind had blown in a year's worth of dirt and grime and firmly embedded it in the furniture. The cupboards and closets needed to be emptied and everything washed and put back, and new curtains made. To my great delight, since I had thought it had been stolen, I found my Singer sewing machine abandoned in a corner. Apparently the handle broke when Karim had tried to carry it off so he left it behind. Now I could mend my curtains. And this time my terrace garden had survived.

Despite my careful planning we had only one frantic day in our apartment before we left for our vacation in the States. I was exhausted. I stayed up ironing until five in the morning, but it really did not matter because I knew the jet lag would do me in anyway when I got to America.

. . .

When the 1979–1980 school year began the children were able to return to *Jamhour*. It was only the second normal school year in Beirut since the onset of civil war in 1975. Now thirteen and twelve, Naim and Nayla participated for the first time in after-school track and field activities. They skied almost every weekend. Naim was a racer, attacking the slopes with speed and precision while Nayla was more careful, preferring a slower, more calculated descent. In December, 1980, they took up karate and would eventually win competitions in their respective divisions.

. . .

Beirut was not constantly at war. During the peaceful times when everything went back to something we could call 'normal,' I was still totally mesmerized by my city. I often refer to it as being like a love affair with someone who was completely out of his mind. But there were so many times when it was a joyous place. That is why I fell in love with it in the first place, and why I stayed. That was why I found it so hard not to believe it would sort itself out some day so that I could again dance at the Caves du Roi and have dinner with friends at Le Vieux Quartier, where the chef prepared his ambrosial Sauce Bolognese and decanted his best *Brunello di Montalcino*, a wine which tasted as if I were kissing the lips of someone I loved.

The glorious calm lasted until the spring of 1981.

8

Pets, Rockets and Snipers

*I*n the spring my container garden was particularly lovely with fuchsia ivy geraniums cascading down white walls. The tall wispy pink laurel, the gardenias and jasmine, yellow and red hibiscus, organdy pink begonias, the fragrant Queen Elizabeth roses, finally had regained all their prewar lushness. I had already given several dinner parties on the terrace, the children were back at *Jamhour* and Foxy Lady had just turned two.

Perhaps she was more high-spirited than most dogs, but no doubt that was because we were a lively family and our personalities affected her behavior. Foxy, unlike other German Shepherds – who generally respond to only one master – had four to whom she was entirely devoted. She primarily depended on Michel for her walks, but I fed her and let her share my bed. She could decipher the sound of the children's school bus out of a street full of traffic when it was still a block away. Her ears would stand straight up like fine-tuned antennae tracking the exact location of the bus. She followed its noisy engine sounds and knew precisely when it stopped in front of our building. At that point she would stand up, walk to the front door and sit there while she waited first for the sound of the elevator, then the giggling voices of Naim and Nayla talking as they ascended. As soon as the children reached the eighth floor Foxy announced their arrival with joyous barking.

On family outings she invariably grabbed the right back-seat window, to the dismay of Naim and Nayla, who were left to haggle over the other window. Her favorite destination was Cornet Chehouan where she enjoyed the freedom to run about. Occasionally we took her to a beach north of Byblos, where we would throw balls to her in the water and make her paddle about to retrieve them.

Foxy did not like suitcases because instinctively she knew they represented a disruption of her life. One Saturday morning when she saw Naim put a suitcase by the front door she leapt up and followed him back to his room. She panicked when she saw Nayla packing too, and trotted nervously into the kitchen. She sat herself down in front of me and stared into my eyes until she caught my attention. There were times when I could not resist teasing Foxy, waiting until the last possible moment to relieve her anxiety so I could hear her excited coyote-like howl. From the kitchen she saw Michel and Naim moving the suitcases into the hallway and onto the elevator. She bolted toward them only to hear Naim say, "Stay, Foxy," as he closed the door. Dejected, she fell to the ground like a discarded mop, laid her head on her front paws and whimpered.

When we were ready to walk out the door Naim called Foxy, made her sit and slipped her leash around her neck and led her into the elevator. She howled all the way to ground level, keeping it up until she was certain she had permission to jump into the car.

However, there were certain days when taking her along was not an option. One was April 15, 1981.

. . .

It started around noon. I was in the kitchen adding the finishing touches to my coq au vin, sautéing onions and mushrooms. I had another half-hour before Michel arrived from the hospital, just enough time to wash and cut the salad and prepare the rice. While the onions finished, I began frying the vermicelli with olive oil. When it was browned I would add the rice, salt and water. Over the crackling sound of hot oil I thought I heard a noise, a thud. I pulled the pan off the fire and listened. The unmistakable sound made my scalp tingle.

"No," I moaned. "Not again."

Foxy's ears stood straight up in response to my cry and she looked at me. "I don't know, girl. Let's go find out."

I turned off the burners under the onions and rice and walked outside. Assuming it was Israeli planes, I went first to the south end of the balcony. They routinely bombed a target in the southern suburbs and called it 'retaliation.' I heard the thud again, but the wind had picked up and it was difficult to determine the precise location. I walked around the balcony faster, and when I turned east I saw the familiar billowing cloud of grey smoke. The bombs were falling near the children's school.

My next door neighbor Andrée also had two of her children at *Jamhour*. When the war began we agreed that one of us would be in charge of bringing our children home should an emergency arise. In spite of an eighteen month respite I knew what needed to be done. I ran to the north side of the balcony just off the kitchen and shouted her name. Her eighth floor apartment, parallel with mine, was only some thirty-five feet away. Her maid came running onto her balcony when she heard my voice.

"Sitt Andrée isn't home," she said.

"Just tell her that Sitt Cathy has gone to get the children from school," I shouted. I thought of waiting for Michel to return from the hospital, but what if he got caught in traffic and took longer than usual getting home? Instead I left him a note on the kitchen table. I turned to run toward the door but tripped and almost fell over Foxy. I had not noticed her trembling in my shadow. I wrapped my arms around her body. "Don't worry, Foxy. I'll be back soon."

I went down the stairs as fast as I could. I never used an elevator when bombs were falling.

My VW Bug was parked in front of the building. I turned the

car around in the alley, drove down Badaro and turned right on Damascus Street. There must have been other cars on the road, but I did not notice them. I do remember slowing down in the middle of the Sami Sohl intersection at the next corner, but the rest – the drive through Fourn ni Chebak, the landmarks I knew so well, the tightly-woven row of stores, apartment buildings, cinemas, and churches along the two lane street – was only a blur.

I did think about snipers and wondered if they were back on the job. Although they had not worked for eighteen months, they had the uncanny habit of reappearing at the first signs of unrest. I kept seeing our friend Father Jerfaneon with a sniper's bullet hole in the front of his head. Did the same fate await me? He was killed in the intersection I was about to drive through, at the end of Fourn ni Chebak.

Jamhour and its spacious grounds sat atop a small hill that dominated the Defense Ministry to the west, the neighborhood of Hazmiya to the south, and the open fields to the east where the Syrian soldiers had settled when they retreated from Achrafieh in 1978. I parked opposite the front door in one of the designated lanes. As I walked toward the main entrance the bombs – as near as I could tell – were falling close to the Defense Ministry, less than a kilometer away.

When I entered the school I heard the muffled sounds of a distant disturbance somewhere down the normally quiet halls of *Jamhour*. I followed the buzz downstairs, past the principal's office and along the empty corridors. The closer I got to the cafeteria, the louder the noise. When I opened the door I was reminded of a boisterous monkey house, only here the occupants all wore the same navy blue and white uniforms. The loud, unrestrained screeches of some seven hundred students venting their nervous excitement were little different from the harsh shrieks of those lesser primates. I scanned the large room for Nayla's teacher, our friend Père Mayet; I knew my children would be with him. I spotted them and waved from the middle of the room. Nayla rushed into my arms and Naim hugged me but then abruptly let go, wanting to tell me how angry he was.

I thought that was good because he could not be angry and afraid at the same time. His teacher had not let them out of the classroom even when a bomb exploded some two hundred feet away.

"Finally, I just stood up and walked toward the door," Naim said. "And you know what? The rest of my class walked out too."

Nayla became silent when she was frightened, and while she rarely cried it was obvious now from the way she tightened her arms around my waist that she was in distress.

"The noise was awful, Mommy. It scared me a lot," she said. She was referring to Stalin's Organs, the Syrian weapon of choice, which fired seven rockets in rapid succession.

I sent Naim off to find Andrée's children. When he returned we bid Père Mayet goodbye and left. Naim insisted on sitting in the front seat, so Nayla was obliged to climb in the back with Nabil and Farid. While they were arranging themselves in the back seat with their book bags, a bomb fell nearby and I heard glass shatter. I told myself if I stayed calm so would they. I got back out of the car, pulled my seat forward and tried to help them, shifting one book bag into the back compartment, the other into the front next to Naim's feet. I was pleading with God the whole time.

When I got back in and shut my door I glanced over at Naim. He was staring at me, reading the fear in my face. Farid, seated to Nayla's right, began joking about where he hoped a bomb would fall, but I missed the punch line. I was too distracted trying to decide the safest way around the Defense Ministry.

As I sped down the main road I got the creepy feeling – the only car on this spacious four lane highway with no buildings on my left, and a ravine to my right – that the bombs were following us and gaining ground with each explosion. Of course they were not specifically trying to bomb my car. The Syrians probably just wanted to take out the road.

What I saw in my rear view mirror was strange; it looked like the road itself was erupting. At first there was just a very small shimmer, and when I glanced back again, everything behind me appeared to explode into the air. I pushed harder on the accelerator.

Another bomb went off at the edge of the ravine on my right. I watched in my rear view mirror as dirt spewed once more into the air like an erupting volcano.

Through all this the chatter in the back seat never stopped, fading in and out of my consciousness as I tried to keep the car on the road and still pay attention to the children.

Farid said something about a school bully crying. The next minute all four children were cheering, "Serves him right."

I thought the third explosion, which seemed to be right behind us, might actually lift the car off the road.

As we approached the next intersection Naim, who had discarded his navy blue blazer and opened his shirt collar, yelled, "Watch out, Mommy, here comes a car!"

I crossed into Fourn ni Chebak and traveled through that neighborhood so quickly that only Naim noticed when I turned left onto Badaro. The three in the back seat finally fell silent when they realized we were in Andrée's garage. I saw her waiting by the door as I drove in. I parked the car, intending to keep it there until the bombing stopped, and walked toward her.

"Why don't you all stay with us for a while, until it quiets down?" she said.

I was about to accept when Nayla said, "Please, Mommy, let's just run and get home, I want to see Poppy."

We walked up to the ground floor and while Andrée and her children continued up to her eighth-floor apartment my children and I went outside. We only had to make a left out the door, cross a small driveway that separated our two buildings, cut diagonally across the sidewalk to the opposite end of our building and turn left. As we crossed the driveway I heard the 'swish' of a bullet pass my ear, and I screamed for Naim and Nayla to take cover against the wall of our building. I was carrying their heavy book bags so they were able to react quickly to the sniper-fire. I assumed he was at his usual vantage point on one of the taller buildings at the end of Badaro Street. With our backs to the wall we were safely out of the field of his scope, since our building sat much farther back from the street than the others. We edged our way along the wall to the front door.

It did not register with me that we were safe until I heard Foxy sniffing under Michel's office door, and her tail batting against the door jamb. Those joyous sounds almost took the edge off the tense afternoon. I know she worked the same marvel on the children because their stiff shoulders relaxed in reaction to her sounds. Before we even began to climb the stairs, Michel's office door opened. Within seconds he and Foxy stood in front of us. Michel could hardly get close enough to give us a kiss because Foxy was bobbing up and down and licking our faces. Michel took the book bags from me and led the way. When we got to the office I collapsed on the black leather couch.

I kept a tin of powdered milk in the office kitchen and asked Michel to make us some hot chocolate. There is something very soothing and restorative about holding a warm drink in your hands, bringing it to your nose and inhaling its aroma. It was the first time I had heard the sound of a bullet that near to me, but there was no question in my mind what it was. I knew instinctively a bullet had come that close. It had happened once to Michel when he was on the balcony watering the plants, and he had described the sound in the same way. But he was alive and so was I, so I put the sniper incident out of my mind.

I had become quite good at storing bits of traumatic baggage I did not want to think about, in retrospect a very unhealthy thing to do. Eventually it got me into a lot of trouble. At the time there was so much going on in our lives, so many life-threatening incidents, that it did not seem helpful to dwell on any of them. Now when I think back to that day, I wonder what would have happened to my children if they had seen their mother drop down on the sidewalk, or I them, without so much as a "Goodbye," or an "I love you."

After a few sips of hot chocolate, Naim and Nayla began talking to their father. They told him what happened at school when the shelling began, and how they got home. Much to my surprise Nayla

A BEIRUT HEART: ONE WOMAN'S WAR

was the first to mention the sniper. "Tell him, Mommy," she said, "tell him about the sniper who shot at us downstairs."

I was pleased that she already seemed to be handling it, because next she complained, "Naim got to sit up front coming home. It isn't fair, Poppy. Next time, it will be my turn. Tell him. He always gets to sit there and I always have to sit in the back," and I knew she had recovered.

"Be glad you were in the back today, Nayla," Naim retorted.

It was one of those moments when I knew what he was going to say before he opened his mouth. I also knew his words would hurt his sister, perhaps shatter her delicate shell.

"If you only knew ..." he continued.

I tried to catch his eye. With my finger to my lips I tried to send him the message, 'please don't tell what you saw.' But he did not notice me.

"Bombs were following us the whole way home. I was watching them in the side view mirror. Some of them fell right behind us. They were breaking up the road. Asphalt was flying everywhere." He turned to Michel, "You should have seen Mommy. She had her foot to the floor the whole time. She could hardly control the car." Then he looked at me, "Isn't that right, Mommy?"

I wanted him to stop. Couldn't he see his sister's distress? Couldn't he see how any relief she might have felt about getting home and surviving a sniper's bullet had suddenly vanished? Couldn't he see how her jaw had slowly fallen open when she understood what a close call we had? When she got up from her chair, walked over to a mattress in the corner and sat down against the wall with her knees to her chest, I had no idea what she would do with this new bit of traumatic information.

Naim did not seem to notice his sister's reaction, but continued talking to his father. But Foxy sensed something was wrong. She got up from her spot in the middle of the room and walking over to Nayla, climbed onto the mattress and sat beside her. I watched the way the dog laid her head in Nayla's lap, the way she looked at her with her gentle eyes. As if responding to an invitation, Nayla began stroking the soft, silky spot on Foxy's head, which she loved to do, and I saw her start to breathe more deeply.

. . .

After taking a break for lunch the militiamen generally got hungry again around six-thirty or seven. As soon as the guns fell silent we went on up to our apartment. I sent Naim and Nayla off to take showers and get into their pajamas. I went into the kitchen. I was hungry, and I was thinking about the unfinished coq au vin and rice which I had to prepare.

The pan in which I had cooked the chicken was on the floor, and a few of the pearl onions and one mushroom had rolled under the oven. Foxy had somehow managed to nudge the pan off the burner.

"Who ate the chicken?" I scowled, looking the dog straight in the eye. The guilty party sank to the floor as if in a faint.

. . .

A few days after the Syrian bombing, we heard rumors of another possible flare-up. It seemed Bachir Gemayal was fomenting a major showdown in Zahle, a quiet Greek Catholic town in the Bekaa Valley some forty miles northeast of Beirut. He was trying to work both sides, Syrians and Israelis, against each other. At the time Zahle and the whole of the Bekaa Valley were under Syrian influence. Bachir knew that Syria would see any attempt to penetrate Zahle as pure provocation. To insure that Syrian President Assad would react, Bachir's men killed some Syrian soldiers. Assad had no recourse but to respond, even if he did not want a fight, and so he fell right into Bachir's trap.

When the Syrians attacked Bachir's forces he publicly proclaimed that Zahle was a Christian stronghold in danger of being captured by the Syrians. The foreign press rallied to support his claim. Headlines read things like, 'Christian minority fights masses of Islam, hell-bent on their destruction.' I do not know whether Bachir orchestrated the entire scheme himself, or if he worked hand-in-hand with Israeli Prime Minister Begin. At any rate Begin stepped in and proclaimed Israel protector of the Lebanese Christians.[16]

Meanwhile the Syrians had stopped bombing Beirut, and Michel suggested I take the children and go to the house in Jounieh for a long weekend, since the schools were still closed. Apparently even the Education Ministry wanted to see what would happen in Zahle and how it would affect Beirut, before making any decision on school closure. The idea of a leisurely weekend at the sea was very enticing, even though Michel was not able to join us. It was particularly appealing because Wadia was in Boston visiting Jacques and his family, Nademe was in Lattakia, and neither was expected back before the first part of July. I did not want to be alone with Naim and Nayla in the big house so I asked Gisèle to join us.

By now I had become very good at packing. I could have the carpets, artifacts, china, and silver packed up and stored in an hour. I kept Michel's black leather briefcase with our important papers and a stash of cash ready for an emergency departure. We had already fled our apartment nine times, so I knew what to take. Despite these past experiences, the list had grown to include a dog, her vitamins, dry food, and toys. No matter how much you love them, pets present enormous challenges in wartime. Decisions on when to leave home and where to seek refuge often depended on who would accept animals. We were lucky we could take Foxy with us to the house in Jounieh.

Gisèle owned a fifteen-year-old parrot named Vico who lived in a cage four feet high and four feet round that barely fit through conventional doors. Vico's cage would not fit in a regular-sized car, so Gisèle had to hire a large Chevrolet Impala to take her to Jounieh.

We met there just before noon. After opening up the house I discovered we had no gas canisters for cooking. We piled Naim, Nayla, and Foxy into the Bug and took off in search of gas and something

---

16 Fisk, *op. cit.*, p. 188.

to eat. To our great surprise all the shops and restaurants were closed in support of Bachir Gemayal and his men in Zahle. I drove on to the post office and put in a call to Michel. Fortunately he had not yet gone to the hospital. I explained our dilemma and my two choices. Either I returned to get some canisters, or he could forget his patients for once and join us for the weekend. My guess is that he was already having second thoughts about staying behind in the hot city. His eagerness to bring the gas, despite having to fight the weekend traffic pouring out of Beirut at that time of day, was a little out of character.

Gisèle was a news junky who held her small portable radio to her ear for some sixteen hours a day in search of the latest battle. That was how we learned, at the top of the hour, that shortly before 2:00 P.M. the Syrians had begun bombing the Christian sectors of Achrafieh, Sin el Fil, Teyouneh and Badaro. I had spoken to Michel around 1:30, but I had no way of knowing if he had left before the bombing began, or if he was caught in a hail of rockets in the mad exodus from Beirut. I was greatly relieved when he strolled nonchalantly in the back door around 2:30; he knew nothing of the bombing and said he had probably left only minutes before it all began. I could finally put my blinders back on. I could forget Beirut, Bachir and Zahle, and concentrate instead on my family and enjoying the warm weather and the beach outside our back door. I took comfort in the children's delight as they played in the sea, and laughed myself silly watching Foxy Lady dog paddle as she tried to keep up with them.

In fact at that moment life was as good as it was going to get, at least for us humans.

From the minute he arrived at the beach house Vico delighted in his new home atop the white refrigerator in the left-hand corner of the living room. With three languages at his command he held court before everyone, including any visitors who walked through the door. Depending on his mood Vico, who was about a foot tall and had a striking red crown atop a gray-feathered body, was capable of insulting our guests in the crudest imaginable language. He knew just about every bad word there was in Arabic to describe someone's mother, sister, and then some. On an average day he imitated a telephone ringing even though there was not one in the house, and he answered it in Gisèle's voice. Sometimes when it struck his fancy he would impersonate her father asking the imaginary caller his name, inquiring how he was, was he sick, was the weather nice, and finally ending with, "Vico is well, thank you." At the end of the day, when he wanted some peace and quiet, he would holler, "Gisèle, Vico dodo" (sleep). She would dutifully cover his cage with a white sheet and move him to a quiet, dark room.

Foxy Lady was Vico's principal preoccupation. Obviously quite aware he was safely perched out of her reach, Vico loved to screech, "Foxy-Foxy-Foxy," in one rapid run-on machine gun phrase. When Foxy heard her name and came charging into the room Vico stopped abruptly. I would have sworn he smiled every time he saw the dog's bewildered expression.

. . .

At least once a week Michel visited our apartment on Badaro to check for damage and water the plants. In our absence our neighbor Mrs. Eid was taking care of our home. She and her family were refugees from Damour, a village in the south which had been ravaged by the Palestinians. I had not been back to our apartment in over a month, so one morning I decided to accompany Michel. We waved good-bye to Naim, Nayla, Gisèle, Foxy, and Vico. It was so nice to close the car door and be completely alone with Michel for a change. I could not remember the last time we had done anything by ourselves. Michel drove while I relaxed with my head against the back of the seat. We talked about nothing in particular, just the idle dreamy ramblings that spill out when one is content.

It was a beautiful calm spring day when we arrived on Badaro Street around 10:00 A.M. Even the mid-morning traffic was reassuring. A delivery truck parked outside Azam's suggested he was finally getting a fresh shipment of *charcuterie* and patés from Paris. In the next block Alfonso would probably have choice tenderloins on his menu again, and gulf shrimp grilled just the way I liked them. Somewhere bread was baking and my stomach reacted to the aroma even though I had just had breakfast. I touched Michel's arm and said, "Smell that? I'm getting hungry again."

"Me, too," he said. "Let's buy half a dozen baguettes to take back to Jounieh."

We had chosen a good time to come, Badaro's day to receive water. It was already flowing into the storage tanks on the roof, so we began to water the plants. While I tended to the ones indoors, Michel attached the hose to the kitchen faucet and began watering the garden. Thirty minutes into what was usually a forty-five minute chore, all semblance of calm dissolved in the metallic sound of wheels rolling over asphalt. Whenever I heard that noise it reminded me of hundreds of sharp steel blades clashing together at the same time.

Our neighborhood had been under the protection of the Lebanese Army, with their tanks positioned on street corners, since 1975. In the past six years we had not only grown accustomed to these tanks, we felt more secure knowing they were there. If the Army suddenly moved their tanks for any reason we knew it signified impending danger. A change in their position meant either that they had received orders to take up battle stations – perhaps on the periphery of our neighborhood to repel an attack – or worse, they had been told to take cover because they would be no match for incoming rockets. In either case we realized that if the Lebanese Army was leaving our quiet neighborhood we had better do the same.

"Let's get out of here," shouted Michel, grabbing my arm and yanking me out the front door. We got as far as the next landing when the first bomb fell, so close the railing vibrated under my hand. Frightened, I stumbled and banged my shoulder against the wall. Michel took hold of my hand and guided me down the stairs, urging me to hurry along despite my painful knees.

"Go on ahead," I finally said. "Please, just go. I'll come down on my own."

"Of course, I won't leave you, don't say such a silly thing."

We had just turned the corner on the fourth-floor landing when the whole building rocked.

"I think we took a hit," I yelled.

Michel suddenly turned around and tried to put me over his shoulder but I resisted. "Please, Michel, you can't do that, darling, thank you very much, but you can't."

I willed my stiff knees to work a little harder. In the next instant something, probably a door, blew into the stairwell just above us from the force of an explosion.

"Jesus," I screamed, "I hope that wasn't our front door."

Debris began filtering down the stairwell and covering us in white dust. We did not stop when we got to the ground floor. Michel led me by the hand down one more flight of stairs to the shelter. He pushed on the door but it would not open. He tried again, then he began banging.

"Mrs. Eid, are you there? It's us, the Sultans, please open up."

From the other side of the door we heard her voice, asking, "Who is it?" wanting to be sure it really was us before unlocking the door.

Mrs. Eid and her husband Elie had transformed the once rat infested, dingy basement into comfortable living quarters complete with bedroom and bath. They had built a wall around the driest section of the basement and closed it off with a door. For electricity Elie tapped into the power source in the concierge's apartment on the first floor, stringing wire down to the basement. Bare light bulbs hung throughout the new room. I remember they swayed and squeaked eerily after each explosion. Like all Lebanese, the Eids were prepared for power outages with a supply of batteries, flashlights, candles, and lots of matches. Mrs. Eid had put together an impressive kitchen, complete with a stove like mine, a refrigerator, sink, and cabinets.

I was struck by the dozens of branches of orange blossoms on the counter. Before I could ask where she managed to collect so many, she knew what I wanted to know.

"Last week when it was quiet Elie drove to Damour. From the abandoned orchards near our old house he cut the fullest branches, just as I had taught him to do years ago. It was such a lovely surprise."

She explained that every spring, at the height of the blossoming season, she carefully picked the delicate flowers and simmered them in sugar syrup, allowing the liquid to reduce to its purest essence before she bottled it. When it was wanted, she diluted it with water to flavor coffee and sweets.

I did not notice the cut on Michel's hand until we sat down together on the worn red velvet couch directly under one of the lights in the middle of the room. When I asked Mrs. Eid if she could spare some water because I wanted to clean his wound, she insisted on doing it herself. This short, round woman found joy in whatever she did. Her smile and incredibly blue eyes – all the more noticeable behind oversized glasses with baby blue frames – spoke the same gracious language. When she had finished with his hand, she put water on for tea. I moved to get up from the couch to help, but she insisted I stay seated. She had her back to me so I could not see what else she was doing. A short time later she returned with a tray of cups of hot tea and a plate of apricot marmalade sandwiches cut into squares. I picked one up and held it between my thumb and forefinger. The Arab bread was warm and I could feel the soft gooey chunks of fruit through the thin bread. I began eating, taking tiny bites. With each explosion outside the flavors seemed to explode in my mouth. How strange it was to be eating such glorious food when bombs were falling around us! I was ravenous; I could have eaten a dozen of the delicate sandwiches.

I sat back on the couch when I finished eating and looked around the room.

"Madame Eid, were you able to salvage any of your belongings from Damour?"

She shook her head, "No, we lost everything. But Nishkarallah (thanks be to God), my family is alive. That is what matters."

"What happened that day? Was it a surprise attack?"

"The Palestinians stormed the village. They took us completely by surprise. Luckily for us a couple dozen *Kataeb* militiamen were home at the time. They began firing back. It was their gunshots that sounded the alarm and saved our lives. We had a lovely old house with a yellow stone façade. It sat at the end of the village facing the sea. When we heard the gunfire, Elie rushed us into his car. He drove down dirt paths through the orange groves until we reached the next village."

"When the shooting stopped did you go back?"

"No, we waited until the next morning. And I wish I'd never gone back. Our house was dynamited. And when we drove to my sister's house, I found her lying on the ground, her legs spread apart. She'd been ..." Madame Eid began to cry.

"The *Kataeb* had all been executed too," said Elie. "From the marks on their bodies, it was evident they had been tortured. It was ghastly. Arafat, when he learned what happened, supposedly wanted to execute the local PLO leader. Even if he had, it wouldn't have changed anything. I saw my neighbors, the way they stared at their dead brothers, fathers, uncles, friends. Revenge was the only thing on their minds. Even our sons Samir and Salim were outraged. And they were only twelve and thirteen at the time."

"The Palestinians did something even worse," said Madame Eid. "They dug up the coffins in the cemetery, shot off the hinges and hurled the bodies around the courtyard. I found my poor mother's withered cadaver in a pile of rubble."

"Can I tell them about your sister's baby?" asked Elie, looking at his wife.

"Da Heelik," (Please) she shouted. "They don't need to hear such things."

Hiding in an underground shelter and listening to the horrifying stories of such courageous people, I was unwilling or afraid to show how scared I was, because I did not want them to think the doctor's wife had no backbone.

It is funny and strange what goes through your mind as you pray. 'Please get me out of here alive, God. If you do, I'll give up my gin and tonics forever.'

It was not the kind of reverent, softly-whispered prayer I said at Mass, but more like the frantic plea-bargain you try if you think you are about to die. I'm ashamed those were my first thoughts but reason is not initially in control. Thankfully my priorities became clearer in my mind a few minutes later.

'Please God, forgive me for my selfishness. Deliver Michel and me safely back to our children. Please God, make the fighting stop so we can leave, and bless my knees so that I can run to the car.'

Around two o'clock, some three hours after the shelling began, Michel looked at me and said, "I think we need to chance it. It sounds like there's a lull in the fighting."

"Yes," I said. "I want to get home to the children."

We told Mrs. Eid we wanted to try getting out.

"Don't do it," she said. "The fighting will start again any minute."

"How do you know?" I asked.

"We just do," she said. "We've been coming down here long enough to know. Just you see, it will begin again any minute now."

We waited a while longer but when the bombing did not start again, it was Elie who finally spoke.

"Perhaps it's time. Perhaps there really is a lull for a few hours. Go ahead, try now, if you really must get back to Jounieh."

Michel started to ask me if I wanted to go upstairs to see what happened to our apartment. I cut him off. "No, let's get out of here."

Elie opened the door for us. "Quick," he said, "go as fast as you can."

"Good-bye and thank you," we yelled as we ran out the entrance to Michel's Fiat, which was parked just outside the front door. The car was covered in a layer of fine white powder and the hood looked as if someone had tried to pry it off. I started the car to make sure no shrapnel had penetrated the engine while Michel removed the larger chunks of cement that had fallen in the way. Like a slalom we wove past piles of fallen debris until we reached the corner of Damascus Street. We could not continue straight as we usually did since snipers controlled the next intersection. We turned right on Damascus Street to the Sami Sohl intersection where we took a left and came out at the Justice Ministry on the *Corniche* Mazra. Instead of driving on the road, which was still in full view of the snipers at that junction, we drove along the tree-lined sidewalk for about a mile. When we knew we were beyond the snipers' range of fire we drove back onto the road. Twenty minutes later we were back in Jounieh.

As we walked toward the front door and saw Naim and Nayla running toward us with their arms outstretched, I began to cry.

"Welcome back from the dead," said Gisèle, herself in tears. News broadcasts had called the bombing 'unprecedented,' the worst Syrian attack to date on the Christian enclave.

. . .

It was two months before the next crisis, and perhaps it was a natural reaction to all the stress of war finally catching up with me. Then again it could have been a consequence of Wadia's return.

One evening in early July, two days after she arrived from Boston, I developed a severe headache. By the next morning it had intensified instead of going away, as my tension headaches usually did. When I was unable to lift my head off the pillow, Michel suspected I had contracted meningitis. He consulted a neurologist friend, Tony Awad, who arrived prepared to perform a spinal tap, since transporting me to a hospital in Beirut was not an option. He had stopped on the way at a small clinic near his house in the mountains to pick up a set of instruments.

Tony brought along his wife Norma, a physical therapist, to assist him. She climbed on the far side of me in the large bed and helped me lie in the fetal position, clasping my knees with my hands, while she held me so I could not move.

I wanted to appear brave no matter how painful it was, but I overheard Tony telling Michel the only needle he could find was larger than those normally used for the procedure. I may actually have stopped breathing as I felt Tony's hand palpating the area around the third lumbar vertebra in the small of my back, and then rubbing the area with an antiseptic. The soothing sensation of something cold and refreshing against my hot skin was only momentary. Tony jabbed my back with a needle that felt like a thick jagged straw cutting through multiple layers of subcutaneous tissue until it reached the spinal canal. When the needle entered the subarachnoid space, the area where there is only liquid, I felt tremendous pressure building up along my spine and I let out a frightened gasp.

Bolts of electric fire shot down my legs. The pain was so severe I began to squirm.

"No, don't move," said Michel.

To make sure I didn't move, he grabbed hold of my legs and helped Norma pin them to the bed. Tony worked as fast as he could to attach a manometer to the needle to measure the pressure in my spinal canal before extracting any fluid. He finally removed the needle about fifteen minutes later. The spinal tap confirmed Michel's diagnosis of meningitis, the treatment for which was complete bed rest.

Gisèle tried to keep me clean, sponging me and gently rubbing my limbs with lotion, but she lost the battle to the heat and humidity. While Michel gave me pain medication, she put cold compresses on my eyes to soothe them and keep out the irritating light. Apart from those few recollections of attempts at cleanliness, my mind drifted aimlessly while my body lay in the sweat-soaked sheets. My head seemed to be inside a long tunnel, and I could not distinguish traffic noise from pounding surf or a talking bird from a passerby on the street. I thought I dreamed Wadia was standing at the end of my bed admonishing me for not making more of an effort to get up.

It was not a dream.

. . .

I have always had a fondness for dogs, perhaps out of spite for a father who forbade us such pleasures growing up, saying it was either him or a dog. I am convinced that as hard as it was to have a dog during a war, Foxy helped all of us survive.

When I was bedridden I knew when Foxy was nearby because she would sit on the floor beside me, attentive as a nurse, resting her head next to my face, offering me her soft spot to touch. It was the way she made us smile with pride or belly laugh at one of her escapades; it was the way she made me angry when she toppled my coq au vin on the floor and ate it; it was the way she tore up the bed, throwing the pillow and bedspread on the floor when I left her alone too long; it was never having the heart to reprimand her; it was the compassion I felt when she cowered under my bed during the bombings; it was the need to cuddle her in my arms and sink my face into her soft fur; it was her greeting us as soon as we opened the door; it was her lick on my cheek that welcomed me home, taking the edge off a stressful day; it was the way she sat on her rump in my car peering out, her paws gripping the partly rolled down window. In war, when life as one knows it is always changing, a pet is a reassuring constant, and it is important to be held to task. That was what Foxy did for all of us.

· · ·

Some two weeks later, when I had regained enough strength, I had but one thought: to take a shower. My face tilted upward, my arms raised above my head, I let the cool, clear liquid run down my body a deliciously long time before I even reached for the soap.

· · ·

Of course I had no way of knowing it, but while I was convalescing the Israelis had been busy drawing up a master plan for a full-scale invasion of Lebanon. The exact date may not have been determined as early as the fall of 1981, but Arafat already knew about the scheme, and he understood that its timing depended entirely on his PLO. The Israelis were looking for an 'excuse' to invade. Over the next six months they provoked the PLO, taunting them continuously along the Lebanon-Israel border in hopes the Palestinians would retaliate. According to the UN, between August, 1981, and May, 1982, the PLO maintained a truce, sponsored by the U.S. and Saudi Arabia, on Lebanon's southern border. On the other hand Israel violated the truce 2,777 times.[17]

As usual, the Lebanese people were the last to know any of this.

. . .

As I recovered, July and August slid gradually into September, the loveliest month of the year in Lebanon, particularly at the seaside. Although things in Beirut were calmer and people were returning home, I had no desire to do so. I was well enough to enjoy the beach, but not strong enough to attempt the all-too-familiar, dreaded ritual of restoring our apartment after a six-month absence, even with Leila at my side.

The announcement that schools would begin the 1981–1982 academic year just one month late on November 1, was reassuring news. When Jacques telephoned from Boston and urged us to leave, insisting the worst of the war was about to begin, we dismissed his concerns. The appearance of stability and calm permitted us to reassure ourselves that our lives had once again returned to normal.

I was again lulled into a false sense of security by my fickle and perfidious lover, Beirut. I fooled myself into wanting to believe we could be happy together.

"He lives in Boston," I reminded Michel. "What could he possibly know?"

---

17 *Op. cit.*, p. 194; UN Records; David, Ron: *Arabs & Israel for Beginners*. Writers and Readers, NY, 1996.

9

People and Rats

I was at a luncheon at Nicole Abouhalka's when I learned of the Israeli invasion, only hours after it began. She had invited about twenty physicians and their spouses to her summer home in Baabdat. It was a perfect day in the mountains. The sun was not too hot for those of us who wanted to sit in Nicole's exquisite garden and soak up its fragrance. The tall jasmine bushes were full of white blossoms, rows of red and yellow roses outlined the perimeter of the grass, and a fuchsia bougainvillea climbed the side of the staircase leading to the veranda. As usual at Beiruti gatherings the women gravitated to one corner to talk and the men to another, everyone content to be in their own little group.

Nicole set out lunch shortly after one o'clock. Her buffet included several Lebanese specialties: *Kibbeh nyeh*, a meat dish similar to steak tartare; *seyyadiah*, whole baked fish smothered in a piquant tahini sauce; and *mougrabia*, a chicken couscous. After we served ourselves we sat at small tables on the veranda or in the garden while her butler served the wine.

Following lunch six of Nicole's guests – three men and three women – gathered on the terrace for coffee and cigars.

George had a family member well placed in the *Kataeb*.

Khalil and Richard knew everyone important in Beirut.

I did not know whether any of the other men seated at the table had influential connections. Khalil was a tall, imposing, somewhat arrogant, barrel-chested man, and everything he said came out sounding bellicose. I had to chuckle whenever he and George got into a discussion. Usually good-natured, they could get very tense. George was the diplomat, the deal maker, the one who could maintain his calm while arguing. I loved it when he wrapped his left arm around Khalil's shoulders and, gripping him as if he were his best friend, held his right hand in the air, pressing his first three fingers together and waving them up and down as he made his point.

"Look," he said, leaning his head close to Khalil's to whisper. First I heard "... Israeli invasion ..." Seconds later I caught "... all Palestinian camps ..."

Everyone else must have heard him, too, because a sudden hush fell over the tables.

When Khalil roared, "Those bastards should all be killed," Nicole's other guests and I got up and walked toward their table.

George explained that Israel had invaded Lebanon that morning. According to his sources the Israeli Army intended to advance twenty-five miles up the coast, and stop just south of Beirut. I looked around the room. To judge from the number of guests nodding their heads in agreement, far outnumbering the few who frowned disapprovingly, there was consensus on Israel's actions. While I could see the necessity of clearing out the nests of PLO, I felt uneasy about what we were agreeing with. I could not clearly articulate it even to myself; maybe it was the unsettling way in which we spoke of eliminating people as if they were vermin. I am ashamed to admit it now, but that was the prevailing attitude in Lebanon in 1982. Our minds were very clear on the subject of the PLO: we were sick of Yasser Arafat. He had boasted one too many times that the road to Palestine led through Beirut. He and his PLO needed to be wiped out, so the Israelis were doing us a favor.

Part of me wanted to believe that, and as long as the Israelis conducted their nasty business in the south, as long as our lives in Beirut were not endangered, we talked comfortably about someone else's battles, someone else's deaths. In retrospect I blush at the naïveté of our thinking; but that was how it was, it was civil war; and we were looking out for ourselves.

"Maybe the Israelis will drop a few bombs on Sabra-Chatila while they're at it," said Khalil, "and get rid of all the vermin."

"That's not funny, Khalil," Nicole said. "Who's going to stop the Israelis from marching right into Beirut? They've already done some pretty awful things to the Lebanese in the south. They're not just killing Palestinians."

"So a few innocent people die," said Richard. "I don't think that's too high a price to pay. Wouldn't you like to see our lives normal again? As long as the PLO is operating out of Beirut, that won't happen."

"Look," Khalil said, turning to Nicole, "it is very simple. Lebanon is not Arafat's country to destroy. Let's get rid of the bastard and his PLO, and if the Israelis are willing to do the job, then I say, 'Ahlan wa Sahlan.'" (Welcome)

. . .

The attempted assassination of the Israeli ambassador in London on June 3, 1982, gave the government of Israel the pretext they wanted to launch an invasion into Lebanon. Ariel Sharon led 'Operation Peace for Galilee.' In two days his troops had advanced all the way to Beirut. On June 6, Israeli warplanes began bombing West Beirut indiscriminately.

The assault on the city lasted sixty-seven days.

. . .

After seven years of war my family and I should have been immune to leaping up, tearing open the doors, and staring in the direction of the latest explosion. But there we were on our balcony in Badaro, watching the Israeli bombers. With our heads tilted back, we shielded our eyes from the sun and looked toward the planes as they sped across the sky.

"There's a Phantom," shouted Michel.

"No, that was an F-16," countered Naim as he snapped its picture. Michel looked at his son, astonished that he could see the distinction. To Michel it was hardly recognizable as a plane. A boy of fifteen, who was fascinated with war, who collected shells and casings, who was familiar with the sound of every type of rocket, Naim knew exactly what he was looking at. Maybe half a dozen planes dove toward specific targets around the Sabra-Chatila neighborhood. They dropped their bombs, they circled the target, they returned and bombed again. The PLO in the camps responded in the only way they could, with anti-aircraft fire. Fifteen minutes later the bombing stopped.

. . .

In the Cairo Agreement signed in 1968 the Palestinians had been given the authority to police their own camps without interference from Lebanese authorities. In the early 1970s President Sleiman Frangie had abruptly dissolved the *Deuxième Bureau*, and the Palestinians took advantage of the resulting lapse in security. With this intelligence-gathering agency no longer a threat, the Palestinians for the first time ventured outside their camps and began policing large areas of Beirut. In some cases they did a respectable job. With America's apparent blessing they patrolled the Ain Mreisse neighborhood around the American Embassy. Lebanon's Jewish community in the Abou Jamal neighborhood hired them to protect their synagogue – the same one the Israelis would bomb and destroy in the summer of 1982 in an attempt to encourage the Jewish community to leave.[18] While the Palestinians appeared to

18 *Ibid.*, p. 325.

A BEIRUT HEART: ONE WOMAN'S WAR

be contributing to the well-being of the city, helping the Lebanese police capture criminals and retrieve stolen cars, they were busily building an infrastructure beneath the city complete with tunnels, underground bunkers and a sophisticated communications network. I never saw these tunnels, and I did not know they were more than speculative rumor until several years later when I read Robert Fisk's book *Pity the Nation*: "The Palestinians built a series of concrete-lined tunnels, stretching some four miles under the camps; they filled them with rockets, mortars and small-arms ammunition. One tunnel ran almost the entire length of the Chatila camp. Eight feet high and six feet wide, it included a series of concrete chambers that housed missiles."[19]

. . .

The Israeli bombing continued the next day and the next, and Michel decided we had to leave our apartment yet again. Every time a one-thousand pound bomb fell a mile and a half away on the Sabra-Chatila refugee camp, the walls, the floor, the air around us, vibrated. We could not carry on a conversation, nor could we hear the telephone ring. My brothers-in-law had sold the house in Jounieh the year before, so our only option was to take refuge with Wadia and Nademe in the apartment in Achrafieh. Since my family's safety came first, I suppressed my reservations about moving in with the two women. War had taught me to put things into perspective and – usually – to be practical.

Because, in the absence of the Israelis, the Christian militias were Arafat's enemy, Achrafieh was routinely bombed by the Palestinians, but it was still safer than our neighborhood. Badaro was not only too close to the Sabra-Chatila camps and the Israeli bombing raids, it lay on the Green Line just two blocks from the dangerous Museum crossing into West Beirut. Achrafieh was two miles away and was a tightly-knit Christian neighborhood whose narrow

19 *Ibid.*, p. 463.

streets and crowded buildings gave one a sense of security, however false.

In the past I might have protested abandoning our apartment, but now I was more respectful of Michel's level head in emergencies and his ability to accurately weigh a potentially dangerous situation. Even though I could be just as rational, I was also just as likely to defiantly resist going to Michel's office when the bombs started falling. Looking back I am not proud of the bad example that set for the children, but as one who insisted war was not going to dictate her life, it seemed a logical position. On several occasions I refused to leave my bed in the middle of the night. I could not face dashing down the dark stairs to Michel's office, particularly if my knees were hurting. I felt I would rather die in the comfort of my own bed than cower in a shelter. One day the bombing was especially bad and Michel, the responsible one, got out of bed.

"Come on, Cathy," he said. "Let's go down."

I rolled over, pulled the pillow over my ears, and went back to sleep. Michel shook me repeatedly. "Come on," he shouted, "the children are already on their way down."

"That's good," I replied. "I'll just die here, thank you. Go on without me."

I did not know it then, but the children were responding with the same defiance to Michel's request. Frustrated when this happened a second time, Michel took me aside one morning.

"Look, you," he said, "don't be so selfish. Didn't you hear what the children said to me last night?"

"No," I answered.

"'If Mommy can die in her bed, so can we.' Our children come first and you know that. Stop this nonsense."

. . .

I fought my domestic war with Wadia like a politician, doing everything necessary to keep things orderly. However, some obligations went well beyond the role of dutiful wife and daughter-in-law. Despite any diplomatic savvy I had acquired, I was never eager to spend any length of time with Wadia, particularly if it meant any kind of intimacy. But since she did not want to give up her bed – which was her prerogative – either Michel or I had to sleep in the extra double bed in her room. Neither of us wanted to take on this dreadful chore because Wadia snored louder than a rusty lawnmower. Michel and I agreed to toss a coin to see who would get to sleep in the living room and I won, I got the couch.

"Sorry about that, darling," I said, laughing, "but you lost."

"Oh, come on, Cathy," he pleaded. "You're not seriously thinking of making me sleep with her."

"Oh yes I am." I smiled and walked out of the room. A little later Michel found me in the kitchen. Naim and Nayla walked in behind him looking very conspiratorial, which made me laugh because I knew what was coming but I resisted and played along.

"Okay, gang, what's going on here?" I asked.

Michel wrapped his arms around me and begged, "Please agree to sleep with my mother."

"No, no, and no." I laughed. "I won that bet fair and square."

"Mommy," Naim said, "you don't want Poppy in a bad mood, do you?"

"Come on, Cathy," said Michel. "You take a pill to sleep anyway. So what difference could it possibly make to you?"

I put my hands on my hips, stared at the three people I loved most in the world, and said, "Oh, all right."

My children were a lot smarter than I. As soon as we arrived at Wadia's, Naim had offered to sleep on a mattress on the floor in the family room, and Nayla told her grandmother she wanted to sleep in her grandfather's old room. Wadia found this touchingly sentimental and told her she could. She never suspected they had ulterior motives.

I gave in mostly because in addition to his mother I did not need a grouchy, sleep-deprived husband. However, Wadia was the clear winner here. She did not care who slept with her as long as she did not have to give up her bed and, once she took off her hearing aid she heard nothing at all since she was stone-deaf without it. So with Wadia's whistle-drum sounds, the bombs, and the artillery fire collaborating in a vile cacophony of wild noises, I was the only one who heard every note. I cannot believe with all my experience of war and survival that I never thought to purchase something as essential as ear plugs that summer.

. . .

I was familiar with Lebanese and Syrian Army tanks, both of which had been patrolling our streets for seven years. The Israeli Merkava battle tank was something altogether different. One day we were having lunch in Wadia's apartment in Achrafieh when we heard a deafening noise, a harsh, rumbling sound which vibrated the French doors leading off her dining room. We were drawn irresistibly onto the balcony by the noise, just as we were by every explosion and every air raid.

The size and sound of a Merkava were meant to intimidate, to instill fear, to extort unconditional surrender. I do not know how tall from the ground it was, but from my vantage point on the fifth floor it looked as though the driver could have hopped off onto any second floor balcony along his path. We watched as it slithered its way down our boulevard, spewing blue-gray fumes out its rear and ripping up the hot summer asphalt like sticky glue, engraving our road with a reminder of its passage in case we might one day forget to be thankful. Daunting, and without regard for anything in its path, it paraded its might shamelessly for all to see, crushing two cars, a large garbage container, and a stop sign before coming to a halt and parking in a nearby field to 'protect our neighborhood.'

Several days later I stood near a Merkava at a nearby gas station while waiting to refuel my car, and my five-foot-six-inch frame came nowhere near the top of its wheels. It was not just the enormous height that was so unnerving; the dark dome of its turret loomed over me, watching my every move, turning with me as I walked around. It was spooky, as if there was no one in there.

That same week Michel and I had a personal encounter with a Merkava. I was driving my VW Bug on our way to our apartment from Wadia's. Just past *Hôtel Dieu* Hospital I had to maneuver the car through a one-way maze of connecting streets before I reached the main intersection of *Corniche* Mazra and Justice Ministry. Apparently the Israeli soldier and his Merkava were in a hurry, and decided to take a shortcut through this same maze of streets. It was our misfortune to encounter this speeding behemoth coming the wrong way toward us. In light of what these reckless drivers did to cars – in the south one callously drove over a car with four family members inside because it was in its way – Michel and I quickly waved our hands out our respective windows, indicating we would be happy to back up. This seemed far preferable to having our children read about the incident in the newspaper the following day: 'A prominent doctor and his American wife unwittingly found themselves in a tight corner yesterday with an Israeli Merkava. Even the amazing maneuverability of Mrs. Sultan's VW Bug could not save them.'

Merkavas aside, as soon as we settled into Wadia's apartment, my top priority was contingency plans for bomb-free days. While Israeli bombs were not falling in our neighborhood, Palestinian rockets were, particularly when the Merkavas – parked in our neighborhoods to 'protect' us – started firing into West Beirut and provoking a response. Those mornings when Michel and I decided it was a good idea to take the children to the beach, I would telephone a number of friends. I always packed a lunch of honey-baked ham and Swiss cheese sandwiches, with some 7-Up and *Amstel* beer in a cooler, and drove to Kaslik, the beach club in Jounieh we had joined in 1978. Those days were some of my favorites; where else in the chaos of Lebanon could five mothers have gathered their combined twelve children and let them run freely to do any number of fun things while feeling confident about their safety and enjoying each other's company?

When we could not go to the beach the children and I prayed the electricity would last at least until eleven at night. Otherwise it was dinner by candle-light, reading by flashlight until we fell asleep, and no movie. Naim was in charge of visiting the local video store to replenish our stash of films. We orchestrated these evenings carefully, keeping our plans secret even from Michel, who routinely went off to bed at 9:00. While Wadia and Nademe watched the Arabic news at 8:30 before going to their rooms, Nayla and I said our good nights, pretending to go off to bed. Meanwhile Naim waited patiently to put down his mattress in the family/television room when the news ended at 9:00. As soon as the house was quiet and Wadia had removed her hearing aid, Nayla and I snuck back into the family room, closed the door, huddled with Naim on his mattress, and watched our film. We had long ago given up such gestures of good will as inviting Wadia and Nademe to watch a movie with us. If the film was in French, Wadia explained the plot to Nademe in that voice peculiar to hard-of-hearing people, and we missed the dialogue. If the film was in English, she asked us to explain the plot to her, and then she would repeat everything in Arabic to Nademe.

. . .

On June 24, 1982, Yasser Arafat was ready to compromise. He asked for nothing more than an honorable exodus from Beirut. Former Prime Minister Saeb Salim tried to broker the deal, but Ariel Sharon did not want a negotiated settlement. He insisted on a humiliating defeat for Arafat.

In Washington, Alexander Haig, Secretary of State under President Reagan, subverted the plan before it even reached the White House, prolonging the siege of Beirut by forty-nine days.[20]

. . .

On July 3 all food and fuel were cut off to the civilian population of West Beirut. On July 4 the water was cut, and the electricity the following day. This was critical for the approximately six hundred thousand residents who had chosen to stay in their homes. Arafat

---

20 *Ibid.*, p. 268.

and his PLO faced no such problems. They had sufficient generators and stores of food in their underground bunkers to last them
for up to six months of siege. When Palestinians fled the south
they were welcomed into Beirut's refugee camps and given food
and shelter. When the poor Shiites fled north to Beirut to escape
the Israeli raids on their homes and villages – the customary retaliation for 'letting' the Palestinians launch attacks from their fields
– they were left to fend for themselves.

. . .

From my mother-in-law's balcony we had front row seats for this
horror show. Night after night I leaned over the balcony looking at
the bombs falling and the lights flashing across the sky. I had no
sense those lights were coming from human beings, it was more as
though Heaven were fighting Hell. I stood there, slightly bent forward, with my arms resting on the railing. Gradually it occurred
to me that neither I nor my children should be watching this; it
was disgusting; it went against everything I believed in; yet there
I was, staying and looking anyway. There were people under those
bombs, and for every bomb that fell someone died beneath it. For
every tracer which shot skyward, there were thousands of bullets
fired at the planes, and every plane – indistinguishable against
the dark sky except for a red light in the rear – had a pilot or two
inside. Presumably they were young men in their twenties, terrified that something was going to fly into their plane and blow
it apart. Maybe they had a ring on their finger and a girlfriend or
a wife back in Tel Aviv; maybe these young men still carried the
smell of their wife's perfume in their hair; maybe they were reserv-
ists called up the day before; maybe they were convinced they were
killing 'terrorists' so it was all right to drop one-thousand-pound
bombs over a dark city where they could not see their targets, if
they had targets at all. And down below on the ground where the
bombs exploded were ordinary people, women cradling screaming babies in their arms, old people holding terrified dogs, a husband frantic because his wife and children had not returned from

an outing. There was complete mayhem across the dark city, and I was watching it all from a balcony.

. . .

Meanwhile, on the political front, Bachir was preparing himself to be a presidential candidate. He had laid the groundwork months before in a pact with Israel's Prime Minister Begin. He agreed to help the Israelis in their military operation in exchange for their help in convincing the American government that he was the best choice for the new president of Lebanon. Ariel Sharon also collaborated with Bachir toward this goal. They were often seen dining at The Retro in Achrafieh, but never when Michel and I were there. When Bachir learned that the Israelis had already killed over eight thousand Lebanese civilians he quietly backed away from the alliance.

It was at this moment when Bachir found the courage to turn his back on the Israelis that we saw in him a man committed to working for the common good of all Lebanese. He made every effort to explain to the different religious communities that his most important aim was to end the civil war. He promised to rebuild a better country, eliminate religious barriers and hire government employees on their merit and not their religious affiliations.

. . .

In reality no Lebanese politician could have accomplished all these things. But we were looking for a leader who possessed the skills of a good housewife, someone who could restore order in his house and act as peace-maker to his extended family. Christians and moderate Muslims alike, we chose Bachir.

. . .

Syrian troops had been occupying East Beirut since 1976. As part of the cease-fire, following the three-month bombardment of the Christian enclave in 1978, Syria had agreed to a partial pull-back. Some of the troops were sent to the area next to *Jamhour*, but most were transferred to West Beirut. When the Israeli army moved into East Beirut in 1982 with their Merkavas and heavy artillery, they settled into the same crowded neighborhoods the Syrians had occupied. When they moved into the Badaro area, they apparently decided our apartment building was suitable for housing officers, and promptly moved in. In our absence Mrs. Eid was acting as caretaker, making it her business to know who came in, and what they wanted. When an Israeli officer arrived to inspect our apartment she called us at Wadia's.

"Dr. Sultan, you'd better come home right away," she said, "the Israelis want to take over your apartment."

Michel assured Mrs. Eid he would everything he could to keep the Israelis out.

Within ten minutes he was dressed, out the door and in his car driving to Badaro. At first he thought he would explain to the Israeli officer that he was a physician who returned to his apartment whenever he could free himself from the hospital. By the time he reached our building he had decided instead to plead the case of a woman whose first name we did not even know. We addressed her respectively as either Mrs. Eid or 'Imm Samir' (mother of Samir, her oldest son). Privately, I called her my 'ange gardien' (guardian angel).

"You can't enter this building," said the Israeli soldier blocking the entrance.

"I want to get to my apartment," Michel replied.

"No one comes in without permission."

Michel introduced himself and asked to see the officer in charge. The soldier left for a minute, apparently to check with someone further up the stairs, then returned.

"You can go up. My commanding officer will see you. He's on the eighth floor."

Michel found a young officer sitting in one of our chairs on the balcony, drinking tea from one of my cups.

"What do you want?" the officer asked.

"This is my apartment. Did you know that?" asked Michel.

The officer shook his head, and listened to what Michel had to say. "You've met Mrs. Eid," he began.

When the Israeli nodded Michel continued.

"Did you know that she and her family were refugees from Damour? They've occupied the vacant apartment just below us since 1976, when the Palestinians destroyed their home. Your presence in our building puts their lives in danger. And, if you'll forgive me saying this, I think they've already been through enough."

The mere mention of Damour caught the Israeli's attention. In January, 1976, the destruction of Damour by the Palestinians had been retaliation for the *Kataeb*'s savage clean-up of the Karantina.

"The Eids fully support your efforts to force the PLO out of Beirut," said Michel. "In fact, two of their sons belong to the *Kataeb* militia, which makes them your allies. One of them suffered a serious gun shot wound to the chest last month when his unit came under Palestinian fire. He is still in the hospital."

Michel told me that when he finished speaking the Israeli officer did not immediately respond. He looked out over the city several long minutes while he pondered Michel's words.

"Now that I think about it," he finally said, "your apartment is much too exposed for me and my men."

Smiling, Michel extended his hand and said, "Thanks, I'm grateful."

The young officer decided to move his headquarters to the corner of Badaro and Damascus Street, opposite the Buick dealership where Michel had shot at the four men while he was on guard duty. We always admired that officer, and Michel kept an eye out for him in hopes of inviting him to dinner; but he never ran into him again.

With typical Lebanese optimism the Buick dealership's show room was full of new cars. When the owner saw the Israelis install themselves, Merkavas and all, on the corner opposite his store front, he knew his cars were in danger. Michel was still in Badaro, talking with the Eids in their apartment on the seventh floor, when he heard the owner yelling. From the balcony Michel saw him – a short, rotund, balding man in his late fifties – running frantically toward the taxi stand a block away. He hired all the drivers there to come and drive away his new cars. Michel said it was hilarious to see eight men running behind this comic little man back down Badaro Street to the Buick dealership. Within minutes the chauffeurs drove away the new cars like a funeral procession with their lights on, presumably to the mountains.

The Israelis installing their guns and tanks in our neighborhood was really no different from the Palestinian fighters they had sworn to eradicate, with their rocket launchers and anti-aircraft missiles installed in villages where stooped old ladies with long, colored dresses and old men in baggy black trousers and fluffy white beards suffered Israeli reprisals.

It was our turn now.

. . .

The children and I were supposed to leave for Washington for a family reunion in July, but I canceled the trip as soon as the air war began. Under the circumstances I thought the choice was very clear: I could not imagine not being in Beirut. While it might have been good to get out of the city for a while, I could not bear the thought of going as far away as the States and possibly being trapped there.

When I decided not to go, I convinced Michel to let me use a portion of the money to remodel our apartment. It did not matter that I never knew from one day to the next if I even had an apartment. My need to believe we would soon be able to return home overrode my common sense. Apparently Naim and Nayla were inclined to play the same game. If I was going to make changes to our home, they insisted on taking part in the decision making. They chose the fabric for their curtains and bedspreads and the color for the walls, and wanted to do the painting themselves.

For the most part we chose our days well and were able to paint for several hours and return to Wadia's without any difficulty. But the one day Michel joined us we had a strange encounter.

We had taken the boulevard down from Achrafieh past *Hôtel Dieu* Hospital and did not discover the mess until we turned the next corner near the Justice Ministry. Every inch of space was covered in cars as far as the eye could see, hundreds and hundreds of them in one enormous traffic jam. All I really needed to do was shift into reverse and back away from the snarl, and Michel was screaming at me to do that. For some inexplicable reason my foot acted on its own, pressing down on the gas pedal and plunging us forward, inextricably fusing us with this enormous rush of refugees trying to get back into West Beirut to check on their homes. All we wanted to do was get to our apartment some two blocks away near the Museum. There was an army checkpoint, which added to the confusion and frustration, because this mass of metal and humanity had somehow to merge from four or five lanes down to one in order to pass through the barricade.

I steered my car into the right lane, intending to ease gradually to the left. I looked over at the woman in the passenger seat next to me. Her car was piled high with luggage strapped on the top. There were four children, all younger than ours, in the back seat. The trunk overflowed, held partially closed with a bungee cord. I could not see what was inside. She smiled and said hello in English.

"Where are you coming from?" I asked. Before she could respond her husband surged forward a car length.

When we caught up again she said, "We have been staying with my brother just north of Tripoli."

We spoke in English. Her name was Nadia. She was obviously a well-educated Muslim woman.

"The bombing hasn't stopped. Why are you going back now?" I asked. This time it was my turn to advance a few more feet.

When we were window to window again she answered, "A neighbor called us yesterday. Our apartment's been damaged." She shrugged. "We're returning home to see what needs to be done."

"There's a terrible rumor going around, Nadia," I said.

She leaned her head out her window to hear, pushing toward me with her elbows.

"People here say the Israelis plan to enter West Beirut," I said. "It'll be awful if they do. Be careful."

Her husband moved the car forward again.

"In case the rumors are true, Nadia, make sure you have a good supply of food and water, and gas canisters." She smiled. She knew all that.

"Allah Ma ak" (God be with you), I said, and waved one last time as she and her husband approached the checkpoint and I neared my street. Of course she did not need my advice.

"Maybe we should make you Supreme Commander of the whole country, Cathy. You seem to have a bit of advice for everyone, even perfect strangers," Michel said, laughing.

My face became hot and I glared at him indignantly even though he was right. That nice woman probably thinks of me to this day as 'that patronizing American nitwit.'

. . .

On August 5, I was with Naim and we had a different kind of encounter. There was no traffic jam, which in itself should have been a warning. For once our building had electricity, so we rode the elevator. We planned to work in my bedroom that morning, and were stirring the paint and laying out the drop cloths when we heard the metallic sound of tanks rolling down the street, which drew Naim and me out onto the balcony. We saw what looked like a dozen Merkavas converging from Fourn ni Chebak and the area around the Justice Ministry toward the corner of Badaro and Damascus Streets, where they stopped. Moments later we heard the Israeli planes. The Merkavas started up their engines as if on a cue from the planes. As the tanks advanced up Damascus Street toward the intersection of *Corniche* Mazra and the Museum, the planes began dive-bombing the area directly behind the Museum. Naim and I moved along the west side of our balcony to get a better view, stopping just outside our dining room. The planes were bombing the race track.

The Merkavas began firing into the field, while the bombs from the F-16s created eruptions across it like mini-volcanoes. After a while it was difficult to see anything, because the area was enveloped in one large plume of dark gray smoke. I was amazed the Palestinians had penetrated this far from Sabra-Chatila, a good mile and a half away.

"They just dug another tunnel," Naim said. He knew everything.

It was reported by Hirsh Goodman of the *Jerusalem Post* that the Israelis took the strategic Museum crossing that day. That was not what Naim and I witnessed.

The Israeli planes bombed repeatedly, but the entrenched Palestinian position never stopped returning fire. The noise was like the final act of some Wagnerian opera with both chorus and orchestra blaring full blast. The PLO proved themselves strong adversaries. The Merkavas could not hold their ground and were forced to withdraw.

The same thing happened to an attack launched simultaneously near Beirut's airport. The Israelis were too exposed, and they lost both positions. My hero Robert Fisk, the correspondent for *The Times of London* who consistently told the story like it was – at least to my way of thinking – said that these two episodes 'resulted in the highest casualty toll the Israeli army had suffered in any one day since the invasion; nineteen killed and ninety-two wounded.' [21]

. . .

Saturation bombing is an efficient way of destroying your enemy without compromising your troops – if there is an enemy. The concept is easy to understand: a squadron of war planes drops bombs continuously over a specified target until the enemy is eliminated. The sound of saturation bombing is difficult to describe. Can you remember the blare of the air raid siren which is periodically tested in your community? If you are too close, the shrill noise causes the inside of your head to hurt and your ears to ring. Thankfully it lasts only a minute or two. Now imagine that siren blaring directly over

---

21 *Ibid.*, p. 298.

your head for nine or eleven or sometimes sixteen hours straight. You cannot turn the sound off, and you cannot walk away from it; the wail is constant. Saturation bombing is worse at night. You can pull the pillow over your ears and try to stifle the noise, but you still feel a vibration, a thud inside your head every time a bomb pounds the ground and explodes.

In a courageous show of support, two hundred fifty thousand Israelis marched in the streets of Tel Aviv to protest their government's unconscionable behavior against innocent Lebanese.

. . .

The Israeli bombing ended on August 21, 1982, exactly three minutes after Alexander Haig resigned as U.S. Secretary of State. Here is Robert Fisk again: 'Haig had given tacit approval for the Israeli invasion in conversations with Ariel Sharon. Throughout the summer the Saudis had sent a series of urgent messages to Washington imploring President Reagan to put pressure on the Israelis. Reagan never received these messages; Haig blocked them at the State Department.' According to Fisk, 'King Fahd of Saudi Arabia warned that his country would withdraw all its investments from the United States at once and impose oil sanctions against the West within hours if the Israeli army was not brought under control. Reagan was at last made aware of the gravity of the crisis and Haig resigned.'[22]

. . .

Arrangements were then made for Yasser Arafat and his PLO guerillas to leave Beirut. The soldiers were to be dispersed to Syria, Jordan, South Yemen, Algeria, Iraq, Kuwait, and the United Arab Emirates. Only unarmed women, children and the elderly would stay behind in the Sabra-Chatila camps.

. . .

---

22 *Ibid.*, pp. 268–269.

On August 22 I went to my apartment to determine what needed to be done before we moved back. I also used the Arabic telephone to contact Leila, to let her know I needed her help more than ever for this eleventh clean-up.

Badaro was desolate. Almost none of the stores had reopened. The Buick dealership was eerie, its showroom windows blown out and its back wall completely gone. Peering through the metal grid gates of Colifichet and Lunettes I saw that they had also lost their windows. Oddly, the stores' names – which hung in large black glass letters across the top of each door – had not shattered. The sidewalk along our building had erupted in an explosion and there was a mound of chiseled stone in our entryway.

Our building had been without electricity since the Israeli saturation bombing. Fortunately, I could see to walk up the stairs in the sunlight, which made patterns on the steps through the broken windows on the landings.

That was how I saw the rat so clearly. It came into the light, and its odd white face shone out at me. Our eyes met briefly, just long enough for some exchange of recognition, before it vanished into the darkness.

Terrified I would see another rat, I touched the walls just enough to steady myself, and watched where I put my feet as I continued up the stairs. Every time I returned after a long absence, I prayed for some kind of miracle, which had yet to happen. On the fifth floor I saw the tail of some putrid animal sticking out of the rubble. On the sixth, when I realized the recently-departed troops had used the darkest corner of the landing as a urinal, I knew there would be no miracle this time either.

Our apartment was in its usual state of disarray, no glass in the windows and the sheer curtains torn as though some vandal had taken a razor to them. For the first time a section of balcony just off Naim and Nayla's bedroom was missing where something had chipped away a large, two-foot wide V. I assumed it was a large piece of shrapnel and left it at that, just thankful that neither of the children was in the bedroom when it hit. I knew of children playing outside, walking down a street with their friends, or simply sitting near a window, who suddenly fell over dead from a shrapnel wound to the head.

I went into the children's bedroom to see if any debris had fallen inside, perhaps onto Nayla's bed which was closest to the damaged balcony. I wanted to get Raggedy Ann, Nayla's favorite doll, which she had asked me to bring back to Achrafieh. When I lifted Raggedy up, I saw black droppings underneath. They were scattered among Nayla's twenty or so other stuffed animals. I wanted to believe the pellets were from mice, but I knew they were from rats. The bedding was rumpled, and it looked as if something had crawled under Nayla's sheet. I felt sick, and my stomach churned with anguish as though the rat had physically assaulted my daughter.

Most of the time I was a reasonable, level-headed person. Sometimes I even admitted to being 'the woman with nerves of steel.' So far I had survived a war, although after fourteen years in Beirut I still had not mustered the courage to kill a cockroach. Imagine rats with their intelligent piercing black eyes and pointed noses, amazingly human in their boldness, nesting in my home! Could even the most thorough house cleaning ever get rid of them? I was not a killer; but in this case I was prepared to make an exception. Any plans I was formulating regarding my rat infestation were put on hold by something far more pressing.

. . .

On August 23, 1982, Lebanon held its presidential election, a glorious moment for Lebanese Christians. Bashir Gemayal – our protector against the Palestinian-Muslim coalition – was going to be elected President of Lebanon. Members of the Lebanese Parliament called 'deputies' elected the president, and it was common practice for them to sell their votes to the highest bidder. Enormous quantities of money changed hands as a means of persuading the deputies to show up and cast their votes for Bashir. Rumor has it that some votes were bought for well over a million dollars apiece, and that the American emissary, Dean Brown, bankrolled the election.

In past elections, Syria had been the power broker but that changed temporarily in 1982.

Parliament initially failed to reach a quorum. Hurried telephone calls were made, with promises of even larger sums of money. Eventually, long after the session should have ended, four elderly deputies were 'escorted' into the Chamber to make up the necessary quorum and elect Bachir.

Some might argue this was far more civilized than the 1969 election when Sleiman Frangie was running for President. During the voting process one of his aides fired a gun inside the Parliament building.

. . .

In the meantime, Naim, Nayla, their cousin Philippe, Michel, Nademe, and I sat in Wadia's apartment in Achrafieh, the heart of Bachir-land, watching the election on television, as were hundreds of thousands of other Bachir fans. We could hardly hear the Speaker count the final votes. The ground-swell of cheers rising out of our crowded Christian ghetto was deafening. People hung out apartment windows shouting to their neighbors, cheering their good fortune. Once the election results became official, the celebrations began in earnest. Ordinary Lebanese, elated by the news, began firing guns from their balconies. The Lebanese have a long tradition of owning guns, but use them primarily for special occasions like ushering in the New Year.

The war changed all that.

Cars so full of people that they were piled on the roofs and hoods, drove through Achrafieh blowing their horns. Militiamen, from their headquarters, from their Jeeps, or from the middle of an intersection, filled the sky with celebratory gunfire for twelve straight hours. I didn't think of how dangerous that was until the next day when I learned five people had been killed.

A few days after his election, Bachir held an open house at his family home in Bikfaya, and invited all of Lebanon. The day after he became President, Bachir had visited every Muslim religious leader and politician and asked for their help in unifying the country. All of them accepted, and came to his open house to show their support publicly. I took Naim, Nayla, Nademe, and Philippe. The crowd was so enormous I wondered if the entire country had actually accepted Bachir's invitation. We were a jubilant, respectful mass of humanity, every one of us caught up in a new mood of hope which could be heard in our voices and seen on our faces. No one seemed to mind waiting patiently in line for hours. What was time when we were about to shake the hand of our savior? Bachir spoke to everyone as though he were greeting good friends. When he saw me his big brown eyes lit up. He smiled and put his hand on mine.

"Oh yes," he said, "I remember you. How could I forget the woman who refused to work at my radio station? I wanted someone pretty to light up my office. My men were so ugly but you still refused!"

I laughed and shook my head. "And you have no idea how much trouble I got into for not accepting that job."

"Oh," he said, "then you're in trouble again because I'm going to make you work for me."

. . .

On August 25, 1982, the U.S. Marines landed in Beirut as part of a multi-national peacekeeping force which included French and Italian troops. Their mission was two-fold: to oversee the departure of twelve thousand PLO guerrillas as part of the cease-fire agreement brokered by President Reagan's special envoy Philip Habib and former Prime Minister Saeb Salim; and for thirty days to safeguard the civilian Palestinian population left behind in Sabra-Chatila. President Reagan hoped these troops would help end the bloodshed in Beirut.

As it turned out that is not what happened.

. . .

With Bachir's election behind us, I made final preparations to return to our apartment. Leila and I scheduled a day for the final cleaning. I was eager to resettle as quickly as possible, because I needed major knee surgery as soon as I could get our lives back in order. Leila had already done a preliminary cleaning, the most important part: she rid our belongings of rat droppings while I washed the sheets, bedspreads and towels. Miraculously the dry cleaner was able to restore Nayla's stuffed animals to their clean, pre-rat condition.

I arrived before Leila. Even the outside of our apartment looked inviting; the landing was clean; the walls were bright; the front door was glossy white with forest green panels. I turned the key and went in. After so many repairs, I had finally discarded the tattered sheer curtains and made new ones for the living and dining rooms. Now everything in those rooms – the marble floors, the sparkling new ceiling-to-floor windows, the rich walnut and cherry furniture, the rebuilt bookshelf, Papa's artifacts, the vibrant Persian carpets, the polished silver pieces on display, the china in its cabinet – welcomed me back.

I went into the kitchen to put some fruit and cheese in the refrigerator. I felt dizzy from climbing the stairs in the heat, so I sat down. Then I heard a sound and stayed very still. My heart began to pound, and I knew in an instant they were there, they had not left. Leila had said they would.

'When we clean an apartment the rats leave.'

She was wrong.

I associated vermin with filth. I rubbed my arms; they felt creepy, as if something was crawling up them. I heard traffic from the street below, I even heard the wind. Then I heard what sounded like words being whispered in muffled voices. I sat up straight. It was obvious where they were, in the hole behind the oven, a perfect place to nest all warm and cozy. Anger replaced fear. "How dare they?" I hissed. They heard my voice and fell silent.

I knew what needed to be done but I could not bring myself to commit the violent act. Leila might have been able to dispose of them, but instead I enlisted Mr. Eid to carry out their execution. He brought along his wife, who carried a sack and a small metal shovel. Standing in the doorway of the living room I watched Mr. and Mrs. Eid walk into the kitchen. Before he closed the door behind him he urged me to go for a walk, or at least wait downstairs. I refused.

I heard a clank and wondered what it was. I realized it was the metal shovel striking the side of the stove.

Then I heard him speaking Arabic to his wife, "Well, there's the first one, maybe it's going to be easier than I thought."

Then Mrs. Eid said, "Oh just wait till you find the mother. She'll fight for her young ones."

There was another clank, and then a squeal.

Mrs. Eid yelled, "There she is, hit her harder!" She screamed a second time, "Hit her again. She's still not dead."

I almost fainted when I heard the sound of the metal shovel crushing the mother rat on the kitchen floor.

Then Mrs. Eid said, "Curious. Look at that white spot between her eyes."

The kitchen table collapsed, and then there were several clanks against the tile wall. Jesus, was he actually chasing the little ones up the wall? I heard a bang against the door, then Mr. Eid said, "There, that must be all of them."

"Yes," said Mrs. Eid, "I think so."

Mrs. Eid cracked open the door just enough to ask for a bucket and some Tide detergent. When they finally walked out, Mr. Eid held the burlap sack of dead rats securely in his hand. I entered the kitchen and saw slight traces of blood everywhere on the white tile walls and the gray marble floor. I thought, 'I will paint it all again as many times as it takes to erase this terrible deed from my house.'

I didn't know why my behavior toward the rats disturbed me. A few days later, sitting on the balcony with a cup of tea, I realized I had created my own little Sabra-Chatila. But rats were rats, not people, and I was not trying to delude myself they were people. Rats are pretty dangerous to have in your house. What unsettled me so much was the similarity in my mind between rats and the PLO. If I found rats deadly, and wanted them exterminated, was it not also perfectly human of me to view a horde of people trying to take over my city with similar malice, and wish them all dead in the same way?

The way in which that rat, with her unique white spot, stepped into the light and identified herself, made me realize some things I had never considered before. At first I thought the rat was a 'he,' but Mrs. Eid knew instinctively she was the mother.

"Look at that peculiar white spot on *her*," she had said.

Looking in the direction of the Sabra-Chatila Palestinian camps I realized with great clarity for the first time that each person in those camps was a 'he' or a 'she,' that most of them were innocent Palestinian civilians who through no fault of their own – aside from being born Palestinian – lived in squalid refugee camps.

I had never thought of them that way before.

10

Hope Lost

U.S. Secretary of Defense Caspar Weinberger visited Beirut on September 1, 1982, the day the last shipload of Palestinian guerillas left Beirut. He declared the peacekeeping mission was 'practically speaking, pretty well completed.' He ordered a Marine pull-out, even though the American government in the cease-fire agreement had obligated the Marines to stay in Beirut for thirty days to protect Palestinian civilians. Because the Marines' departure effectively terminated the entire peacekeeping mission, the French and Italian troops withdrew as well. In the same cease-fire agreement, the Israelis had assured the Americans they would not enter West Beirut if Arafat and his guerrillas agreed to evacuate the city.[23]

On September 11, 1982, the Marines left Beirut, seventeen days into their thirty-day peacekeeping mission.

. . .

---

23 *Ibid.*, p. 351.

On September 14, we moved back to Badaro. The children and I ate an early breakfast with Wadia and Nademe, and were at our apartment before eight. My handyman Ibraham was already there with his crew, making last minute adjustments to our new water system, which ended up taking most of the day. Leila had let them in. She had stayed the night so she could give the balconies one last scrubbing, and clean the floors and kitchen before we arrived. Naim and Nayla were so excited to be going home to their newly decorated bedroom – the walls Swedish blue, the curtains pumpkin and the bedspreads navy blue – that they actually offered to clean out their drawers and desk and reorganize their closet. Before they tackled that, I asked them to re-shelve our five hundred hardcover comic books, while I went to Wadia's to retrieve the last of our belongings.

I had the box in my arms, and was ready to leave my mother-in-law's, when a powerful explosion shook the building. I set my load on the dining table and rushed to the balcony with Wadia and Nademe. A cloud of thick smoke was already moving over the neighborhood. Leaning over the railing I could see people pouring into the street. One woman in particular kept pulling at her hair, grabbing great clumps with her fists and shouting something unintelligible. She repeated it again and again, like the verse of a prayer, until we finally understood: "It's the *Kataeb* building. Bachir is inside."

I knew the building well, it housed the radio station. I remembered the small sound-proof newsroom in the middle of the building where I had sat to deliver the news. Bachir would have been in his office directly below that room.

As President-elect, he insisted on personal contact with his supporters. Despite grave security concerns, he went to his Achrafieh headquarters every Wednesday for a neighborhood meeting. The room was full that day, and Bachir was standing in the middle of the room surrounded by well wishers, when a two-hundred-pound bomb detonated in the ceiling directly above him. The entire building collapsed. Reports throughout the evening insisted he was still

alive. Mrs. Eid's youngest daughter Nounou, who was in the building at the time of the explosion, escaped with only minor injuries;
so we were hopeful.

Michel and I attended a dinner party that evening where we talked
of nothing else. Our host, Joe Chahine, called one of his colleagues
at *Hôtel Dieu* Hospital, where they had supposedly taken Bachir, and
was given every assurance that Bachir had survived the explosion.

On September 15 we turned on the radio as soon as we awoke.
Classical music, a Lebanese sign of mourning, was playing on every
station. We knew instantly: Bachir was dead, our dreams shattered,
our hope lost. In the silence of that early morning hour, an Israeli
F-16 flew low over the stricken city and tipped its wings in tribute
to a fallen hero.

On September 18, 1982, four days after Bachir's murder, between
fifteen hundred and two thousand men, women and children were
found massacred in the Sabra-Chatila camps. The numbers are
vague because no one knows precisely how many were killed. Lebanese government figures showed seven hundred sixty-two bodies
recovered, but official estimates concluded that at least double that
number had already been privately buried.

The massacres had begun on the night of September 16, when
about two hundred militiamen sent by Israeli Defense Minister
Ariel Sharon entered the camps. They were a carefully organized
coalition of Bachir's Christian Lebanese Forces and members of the
South Lebanese Army, Israel's proxy in their self-proclaimed 'security zone' in southern Lebanon. The Christian militiamen were
under the immediate command of Elie Hobeika, one of Bachir's
commanders. His men were chosen from the Damouri Brigade,
one of the more extreme elements of the Christian militia, from
Damour, the Eids' village in the south, ravaged by Palestinian guerrillas in January, 1976.[24] These young men had seen their family
members slaughtered and defiled, their homes destroyed. Hobeika

---

24 *Ibid.*, p. 387.

and his men were under the command of General Amos Yaron, Director-General of the Israeli Ministry of Defense.

For thirty-eight hours, from the evening of September 16 to September 18, Israelis stood guard outside the camps to prevent anyone escaping. Planes dropped flares to aid the militiamen inside the camps.

The victims were unarmed Palestinian civilians, the same people I had cursed and wished dead, and had only recently come to realize were individuals and fellow human beings.

They were all dead, exterminated just like my rats.

Before they left the camps on September 18, the militiamen bulldozed the bodies into heaps, pushed them into shallow make-shift graves and covered them with dirt.[25]

Robert Fisk revisited the Sabra-Chatila massacre in a 2003 article for *The Independent*. After spending several weeks in Israel, he became fascinated by Ariel Sharon's repeated reference to the Palestinians as 'murderers, terrorists.' Mr. Fisk had heard Sharon use those words before. 'I called up an old friend with a talent for going through archives. I gave her the date that was going through my head, 15 September, 1982, the last hours for up to two thousand Palestinians who were about to be murdered in the Sabra and Chatila camps in Beirut.' She was able to locate the September, 1982, Associated Press release. 'Defense Minister Ariel Sharon, in a statement, tied the killing (of the Phalangist leader Gemayal) to the PLO, saying that "it symbolizes the terrorist murderousness of the PLO terrorist organizations and their supporters." ' A few hours later Sharon sent the Phalangists into the camps. Fisk goes on to say, "Reading that release again, I felt a chill come over me. There are Israelis today who feel as much rage towards the Palestinians as the Phalange felt 19 years ago. And these are the same words I am hearing today, from the same man about the same people. Why?"[26]

---

25 *Ibid.*, p. 364.
26 Robert Fisk, "Travels in a Land Without Hope," *The Independent*, August 29, 2001.

Could it be because we still have no leader wise or courageous enough to sit the warring factions down and demand some sensible humane solution?

. . .

Shortly after the massacre, Michel and I met Mrs. Eid waiting for the elevator. As people everywhere were discussing the Sabra-Chatila carnage, it was perfectly natural for Michel to say, "Wasn't that a tragedy? It makes me so ashamed of being a Christian."

Then he asked, "Have you heard from Samir or Salem? Did they know anything about the killings? What were their reactions?"

Mrs. Eid paused a long moment without answering.

"They didn't do any of the ... They weren't in the camps, were they?" Michel asked very carefully.

Mrs Eid stood only about 5' 2" and in order to look directly at us she had to tilt her head back. Her luminous blue eyes swelled with tears.

"Yes," she replied, "they went into the camps."

There we were, face to face with the woman who had sheltered us during bombardments, killed rats for us, taken care of our home and garden in our absence, the same woman who had lost everything. Yet she still had so much love and compassion that her heart cried for those who had once been her enemies, some of whom her own sons had probably killed. Humbled by Mrs. Eid's humanity I hoped I would learn to see more clearly with my own heart.

. . .

Michel's Palestinian secretary Freyha lived in an apartment building near the Sabra-Chatila camps. When she came to work on Monday morning, I was curious as to what she knew about the massacres.

She had heard the machine gun bursts, which had lasted almost two days, but it was the screams, she said, the voices of children crying, of women pleading, which still haunted her. "I was too terrified to even pull open the blinds and look out," she said. "But it's the voices I heard, the pain in their pleas that I'll never forget."

It was not until late Saturday morning, when the camps fell silent that she dared crawl onto the balcony and peer through the railing.

"There was a foul, almost sickeningly sweet smell in the air," she said. "And the flies – there were great hordes of them everywhere. That's when I knew something awful had happened."

She was deeply moved by a group of young boys who looked as if they had been playing one of those games where children huddle together over a ball, arms linked, shoulders touching; they had fallen together in a pile. Their faces looked as if they had been daubed with dark red finger paint. A small girl lay on her side in an alleyway a short distance from the boys. Freyha thought at first it was someone's doll. Her dress was blotched with blood and dirt. A crimson halo encircled her head.

Around mid-morning, she saw a group of journalists enter the camp. One of the men climbed onto a huge pile of dirt to get a better view. The mound looked about ten feet high. He struggled to reach the top, holding out his arms to steady himself as he went.

"Have you ever seen someone try to walk across a trampoline without falling?" She asked, laughing. "That is how he looked."

The man slipped and lost his balance. Trying to catch himself, he grabbed hold of a dark red rock – the color of much of Lebanon's rich soil – which protruded from the mound of dirt.

"It wasn't a rock," she said. "It was someone's bloated stomach."

Horrified, he let go, lost his balance and tumbled to the ground.

Ironically, the Muslim politicians could not allow themselves to be seen to condemn the Maronite Christians' participation in the camp massacres, since Parliament – of which they were members – now had to convene to elect another Maronite as President to replace Bachir. The old-line politicians viewed Bachir's brother Amine as a reasonable compromise. Amine had been a Deputy in the Parliament for a number of years. In many ways he was Bachir's opposite, rigid where Bachir was wily, aloof where Bachir had been magnetic and charismatic. He portrayed himself as a champion of compromise and conciliation, in contrast to Bachir's propensity for crushing his opponents. Amine had nothing but contempt for the *Kataeb* thugs under Bachir's command, and he was innocent of any ties to Israel.

On September 21, 1982, one week after his brother's assassination, Amine Gemayal was sworn in to serve one six-year term as Lebanon's new president.

But no one cared.

We were much more interested in the bomb an Israeli plane had dropped on the Lebanese Army Ammunition Depot near Fourn ni Chebak, shortly before Amine took office. Naim and I were moving furniture around in my bedroom. Even though Leila had her radio on in another room, I heard the plane overhead. Within seconds a series of powerful explosions reverberated across the city. So insatiably curious were Naim and I that we tried to dash outside, only to find ourselves thrown sprawling on the bedroom floor by the hot blast, staring eye-to-eye with Foxy who had wisely scuttled under the bed.

An eerie darkness, from the great puffy mushrooms of smoke from the explosions, settled over the city. Some believe the Israelis were delivering a message to Amine that day, a reminder that if he was not yet a supporter of Israel, as his brother Bachir had been, perhaps he should become one, and quickly

Eight days after Amine was sworn in as President, the U.S. Marines crept back into Beirut as the American government tried to repair the diplomatic damage their early departure caused.

Over the course of the next six months it would fail miserably.

. . .

After four months of almost constant emotional turmoil, I was exhausted from the cumulative effects of the Israeli invasion, the nonstop air raids, the saturation bombing, Bachir's assassination, the rat killing, the Sabra-Chatila massacres, meningitis, and constant knee pain. Then there were the three and half months of sharing Wadia's bedroom, listening night after night to her whistle-drum snoring. I had reached one of the few times in my life when I thought I could not handle another calamity. I was in crisis, and I knew it. I suffered from fatigue that never went away, even after a good night's sleep, something I had never experienced before, and I needed major knee surgery.

One does not usually look forward to such things, but in my state of distress, I did. I saw it as an opportunity to get some rest. When I mentioned that around Michel he just shook his head and called me his 'woman with the nerves of steel.' He did not know that in order to stand, to cook, to walk up and down eight flights of stairs, to help Leila clean, I was taking a double dosage of pain medication. He also seemed to forget that I had already had twelve knee surgeries. So what was one more? I wanted some relief, but more importantly, I wanted someone to take care of me for a change.

Leila could do that better than anyone I knew, and I gladly handed over all household duties to her. The only thing she asked me to do was decide the day's lunch and dinner menus. She took care of everything else.

. . .

I remember waking up in the hospital room after the operation and hearing English being spoken. It was Fay. She was talking quietly to the children in the corner. The last thing I heard before falling back into medicated slumber was something about lunch the following day. When I awoke later I heard different voices, this time speaking French. I opened my eyes to see Sonia, Hoda, Myrna, and Lina leaning on the bed rails, talking softly and waiting for me to wake up. When Sonia saw me trying to open my eyes, she leaned toward me.

"Can I get you anything, Cathy?" she asked.

I smiled, shook my head, and fell back into a state of morphine bliss.

Michel's sister Andrée literally moved into my hospital room. She had a bed brought in and spent five nights with me. After the first few days, when I was more alert and less inclined to fall back to sleep every time I opened my eyes, we talked, or, rather, I listened. Andrée was a raconteur who could weave together a story every bit as fascinating as Scheherazade's, and she could make me forget my pain in the telling.

My brother-in-law Raymond had lumbar disc surgery the same day as my knee surgery, so we were in the same hospital one floor apart. Wadia visited her son daily, but never found time to visit me. Ten days after my discharge, she did call me at home to see if I needed anything.

Michel was very disappointed by his mother's behavior, and one day I overheard him talking to Andrée. "Do you know when she finally called my wife?"

I never asked him if he confronted Wadia about the incident. I simply did not want to know. It was I who accompanied Wadia on her doctor's visits, took her shopping and never said 'no,' never said 'sorry, I am too busy.' Out of anger and hurt I resolved to no longer be available to do those things; I was very mistaken to think I could so easily relinquish my duties as an accommodating daughter-in-law.

. . .

My friends were as jealous of me as Wadia and Nademe were. Everyone knew how good Leila was at whatever she did, and they all wished she worked for them. Leila's greatest talent was cooking. While I was recuperating, word spread quickly that Leila made incredibly good cookies.

A *Sablé* is a three layer round butter cookie. The top and bottom layers are cookies with a distinctive petal edging. The top piece traditionally has a round hole in the middle, the trademark of the authentic *Sablé*, cut by a special mold which is pressed over the dough. After they are baked, these two layers are glued together with thick apricot marmalade, and the chef-d'oeuvre is then generously sprinkled with powdered sugar.

Leila served these delectable goodies with freshly-made lemonade. No matter how hard she worked, Leila never made enough cookies or squeezed enough lemons. Even on days when we expected no visitors because there was no power, we were always surprised. One afternoon when my French friend Catherine called, she was told not to come because we had no electricity. She came anyway, in a foot cast, walking up the eight flights of stairs. She and her archaeologist husband had been moving heavy marble pieces in preparation for an exhibit when one fell on her toe. I am still not sure after all this time if she did not really come for some of Leila's *Sablés*.

On September 26, 1982, Israel withdrew its troops from Beirut, and moved them to the Chouf Mountains south of Beirut, a region shared by Maronite Christians and Druze. Both groups had been attracted to this region as a refuge from the Sunni rulers of the Ottoman Empire. During the civil war, Druze fighters had driven most of the Christians out of their villages. Once entrenched in the Chouf, the Israelis allowed the Christian Lebanese Forces to move back in. Knowing the history of the region, they knew this would re-ignite a one-hundred-forty-year-old vendetta between Maronites and Druze. As anticipated, the Lebanese forces tried to reestablish their control over the region with the same tough tactics they had used elsewhere, but the Druze fought back. Within days, the well-armed Druze militia had defeated the Christian forces and trapped the remaining Maronites in pockets of resistance in the hills. The Israeli Army was the only thing that stood between the Maronites and the Druze.

This precarious situation lasted almost a year until the Israelis abruptly pulled their troops out of the Chouf in September, 1983. Their withdrawal ignited a particularly ferocious battle between Maronites and Druze which forever altered our lives.

. . .

One evening in early January, 1983, shortly before calling everyone to dinner, I walked into the corridor to get a platter from the closet. I caught sight of Nayla walking into the bathroom with her father's gun in her right hand. She went inside and closed and locked the door before I could reach her. I heard her sobbing, and yelled to Michel and Naim for help. We pleaded with her to open the door but she refused, continuing to cry with a sorrow that ripped open my heart. Finally, Michel convinced her at least to talk to us and tell us why she was so upset, even if she did not want to open the door. Eventually she turned the key and Michel went in, put the toilet cover down, and invited Nayla to sit on his knees with his arms wrapped around her. Naim and I stood waiting outside.

At Michel's gentle urging, she began to talk. It seemed that several of her classmates had recently given parties, and she had not been invited to any of them. She hated being excluded. She had only two friends, Susie and Sylvia. None of the boys in her class liked her, they were intimidated by her. Aside from her two friends, she did not like the other girls in her class because they were immature. And while one part of her wanted to act stupid like them in order to be accepted, the other part was not willing to try to be someone she was not, just to fit in. Michel spoke in whispers, his voice so sad and tender it made me cry. He told her he had faced similar problems when he was her age.

"No matter what, Nayla, never compromise who you are," he said. He assured her that she would eventually find mature and intelligent friends.

Michel took the gun out of Nayla's hand and slipped it in his pocket. Later he hid it in a locked closet.

A few days later I asked Nayla why she took the gun into the bathroom. "Did you intend to use it?" I asked.

"No," she replied, "I just wanted to get your attention."

Michel insisted that Nayla's crisis was due to adolescent hormonal imbalance, and I chose to believe him, which was far more palatable than pondering the possibility of a more serious problem.

. . .

It was a strange winter and early spring. For the first time in twenty years it snowed near *Jamhour* in the suburbs of Beirut. There were such massive amounts of snow on the ski slopes that it took a week to clear the parking lots and groom the trails before we could use them. Israeli tourists, identifiable by their blue license plates, visited Beirut that year. For the first time ever, Lebanese were allowed to drive into Israel. U.S. Marines patrolled the city streets while the Sixth Fleet, with frigates and cruisers, patrolled the coast. If the American presence did little else, at least it brought investors back into the country. The Lebanese pound, which had fallen to six pounds to the dollar, went back up to three. In the midst of this strange time of economic growth and noisy optimism, we consciously chose to forget that none of our problems had been solved, that Lebanon was still carved up between Syria and Israel.

People develop amnesia in war.

. . .

On April 18, a suicide bomber drove his truck, loaded with five hundred pounds of TNT, into the main body of the American Embassy.

I had visited the building five days earlier to renew my passport. Samir, the Lebanese employee in the consular section, whom I had known since 1969, helped me that day with my paperwork. That was the last time I saw him. He and fifty-eight others, seventeen of them Americans, died in the blast. I think of Samir often because I owe him my life. He was the one who had suggested the children and I become Lebanese citizens. I was very grateful to Samir when the war began and I was able to show my Lebanese ID card instead of my American passport at checkpoints.

The American Embassy was in three sections, a seven-story central administration building with a wing on either side. There were no cement barriers at either end of the entrance, and the suicide bomber was able to drive his truck into the circular driveway off the *Corniche*, and into the building. The blast was so strong that a car traveling past the Embassy at the time of the explosion was blown off the road and into the sea. In the visa section the unsuspecting Lebanese who had queued up all morning to apply to visit the United States, were burned alive in the blast. The CIA's Middle East station chiefs were inside the Embassy at the time of the explosion. In the aftermath, experts wondered if their meeting had not been called to discuss the recent arrival of Iranian-backed Hezbollah Shiite fighters in the Bekaa Valley, who were about to declare an 'Islamic Jihad' on the West.[27]

. . .

During those years there was a great deal the American government did not understand about the Middle East, and Lebanon in particular. It certainly did not understand that Lebanon, due to enormous social inequities, was emerging as a place where centuries of Arab resentment of the West were beginning to find voice and direction, where the ideology of Iran's Ayatollah Khomeini would take root and produce a unifying voice against America.[28] Sadly, with the invasion of Iraq in 2003, nothing has changed, America has not altered its policy in the Middle East, and violence and hatred toward the West have found an even stronger voice.

The peace treaty signed by Lebanon and Israel on May 17, 1983, was a perfect example of American ineptitude. Brokered by the United States, the agreement was centered around a series of clandestine understandings between Israel and Lebanon. It pledged a phased Israeli withdrawal from all of Lebanon, based upon a simultaneous withdrawal by Syria. Free of foreign intervention, the Lebanese government could pursue a formal peace with Israel. The agreement had one enormous flaw: the Americans failed to inform Syria's President Assad of the deal. Assad enlisted the Druze in the Chouf to bomb Christian East Beirut, to punish the Gemayal government for their collusion with America and Israel.

I had just left the hairdresser's a block and a half from my apartment when I heard the explosions. The morning news had

27 Fisk, *Pity the Nation*, pp. 478–479.
28 Fisk, Robert: *Pity the Nation The Abduction of Lebanon*. Atheneum, NY, 1990, pp. 443, 469.

announced that the French contingent of the Multi-National Peace-keeping Force would be blowing up mines – left around the race track by the Palestinians – all day. Since the track was just two blocks from our apartment, I assumed the blasts were from there. I stopped at the green grocer's to buy lettuce for lunch, and didn't think anything of his curious gaze. At Azam's, I was surprised to find he was out of French bread.

"Didn't you bake today?" I asked.

"Oui, Madame," he replied, "but you know how frantic people get when bombs start falling. They buy everything I have."

"Those aren't bombs," I said, as I laughed and turned to leave. "The explosions are from the mines. Didn't you hear the news this morning?"

I was so confident the baker was wrong, that when I saw Michel's car parked in front of our building I just assumed he had returned early to see patients in his office. When I opened the front door of the apartment I thought it odd that neither Foxy nor Leila greeted me. I had just finished searching the apartment when Michel burst through the door.

"Cathy, what are you doing up here?"

"Why are you so excited?" I asked. "Where are Leila and Foxy? Did something happen to them?"

"Have you lost it completely? Don't you hear the bombs?"

"Bombs? I thought it was …" Before I could say another word, I remembered Naim and Nayla.

"I've got to get to Jamhour." I turned to get my purse and almost bumped into Michel, who grabbed my shoulders.

"Relax. Andrée has already gone to get them."

I fell onto the nearest kitchen chair and began to cry. "How can I relax when my children are dodging snipers and bombs? It should be me driving them home. Then I wouldn't have to sit here worrying."

"Come on, my nerves-of-steel lady," Michel said, helping me up. "Let's go to the office."

My knees hurt so much I could hardly walk down the stairs. Leila went back to the apartment to get us some food, I swallowed my pain pills, got as comfortable as I could on the leather couch, propped my knees up on pillows, and waited. Half an hour later Foxy suddenly leapt up, ran to the door and started to sniff. When her tail began to wag, I knew the children were safely home. I jumped up, forgetting my painful knees, and ran to open the door. Nayla broke loose from my embrace and threw herself on the couch. Naim, rarely at a loss for words, just shook his head when I asked how bad it was.

The Chouf battles could not have come at a worse time. Michel was scheduled to leave the next morning for America for six weeks of medical meetings, a refresher course at the University of Wisconsin, and a visit with his brother Jacques in Boston. I was certain he would cancel his trip in light of the bombing. As the afternoon wore on, and the bombs continued, he did not mention his plans. Finally, when I could no longer stand the suspense, I said, "Well, I suppose you'll cancel your trip, won't you?"

"No," he replied, "I'm still going."

He had everything planned. His sister Andrée and her husband Ernest were in Paris, so Michel decided we should go stay at their house in Achrafieh.

"Tomorrow morning I'll take a taxi to the airport from there," he said.

I started to ask, "How can you think of leaving?" but there was something about his expression when he looked at me that reminded me of the trembling stork in Cornet Chehouan that wanted to be somewhere else.

"I think that's a good plan," I said, puzzling over what I would do for six long weeks alone with my anxiety.

Michel made me promise that we would stay at Andrée's until the bombing stopped. That was easy when I considered the intensity of the battles in our neighborhood.

. . .

After five days at my sister-in-law's apartment, where her maid Hasna cooked and cared for us, the children and I returned home.

In Michel's absence I thought we had all handled this latest round of fighting quite well. So when classes resumed I was surprised when Nayla refused to get out of bed.

"I can't go to school, Mommy," she said. "Please don't force me to go."

"Okay, darling, you can stay home today."

"No, Mommy, you don't understand," and she began to cry. "I can't go back there again, ever."

After she had fallen back to sleep I called Michel at his brother's in Boston.

"She's just being capricious, that's all," he said.

His words reminded me of the gun incident, and how I had agreed with his interpretation of her behavior. This time I decided to trust my own instincts. After our conversation I called Elie Karam, a psychiatrist who was a friend and colleague of Michel's. He promised to come see Nayla later that afternoon.

After he spoke with her, Elie came into the living room and sat beside me. When he saw how distraught I was, he realized I could not handle any harsh clinical terminology. He chose instead to describe Nayla's depression as a form of self-preservation.

"She has closed off her mind so she no longer has to exist in the brutal reality around her."

In a serious moment like that, when you think your whole world may just have collapsed, you are frightened your daughter may never recover, and the support of your husband is three thousand miles away, you do not mind being given such a simple explanation. Elie thought it best if she were started on medication.

. . .

I almost wished Michel had stayed in the States, since he returned as depressed as Nayla.

"How can you come back to me in such a state?" I asked.

"I can't help it," he said, "I didn't hear a single piece of encouraging news about Lebanon the whole time I was there."

Most of Michel's information came from our friend Mike C., whom we had always assumed was a CIA operative. Considering America's track record in the Middle East, and Beirut in particular, I wondered aloud why he would believe what Mike said, when his so-called expert opinion came from an agency incapable of protecting its own men who died in the Embassy blast.

I looked Michel straight in the eye. "Is there something you haven't told me yet?"

"Like what?"

"Have you turned your back on Lebanon? Have you already decided we're emigrating to the States and you just haven't told me yet?"

"No, certainly not."

"Then why else would you choose to believe all that stuff about Lebanon? Your brother has been calling us from Boston for years urging us to leave. Every time he called we'd laugh and say, 'What does he know?' What's changed now? I'm not going anywhere and neither are you. Are we always in a war? No. Don't we also have normal times?"

He nodded.

"So do me a huge favor, Michel. Don't give me any more doom and gloom crap."

I walked over to the telephone.

"I'm calling Elie Hayek to invite him and Eva over for a drink this evening. He has his hand on the pulse of this city. He'll tell you everything's going to be all right."

. . .

Sometimes depressed patients have to change their medications several times before they find the one which produces the best results. When there was no significant improvement in Nayla on the first drug, Elie started her on a new one. Once the patient is on the right medication, it can take up to two weeks before there is any noticeable change, a painfully long time to wait when you are desperately looking for even the slightest sign of improvement. Nayla went for days without eating, she slept a lot, and even when awake she was distracted. I wanted to ask her what she saw in that other world, but I think I was afraid her answer would be, 'Nothing,' and that would have frightened me even more. Nor did she want to see her friends. At first they called trying to get her to come to the beach with them, but after awhile they stopped. Then, I do not know why – maybe it was just a good day – we got lucky. Her two best friends, Sylvia and Susie, turned up at the front door unannounced.

"Mommy, did you invite them?" Nayla asked.

"No, darling, I didn't know they were coming."

She burst into joyous laughter, and my heart skipped a few beats. Just as abruptly the following day she crawled back into some dark chamber of her psyche. Sometimes I became paranoid when I saw her looking out at the balcony. In my mind's eye I could see her suddenly climbing up on the railing and jumping off, and I would look over the edge and see her spread-eagled on the road below, gone just like that.

Each time Nayla had an appointment with Elie, I sat on a brown leather couch in the corner watching her. Sometimes she replied in soft whispers to Elie's gentle questions. Other times she gazed blankly past him, apparently unaware he was even there.

On one particular visit, a profoundly heavy sadness came over me. At first I thought it was rooted in my fear that Nayla might never recover. Instead, it was the realization of my own depression. I envied my daughter's ability to withdraw into a peaceful world where she had no responsibilities except a few for herself. But I had to be everyone's rock, 'the woman with the nerves of steel,' and I could not escape. I began to cry.

Elie came and sat beside me. He thought I was crying for Nayla, and he reassured me she would recover. I nodded as he spoke, trying to say something, but I could not force myself to be as honest as my daughter.

. . .

Approximately thirty percent of children Nayla's age suffered from depression at one time or another as a result of the war. Her cousin Philippe, and Andrée's maid Hasna, were also being treated for depression at the same time. When I took Nayla to her appointments, it was rare when I did not see several people I knew, there either as patients or accompanying a loved one.

To our great relief, after three weeks on her new medication, Nayla began to show signs of improving. Michel and I agreed this would be a good time for a change of scenery. The children and I had not been abroad in four years, so I decided to take them to the States for a two-month holiday to visit family and friends. Elie thought this was the best possible treatment for Nayla, and so we planned to leave at the end of June as soon as Naim finished school.

. . .

The Marines did not go back to America in the summer of 1983. Some of them never left Beirut. At 6:20 A.M. on Sunday, October 23, six months after the American Embassy had been destroyed, a suicide bomber drove four thousand pounds of explosives past the guards at the Marine compound near the Beirut airport. The explosion leveled the four-story Battalion Landing Team headquarters, killing 241 Marines. At approximately the same time a second suicide bomber drove into the headquarters of the French contingent of the Peacekeeping Mission, killing 58 French paratroopers. The young American on duty at Marine Post 7 that morning could not fire at the suicide bomber because – like all Marines on duty anywhere in Beirut – he was not allowed to carry a loaded weapon.

After all, they were on a 'peacekeeping mission.'

11

Turmoil

*M*y now fifteen- and sixteen-
year-old children and I left for America the first week of July, 1983.
I could hardly believe we were actually about to go on vacation for
the first time in four years. While it felt strange to be leaving Michel
for such a long period of time, he was pleased that we were going,
and did not mind taking Foxy and moving in with his mother. In
spite of my carefully laid plans our departure evolved into a tense,
risk-filled adventure.

Our flight on the Lebanese-owned Middle East Airlines was
scheduled to leave Beirut at 11:40 for New York via Paris. I made
arrangements with George, the local taxi driver whom I used frequently, to take us to the airport. I did not want Michel to accompany us because the Syrians, still occupying West Beirut, were
manning barricades on the airport road.

Our bags were packed, and we were practically out the door,
when our travel agent Akram Itani called in a panic.

"Michel has to accompany you to the airport," he said. "There's no way around it. The Syrians are not letting women and their children leave unless their husbands are present to sign a release."

When I told Michel this he sat down in a chair and the color drained from his face.

"I have a bad feeling about this, Cathy, I don't know why. This would just do it, wouldn't it? What if my name is still on one of their lists?"

When George came to the door to help us down with our luggage, I told him that Michel had to accompany us to the airport.

"Don't worry, Madame Sultan. This time of day it's too busy on that road to stop anyone."

George was wrong. Despite heavy traffic, the Syrian soldiers were stopping cars and demanding to see ID cards. When it came our turn, the soldier looked hastily at mine and the children's and handed them back. When he saw Michel's Syrian birthplace he held onto his ID and walked off to show it to his superior seated inside the guardhouse at the side of the road. Michel threw back his head and closed his eyes while I watched the two men who appeared to be checking his name against a list. After what seemed the longest minutes of my life the soldier turned and walked back across the road. His superior rose and stepped outside the door. He wore sun glasses, so I could not see his eyes, but I would have sworn he was staring at our car, waiting. At that same moment I felt a pinch on my left arm, and I flinched. Nayla, seated between Michel and me, was watching. She did not say a word, but the twist of her hand asked the question, 'Shoo?'

I shook my head that I did not know. When I glanced back outside my eyes met Naim's in the side view mirror; he knew. The soldier made his way back to Michel's side of the car. I felt certain he was going to say, 'You're under arrest.' I stopped breathing and waited. Without so much as a 'Ta Faddel' (here), he handed Michel his card and with a slight tilt of his head motioned us to move on. No one spoke; but we all exhaled simultaneously.

After Michel had delivered us safely inside the airport, he still had to face other Syrian barricades on his trip home. While we were unloading the bags we discussed how to get Michel back to the hospital. George was to drop him there and call Wadia to tell her he was safely back. Because it was difficult to get through to the hospital switchboard, I decided I would call Wadia once I passed the last security check.

Before I boarded the plane, I tried several times to phone Wadia, and each time her line was busy. When our flight had been called, I tried one last time to get through, not succeeding but pretending I did, somehow managing to convince Naim and Nayla I had spoken to their grandmother. They were greatly relieved to learn their father had crossed back into East Beirut. Of course I knew no such thing, and I was close to tears by the time we boarded the plane.

"What's the matter, Mommy?" Nayla asked.

"It's just a tension headache, darling," I answered, "get your Walkmans and books out and relax while I try to sleep it off. I'll feel much better by the time we get to Paris." I took some aspirin and prayed that Michel was safe.

At Orly Airport in Paris, an employee of Middle East Airlines explained how I could purchase a telephone card. I told Naim and Nayla I wanted to reassure Poppy that we had gotten to Paris, and I dialed Wadia's number. I was so terrified to hear he had never returned that my hands shook. The telephone rang once, then a second time. Drops of perspiration formed on my forehead, and blood pounded in my ears. Would no one pick up? I was overwhelmed with relief when Michel answered on the third ring.

"I'm all right," he said, "but I almost wasn't. I got stopped again and I thought for sure they'd haul me off. But I'm safe. I'll never go over there again."

"Oh Michel," I cried, before I remembered my children standing beside me, "please take care of yourself. We send you a big kiss, and we'll call you from New York."

I hung up, thinking I had cleverly deceived my children. Naim glared at me.

"You lied to us."

"Yes I did, darling, but it was only so you and Nayla wouldn't worry."

I glanced at Nayla who was standing rigid, staring at her brother. The only things moving were her fingers, pulling at the hem of her skirt.

"Let's see if I got this straight, Mommy," Naim said. "The Syrians stopped Poppy on the way home. Right?"

I nodded.

"Where would they have taken him?" asked Nayla.

"Where do you think," Naim replied, "to Palmyra. Don't you remember? That's where the underground prison in the desert is. It's where everyone dies."

As Naim spoke I watched my frail stork, the color draining from her face as she reacted to something else which had been following her, of which she had been unaware. I flashed back to the time I rescued them from school in my Bug and the bombs were dropping on the road behind us as we tried to get home, the day of the sniper. As all these thoughts collided in my mind, I understood it was not always her own life about which she worried, it was also the possible loss of a family member, in this case her father. All the near misses came down on me like the collapsing roof of a house.

Suddenly I just wanted to run. I was too tired to cope with this insanity. I needed someone to take care of me. I could no longer think coherently. How could I? There was nothing normal about what I was doing, or how we lived. I did not even know how I managed to survive each day. It was either luck or habit when I did anything right.

It was all I could do to get on the plane with the children.

. . .

I was totally unprepared for the mayhem outside JFK Airport in New York. When we came out of customs, the mob waiting for family and friends was caged behind a floor-to-ceiling chain link fence no more than twelve feet from our faces, rattling the metal like convicts demanding release. A few men were actually climbing the fence, shouting, waving, trying to get the attention of those still inside or exiting with us. After a four-year absence this was not the America I remembered. I found something else equally as strange: I was in the country of my birth, yet I heard more assorted world languages than I heard English.

My anxiety increased when I did not see my sister Sheila waiting for us outside. I had not realized our plane was forty minutes early, as Naim discovered when he reset his watch. We waited for my sister in an air conditioned hall with a view of the street. When she still had not appeared after half an hour, it occurred to me to phone her. I searched in my purse for her number, but I had forgotten to write it down. I should have known she would eventually arrive, but my heart started to race, and just when I thought I would burst into tears Naim cried, "Look, Mommy, there she is. There's Sheila," and he ran to greet her.

My snobbish little self – the woman who had matured into a sophisticated clothes-conscious Beiruti – saw my sister as still the hippie she was in the 60's. What a little snot I was, in light of her kind and generous invitation to visit her and her husband Luis, to care about her long, full skirt, short sleeved blouse and Birkenstock sandals.

. . .

After a week of museums, shows and shopping in New York, the children and Sheila and Luis and I joined my parents, our other two sisters, one brother, and all their families for a week-long reunion. My father had found a large house right on the ocean in Virginia Beach, and each family paid a share of the rent and food.

On our last visit four years before, my parents had disappointed me severely by picking us up at the airport, taking us back to their two-bedroom apartment in Arlington, Virginia, and leaving for a previous dinner engagement with friends. In Beirut my family would never have done that.

"You don't mind, do you, Cathy?" My father said. "We thought you'd be tired and want to sleep."

Of course what I really wanted was to be with my parents, having traveled half-way around the world to see them.

On their visit to the Middle East, we took my father to Palmyra to see the Roman ruins, and he did not want to go on the sunrise walk in the desert – despite that being the principal reason we had traveled six hours by bus from Damascus – because he had forgotten his hat, and was afraid his hair would fly around. It was ironic that now he chose to come to Virginia Beach, where it was always windy.

Nothing had changed this time.

My mother had the radio on in the kitchen to catch the news and weather, as she did every morning. From the dining room, where I was having breakfast, I heard the word 'Beirut.' I rushed to the kitchen and turned up the volume. My father, following right behind me, switched off the radio in the middle of the story.

"I'll have none of that, Cathy," he said. "I don't want you bringing Beirut on this vacation."

. . .

Naim spent his week in Virginia Beach almost entirely in the water, swimming and riding waves with his cousins and uncles. My sister Donna's new husband, Dick, rented a boat two different days and took Naim – with whom he had developed a remarkable rapport – and my brother Joe deep-sea fishing.

One day Dick organized a canoe trip down a local river. Nayla and I shared a canoe, which was a mistake, since neither of us knew anything about paddling. She sat in the front and I – wearing my fancy Dior sunglasses, which were a birthday gift from my children – sat in the back, trying my darnedest to keep the canoe straight in the water. Naim was in the lead with Dick, while Donna and our other sister Barb trailed behind us. Going over some tiny rapids, our canoe capsized. We were not wearing life jackets and Nayla and I plunged into the water; it was not deep, but it was cold, and fast and full of silt. When we hit the bottom the silt was stirred up and rose in the water, blinding us. I came sputtering to the surface, annoyed that I had lost my sunglasses, but laughing because I was having so much fun, in spite of a pounding heart. The canoe was spiraling off by itself down the next rapids, and Dick and Naim were giggling their heads off and trying to grab it. I looked around for Nayla but couldn't see her. I had an anxious moment before she shot up out of the water like a geyser, screaming, her eyes huge and her pupils black. I rushed over to her and took her in my arms.

"You're safe, darling. You're safe and you're going to stay safe."

Looking over Nayla's head I saw Naim wading toward us in the water. He gathered both of us in his arms and held us tight.

"Mommy says I'm going to be safe. Am I?" Nayla asked her brother.

"You are, Nayla," he said, crying.

. . .

The children and I returned to New York so we could see more Broadway shows. At Nayla's request we saw *Cats*, and a ballet at Lincoln Center. We could only find two tickets for a matinee performance of *Amadeus*, so Nayla and I went. I was looking forward to the play, which my friends in Beirut had urged me to see. Our seats were front row balcony. Once the lights had gone out and the play began, as the music filled the theater I found myself thinking about Beirut, and about Bachir and Tony Frangie instead of Mozart and Salieri. I told Nayla I had to go to the toilet and left my seat, sobbing. People glanced oddly at me as I made my way toward the exit. They probably thought I was crazy. I tried to calm down, and a few minutes later I returned to my seat, but sometimes the intensity of the play swung me right back to Beirut and I had to reach for another Kleenex.®

As we drove back to Sheila's apartment, I watched the odds and ends of life rush by: a man with a bottle in a doorway; a prostitute in red satin walking in amazingly high, pencil-thin heels; near the park I saw a young man snatch an old woman's purse, and no one reacted. Right around the corner from Sheila's apartment, a policeman was holding a gun to a man's head while he fumbled for his handcuffs. Something was very wrong. We pulled up outside my sister's brownstone, and there was a man standing on the steps. He stared at us, and it was as if a bomb went off in my head.

The sleeves on his white T-shirt were rolled up nearly to his shoulders, showing large, firm biceps. It was him, it was the man who had tried to rape me twenty years ago in Washington, I was convinced it was him. I must have been completely off my head. I could not get hold of myself. I slid down into the seat gripping my daughter's hand.

"Mommy, what are you doing?" Nayla asked. "You're hurting me!"

"Nayla, je ne peux pas bouge" (I cannot move), I whispered. "C'est l'homme, c'est lui, c'est l'homme qui a essayer de me voler. Je sais que c'est lui" (it's the man, it's him, the man who tried to rape me, I know it's him).

"Mommy, what are you talking about?"

"En français," I said, pointing to the taxi driver.

"Give me your billfold. Let me pay the fare."

She gathered up our bags, and helped me out of the cab and into the building.

Later, after Nayla had put me to bed, she came and sat beside me. I told her what had happened at Providence Hospital in 1965.

"Mommy, there is no way that could have been the same person. This man was perfectly harmless. Didn't you see how he moved as soon as he saw us approaching?"

"Yes, darling, but ..."

"Mommy, you shouldn't let yourself get so upset."

In the war I had been the steady, unfaltering housewife keeping it all together. Was I going to come completely undone now that the pressure was off?

On our last day in New York, Nayla, Sheila and I had lunch at an outdoor restaurant in the South Side Harbor neighborhood. Nayla appeared to enjoy herself. She liked a gray two-piece outfit in an Ann Taylor store, so I bought it for her. From there we strolled around Wall Street, and did not return home until shortly after 4:00.

Nayla went into the bedroom to put her package away. About ten minutes later I walked in to find her sitting on the side of the bed, tears streaming down her cheeks, a bunch of pills in her hand. I walked over calmly and sat beside her. I kissed her head and pulled her to my chest, and she began to sob. I asked her if she intended to swallow all those pills, and she said she did not know. Sitting there on the bed next to Nayla, I was again reminded of the frightened stork lying on its straw bed in Cornet Chehouan.

. . .

On the morning of September 1, 1983, I arose early, too excited to stay in bed. Our bags were packed and we were going home, scheduled to fly Middle East Airlines that evening from JFK back to Beirut via Paris. I was glad my parents had gone to work so we could have a leisurely day to ourselves. We had been staying with them in their two-bedroom apartment for the past week. The small quarters did not bother me; nor did sharing a bedroom with the children; my father lifting the newspaper in front of his face whenever he saw me – so I would not irritate him with news from Beirut – and my mother acquiescing in his behavior, refusing to tell him to stop acting like a child, *did*. How awkward and absurd it all was. I could not wait to get out of my parents' apartment and back into the dysfunction of Beirut. I might die there, but until I did I could handle just about anything, except a visit with my parents.

Around noon Michel called. Instantly I knew from the sound of his voice that something was wrong, that perhaps someone had died.

"You can't come home, Cathy," he said, "it's started again."

"What are you talking about?" I asked, sinking slowly into the armchair near the telephone, as my legs turned to rubber. I knew what he was going to say.

"The war, it's started again."

"We just spoke two days ago, Michel, and everything was fine then. What's happened?"

"The Israelis abruptly pulled out of the Chouf and the whole thing flared up again. It is unbelievable, Cathy. This is the worst it has ever been. The bombing has been going on now for two straight days. There's no end in sight."

"I'm going to call the airline to see if ..."

"Cathy, listen to me. MEA has canceled all flights. Its planes are grounded. It's only been two months and already you've forgotten? When bombs are falling, planes don't fly in or out of here."

I tried to sound reasonable. "Then what should we do?"

"From the looks of things, you'll have to stay there awhile," he said. "Maybe you should put the children in school. Call Jacques. See what he suggests."

"Michel, this is all too much. I can't think right now. I'll have to call you back."

I had no time to collect my thoughts, no time to sound like an adult in front of my teenaged children; they could tell from the tone of my voice that something had gone terribly wrong. A large double window looked out on woods, and green grass, and patches of red salvia, yellow roses, and purple veronica. I wanted to be down there, I wanted to go for a long walk, maybe even walk away to some very distant place, any place so I would not have to be in that room at that moment and say what I had to say.

Naim and Nayla understood the part about remaining in America temporarily, but they objected to the rest.

"No!" Naim shouted. "I know what you're going to say. It has something to do with starting school here, right? Don't say another word. We are not going to school here."

"It could be weeks, maybe months before we can ..."

Naim cut me off. "So what?" he cried, his voice cracking.

Suddenly, like the time she shot out of the murky river, Nayla cried out, "Oh please, Mommy, please don't make me go to school here."

The terror in her voice was like a knife cutting into my heart, and I sobbed. The young boy who had spoken so offhandedly about bombs tearing up roads behind him, about Palmyra, about the dead bodies in the street, was crying too.

I had no time to grapple with the intricacies of an indefinite stay in the States. I had to decide as quickly as possible on a course of action. I knew two things: we could not live with my parents, and the school year had already begun. I wanted to run to my grandmother for her sound advice, but she was quite ill. Unsuccessful cataract surgery had left her blind. The idea of not being able to read, and do things for herself, was too much for her to bear. She gave up wanting to live, took to her bed and already had begun to deteriorate physically and mentally.

Grandma Catherine was ninety-five when she died in September, 1984. While I should have rejoiced at her beautiful long life, I was not in the right frame of mind to see that clearly. Having no other family members to whom I could turn, I needed her support and sound advice more than at any other time in my life. Just as Michel did with his father, I had the foresight to write a letter from Beirut to my grandmother before she died. I told her how special she was, and how blessed I felt to have such a caring person looking after me. I take great comfort from that.

. . .

After consulting my brother-in-law Jacques in Boston, we decided to fly there two days later. Jacques' good friend Joe Soussou – who had shared our apartment when they were studying at MIT – insisted we come live with him and his family until we could return home. Jacques enrolled the children in private schools, Naim in the Jesuit-run Boston College High School, Nayla in the Newton Country Day School, because it was small and well-respected for the personal attention it gave its female students.

Joe and his gracious wife Helen converted the third floor, part attic, part game room, into Naim's quarters. Nayla and I shared a spacious bedroom with a double bed on the second floor. This became Nayla's cocoon, and she rarely wanted to leave it, neither to eat nor to socialize with the household, to the point that her isolation offended the Soussous. They thought she was being capricious, which brought back Michel's earlier words. Joe came right out and asked me why she was so impolite when they were doing everything they could to make her feel at home, and my brother-in-law complained she was moody. It never occurred to either of them that Nayla was suffering from war-related depression. Jacques' son Joe still had nightmares from his only exposure to the war, a taxi ride he took from Jounieh to the airport in Beirut in 1978. Yet Jacques was unwilling to accept the fact that Nayla, who had lived eight years under the bombs, could be depressed. It is human nature to distort the truth and interpret it the way we want it to be. We require hands-on experience in order to comprehend the depths of despondency to which a person in deep depression can fall. In their defense, the Soussous had never lived in a war, so it was difficult for them to understand the traumas my children and I carried in our hearts, the longing we felt for the good part of what we had left behind.

Several times it occurred to me we might as well be speaking to each other in mutually incomprehensible languages. They thought it odd that I was astonished every time hot water came gushing out of a faucet. They had no way of knowing we had lived without such luxuries for eight years. I thought they were silly to complain about missing their favorite television program when an electric storm cut the power. We had lived through most of the war without electricity.

The Soussou family tried to accommodate us in every possible way. Helen loaned me her car to drive Nayla to and from school every day. When my frail little stork kissed me good-bye as she stepped from the car, we both knew she would say hardly a word at school. My daughter, with her peculiar personality and her war-torn brain, just could not reach out and connect to anyone new. At the end of the day it tore at my heart to see the same sad face walk out of school and climb into the car without having spoken to another girl all day.

. . .

Helen was about to begin her Masters' thesis when we moved into their house. She had known me as an active woman and now she saw me in crisis, with nothing to do. Very cleverly she suggested I might do the shopping and cooking. Now I had something around which to construct my day. She also encouraged me to join her exercise classes, which were held in a small studio in Cambridge. Helen had told the owner, Dorothy, that I suffered tremendous anxiety, and she began teaching me how to relieve the tension through exercise. In addition to my painful knees, my sciatic nerve was shooting sharp pains down the back of both legs.

"A sign of extreme stress," she insisted.

Through working with Dorothy I learned to listen to my body's needs, and while it did not yield immediate results, I began learning the life-long process of stress management, although what had taken eight years to develop was not going to disappear in a matter of weeks or months.

Naim was different. Instead of letting his pain consume and destroy him he converted his anger into a determined attack on academic challenges, the harder the better. He made only one concession at Boston College High School. He began as a junior, not as a senior. According to the Jesuits, the extra year would give him adequate time to adapt to the American system, prepare for the SATs and choose a good college. When Naim's advisor suggested he take less challenging classes his first year, he insisted on taking the heaviest possible load. He spent three hours a day traveling by bus and subway to and from his school in Dorchester. Although Naim kept to himself as much as possible, he did allow me to prepare his breakfast and send him off with a kiss. He left by the back of the house just off the kitchen. I stood at the door and watched him cross the yard to the sidewalk on Garfield Street. It is the saddest image I have of him: his head is down, his shoulders bent forward as though carrying a tremendous load, trudging away from me. At the top of the hill he turns his face, full of pain, to see if I am still at the door, and he waves. I wait for that moment to blow him a kiss, to wave a last good-bye.

After he returned from school and had eaten a snack he would retreat to the third floor and not reappear until dinner time. It broke my heart that he would not talk to me or let me console him. He knew how deeply depressed I was before the rest of the people in the house, and realized how emotionally overbearing I had become, and how difficult it was to be around me.

The only bright spot in our week was nine A.M. every Saturday when, each on our own phone, we got to speak with Michel. Beforehand we were bursting with questions, but always ended up asking the same ones: 'How are you?' 'How is Foxy?' 'Can you still get to the hospital?' 'How bad is it?' 'Any sign of a cease-fire?' and most insistently, 'When can we come home?' The sound of his voice had to be enough to get us through the week until the next Saturday.

The constant worry for Michel's safety and the separation from him and my friends were far more difficult than any hardships or dangers I had endured in Beirut. As nice as my old friends in Boston were, they had no way of understanding that the difficulty I was having adjusting to their world was because I had been living in a war for so many years. They had no idea how to respond to my tears at the very mention of Michel or Beirut, so they stopped asking questions; eventually they avoided me altogether. Apparently I had learned nothing from that time in Greece, when Gino and Nancy got tired of my constant babbling about Beirut.

It took me years to discover that I was totally out of control, which my Boston friends had obviously realized. My emotions were tangled up in every word I spoke, and I must have seemed like a bomb about to explode. My friends did not have the heart or the words, to tell me the truth about myself. I had to figure it out at my own pace. But Naim knew, and so did Nayla. When she told me that her friend's mother found me 'somewhat hysterical' at a dinner party we attended, I did not understand what she meant.

As I reflect on that evening I see the Cathy that was, a woman who talked constantly about the war, and coolly described our reactions to different sounds.

"We never took machine gun fire too seriously," I explained, "even when it was nearby. And unless rockets fell directly on our neighborhood, we huddled together in front of the bathroom window and watched them falling around us." I was desperate for everyone to know, to understand and share our experiences.

I remember the looks on their faces, and the nervous glances they exchanged. Obviously, there was something seriously wrong with me.

. . .

I often wonder what would happen if another major crisis befell my life, if I suddenly lost Michel or one of our children. Would I have the mental fortitude to handle it, or is emotional trauma like a permanent short circuit which cannot be repaired? Would I go to the edge of the precipice faster than someone who has never been there before, or would I be able to step back and take control of the crisis before the panic-demon takes over, because I have lingered there so many times?

That seemed to be what I saw happen to my dear friend Edith in June, 1999, when we all took our annual tour of Northern Lebanon. Edith had lost her youngest child, Katia, in 1989. She was electrocuted when her hand touched a dangling live wire broken by celebratory gunfire the night before. As always, we stopped in the village where Katia died. We lit candles at a roadside shrine to the Virgin Mary, which Katia's friends had erected in her memory. As we approached the shrine, a profound sadness enveloped Edith, and for a moment, before she could speak, I felt her fighting back her monstrous sorrow. Then, with a wonderfully dignified control of her emotions, she stepped away from the edge of the precipice.

Once again she had escaped the panic-demon.

. . .

While I was in Boston, Michel sent me a sketch of himself. The white paper was blank, except for a small square cage in the far right-hand bottom corner of the page. 'Me,' was printed next to it.

In my mind I could see him constantly. He was crossing the Ministry of Justice intersection on his way to the hospital when his car stalled, and a sniper killed him. Or he was walking Foxy when the bombs began to fall, and both of them were hit and lay bleeding in the street. Or he was upset and yelling at a *Kataeb* militiaman blocking the road, and the man walked over to Michel's Fiat, pulled him out, and beat him senseless.

There was no limit to the ways I saw him die.

One day Jacques' wife Linda asked me if I had heard from Michel, and I burst out crying.

"Christ, Cathy," she said. "I can't say anything to you. All you do is cry."

. . .

In one of the Saturday phone calls in early November, Michel announced he was coming for a visit. Naim asked him to come over Thanksgiving when he and Nayla had vacation. Michel asked if I wanted anything from our apartment, and I suggested he bring my red and gold tablecloth and napkins from Damascus. I wanted a souvenir of our lives in Beirut, something typical of Arab culture, since I was not sure I would ever see my belongings again.

. . .

Michel brought a large dose of reality with him. The situation in Beirut was so unstable, the battles still so frequent, that we could not hope to return home anytime in the near future. It was also evident we could not continue to impose ourselves on Joe's family. Michel agreed that we should rent a small apartment and buy a car. Jacques found a Chevrolet Cavalier, and I found a two-bedroom apartment on Summer Street, a few blocks from Jacques and his family.

Michel stayed long enough to help us move into our apartment, and left for Beirut shortly before Christmas. I was hurt that he chose to spend the holidays with his mother, but long ago I had stopped making an issue of things like that. He said he would not return until the end of May or early June, close to the end of the school year. That made me cry.

"Hang in there, Cathy," he said. "You've got to be strong for all of us." He explained the way he saw things. "It makes much more sense for me to spend what little money I'm making in Beirut supporting you all here. Why put money into a plane ticket when we have expenses like tuition, rent and car payments? Maybe you'll want to take a small break, go skiing in Vermont. Didn't Donna and Dick ask you all to join them?"

While that made sense it made nothing any easier. Five months is a long time to worry about someone you love. I tried to put on a happy face for everyone's sake, to turn each day together into a celebration of sorts. Afternoons were our private time. Other times we took long walks, talked about Beirut, and caught up on news of our friends. We would pick up Nayla from school, and meet Naim coming out of the subway at Harvard Square. On weekends we went to Jacques' house in New Hampshire, where we hiked in the woods and watched Naim and Nayla ski a nearby slope on what seemed the coldest days of the year.

Michel left on December 21. After dropping him off at the airport, I stopped by Jacques' to return the keys to the New Hampshire house. Linda was preparing for a Christmas party that evening to which the Soussous were invited, but we were not. I was terribly hurt and could not understand why she had not included us. She knew Michel had just left, and how upset we were by his departure. All this was swirling around in my head; but it did not include that one thing I had not yet figured out about myself.

I was grateful Sheila had invited us to New York for Christmas, or I would have gone mad. I was thankful I had the resources available to leave Boston, to spend the holidays with her, or to endure an indefinite exile in America. So many people in similar situations do not have the luxury of that leeway. I continually thank God for the lucky chance which brought me to marry a man with a successful career.

. . .

At the end of February, 1984, Michel phoned to say that he would be arriving in Boston on March 4. Saba and Jackie Nader, good friends as well as patients, had asked him to accompany them to Boston for a medical check-up at the Lahey Clinic, where Michel had trained.

Fate used the Naders to change our lives forever. Their visit to Boston coincided with Lebanese peace talks in Lausanne, Switzerland. Leaders from each of the warring factions were attempting to reach some sort of political solution. Saba knew everyone at the talks, and every night when he and Jackie returned to their hotel, they spoke with their friends by telephone. Michel and I did not know this until our last day together, when Saba and Jackie invited us to lunch. It was my birthday. I was driving, and we stopped at the Ritz Carleton to pick them up.

When we arrived at Anthony's Pier 4, Saba greased the maître d's palm to get us a window table. For a brief moment I was back in Beirut and loving it. I was with sophisticated friends who knew how the system worked, and were not afraid to very discreetly slip someone a few dollars in order to get what they wanted. Saba was the perfect, attentive Lebanese host, and knew the precise moment to turn to Michel and say what was foremost in his mind.

"I want you to listen carefully to what I have to say," he said. "I have spoken with my friends in Lausanne. Our pompous politicians are making ludicrous statements to the press promising reconciliation, but it isn't going to happen. The talks have failed. Things in Lebanon are hopeless, Michel. If you have a chance to practice medicine in the States, stay here. As your good friend, I urge you not to go back to Lebanon."

. . .

After we had dropped Saba and Jackie off at the hotel, I found my way back to Storrow Drive, the most direct route to our apartment in Watertown. It was not yet three P.M., and the traffic flowed at a relatively smooth pace, which rarely happened in Beirut except late at night. As many times as I drove Storrow I was still surprised that I was in Boston, driving along the Charles, not in Beirut, driving along the Mediterranean. I never thought about America in that way when I was in Beirut. When I was there I felt I was home, and never wished I was in America. I suppose that was strange since I was a foreigner in a foreign land, but it felt much stranger to be back in America, a land I was supposed be a part of and know, but had forgotten.

So we were driving along the Charles River, one of the most scenic routes in Boston. Mid-March was too early in the season to see the familiar flotilla of small sailboats that graced the Charles, but Harvard's rowing crews were out in their sculls pacing each other. Along the sea in Beirut, few seasonal changes were noticeable, and there was a constant flow of seafaring vessels in to and out of port. At night the gas lamps of small fishing boats dotted the shoreline like stars fallen to earth.

In Boston it was almost St. Patrick's Day, and the Irish were drinking green beer and wearing green carnations. In Beirut the white St. Joseph lilies were blooming, and it was Lent and perhaps Ramadan, depending on the Muslim lunar calendar. On Storrow Drive motorists at least drove courteously, even while disregarding the speed limit. In Beirut, where there were no speed limits – or none to which people paid attention – motorists drove like shrewd race car drivers.

These contrasts swirled around in my head until the reality of what Saba had said struck me. I pulled abruptly into a parking area along the Charles, expecting Michel to comment on my reckless maneuver, but he said nothing. It was as though he was expecting me to explode, and as long as he remained silent I would not, but I did. A nearby bridge over the Charles was supported by two massive stone arches whose reflection on the water formed the top of a heart.

It was mine, and it was broken.

"That's it, isn't it?" I cried. "We aren't going back. That's the end of my city. I just can't believe it. I think I might die if I have to live here."

Michel put his arm around me. "Calm down, Cathy. You are surely not going to die. You'll be just fine."

"No, I won't," I whimpered.

My head throbbed as if someone were pounding on it. The more I cried the more the pressure built up. I felt like a balloon with too much air in it, ready to burst, but I could not stop crying. The sadness inside me was too huge.

Michel said, "Cathy, listen to me."

"Let me be!" I cried more. I have no idea how long it was before he called my name again; when I opened my eyes everything was blurry.

"I'm blind!" I sobbed.

"It's not your eyes, silly," he said, laughing. "It's been raining for a while and you've done a splendid job of fogging up the windows. Your eyes are fine. Give them a rest now, okay?"

Somehow I managed to get a grip on myself and drive to Nayla's school and bring her home. Michel and I waited until Naim got home before we told the children the news. I asked Michel to tell them.

He explained, step by step, what we had learned from Saba. He was saying, "Staying in the States is the only logical thing to do," when Naim stood up, ran to his room and slammed the door.

Michel turned to Nayla and said, "Don't you see, Nayla ..." but she was already sobbing on the floor. I sat down beside her, took her in my arms and rocked her for a long time before I felt her go limp against my chest. I looked up at Michel. I think in that brief moment he saw the woman who was his rock, the 'woman with the nerves of steel,' begging for his help and about to lose her mind. He got down on the floor and crawled in between Nayla and me, and gathered us into his arms.

"Things will get better, I promise. I won't leave you ever again."

EPILOGUE

$\mathcal{M}$ ichel asked his former boss, Dr. John Morrissey at the University Hospital in Madison, Wisconsin, to help him find a job. When Dr. Morrissey went to his office the next morning he found a letter on his desk from Dr. Steve Immerman, spokesperson for a group of independent physicians in Eau Claire, Wisconsin, which was looking for a gastroenterologist. Dr. Morrissey telephoned Dr. Immerman and told him he had a particular physician in mind.

Michel had obtained his license to practice medicine in Wisconsin in 1977, so he was able to start work immediately. I was not disappointed, because I remembered Wisconsin for its orderliness, for its forests and natural beauty, its clean air and water. If there was any place I longed for – besides Beirut – it was just such a peaceful place.

While we assumed he would be successful, there were no guarantees. It was excruciating for Michel, at age forty-seven, to borrow fifty thousand dollars from a local bank; he had never been in debt.

Naim did not move with us to Eau Claire, but stayed to finish his last year at Boston College High School. Nayla, on the other hand, spent two very unhappy years in Eau Claire.

Each of us reacted differently to the trauma of being forced to leave Beirut. One of the things that still upsets Michel, to the point he cannot speak of her without tears coming to his eyes, was unintentionally abandoning Foxy. It was as if his grief over the senseless war, his loss of country, family, and friends, was all symbolized by having to leave the dog behind.

This is illustrated by what happened when Wadia decided to pay us a visit, a week after we arrived in Eau Claire. She insisted on coming, despite our explaining we were still in the process of moving in, and not ready to accommodate her.

She stayed six weeks.

Wadia expected fanfares and red carpet treatment when she arrived. Our less-than-enthusiastic welcome got us off on the wrong foot. Apparently she decided to get even as soon as possible.

Michel, understandably preoccupied with his new medical practice, counted on me to cater to his mother's whims, a task on a par with listening to her rusty-lawnmower-like snoring from the adjacent bed all those long years ago. The challenge was to rise above statements like, 'Since it's your job to entertain me, what are we going to do today?'

In a small, rural Midwestern city, where I was myself a newcomer, it took enormous inspiration to plan any activity which would appease Wadia. Mostly we shopped. Occasionally we ate at a restaurant she did not appreciate, or saw a movie she could not understand.

One of the first people I had met in Eau Claire was a kind Syrian woman, who invited my mother-in-law and me to lunch one day. While conversing with this lady, Wadia commented that her husband was a better person that she was. My new friend took offense at this remark, and told me so.

"She does not even know my husband. How can she say such an outrageous thing?"

Michel was very upset when he heard about this: the woman's husband was his greatest source of patient referrals.

On another occasion, Wadia told this same friend that I had broken any number of precious objects in her Beirut apartment, including her antique chandeliers. As hard as it was, I knew from long experience not to provoke her when she was bored and trying to create a crisis. That evening, when Michel arrived home and insisted on resting before dinner instead of visiting with his mother, Wadia found her long-awaited moment.

I can still her sitting at the corner of the kitchen table, her chair adjusted so she could closely observe my every move, and offer suggestions on how to do things better. Although my new hairdresser had colored her hair jet black just five days earlier, white roots had already begun to reappear around the contours of her face. Michel arrived at the table as I was serving the rice salad and sliced beef. Wadia had already helped herself and started to eat.

"Did I ever tell you how we got rid of Foxy?" she asked, turning to Michel. He shook his head.

"As soon as we knew you were not coming back, Nademe found Foxy a new owner. Within a week she was right back at our door. She barked and that's how we knew she was there. When Nademe opened the door Foxy rushed in and ran down the corridor."

"Arrête, je ne veux plus entendre," (Stop, I don't want to hear any more) cried Michel, getting up from the table and walking out of the room.

Wadia laughed and went on in a louder voice, "And she ran into your bedroom and hid under your bed."

I could hear Michel erupting into convulsive sobs behind our closed bedroom door.[29]

. . .

---

29 We were never able to ask Wadia any more details about Foxy's fate. For many years Michel could not hear Foxy's name without getting tears in his eyes. While we have no idea of what really happened to her, we were finally told she had been given to a young boy.

After Wadia left, the next few months in Eau Claire were, in some ways, like 1977, when I had to refurbish my apartment after I returned to Beirut. I got so immersed in decorating our rented townhouse, I almost enjoyed it, probably because I did not have to think. Most days I worked to the point of exhaustion, so by the time I cooked and served dinner, and visited awhile with Michel and Nayla, I was too tired to remember that the telephone had not rung. I had made a few new friends whom I could have called, but they would not have understood why I was acting like a love-sick woman forced to leave her lover.

In the mornings, Nayla grabbed a quick breakfast before I drove her to school, and Michel prepared for his busy day; evenings were our only family time. Michel usually got home from his office around half past five, exhausted after a strenuous day. My welcoming smile did nothing to elevate his mood, and he retreated to our bedroom to rest before dinner; and so began a typical evening at our house.

Nayla's personality was similar to her father's; she was sixteen, depressed, had no friends, and was attending her third new high school in three years. Add me to this unhealthy mix: because of my own depression I habitually glossed over the thing that was fundamentally wrong with all my relationships.

By six-thirty our dining room had become a war zone, Beirut all over again. Nayla arrived at the table a few minutes late. Michel was already seated.

"Where were you? Your mother called you five minutes ago."

Nayla did not answer, and sat with downcast eyes. I began talking to Nayla, trying to pretend nothing was wrong.

"Did your English teacher like your essay, darling?"

Michel's hands rested on either side of his plate; he had not touched his food.

"What kind of behavior is this?" he shouted. "I work hard all day long and I can't even have a pleasant meal. Everyone ignores me. My daughter won't answer a simple question. Instead of correcting her, you encourage her," he roared, glaring at me.

Abruptly he stood up and walked out of the room.

While Michel fumed in his bedroom, I spoke to Nayla in hers. She was lying on her bed.

"Please, darling, can't you just go and say you're sorry?"

"Sorry for what?" she asked. "Sorry that he lost his temper? Sorry that he can't understand that I have feelings, too? I don't exactly find life easy right now either, you know."

"But darling, it doesn't cost you anything to say you're sorry."

"Yes it does, Mommy," she replied.

"Then just walk up to him and give him a kiss without saying anything," I insisted.

"Mommy, just because that's how you've always handled your arguments with Poppy does not mean it's the right way. You should not have to apologize for something you didn't do."

"Don't judge me for the way I choose to handle your father, Nayla. It may not appear to be the right way, it may even be an unhealthy way to deal with a relationship, but it's the only way I know to hold everything together. You're always saying 'if only people in Beirut could get along.' Well, you're talking about me. You're talking about what I do, about compromise, about putting my ego aside for a time and saying, 'Okay, I'll swallow it. You're right, I'm wrong. Let's just forget it and move forward.'"

Nayla did not answer, so I went on.

"If everyone had the same attitude, think how many problems we could solve. If people were willing to compromise, maybe we wouldn't even have wars. I don't know what else to tell you, darling. I don't even know what my role is anymore. Is it just to keep you two from each others' throats? Is that all I'm doing here?"

"I feel sorry for you, Mommy," she said. "It's not your fault, it's his."

"Well," I said, "he's just like you. He's depressed too. Look at the stress he's under, at how hard he's having to work. He's not even in his own country. At least you were born here. How do you think he feels having to start all over at forty-seven?"

"I don't know, Mommy," she replied, "but I think he could handle things better than he does. He should be more grown-up. He's more of a baby than I am."

Nayla turned her face to the wall and began to cry, while I sat on the edge of her bed and rubbed her back. I wanted to tell her how much I was like her at this age, except her angry attention-seeking was not about the lack of love and affection, it was about the pain of leaving Beirut and her friends, and the difficulty of adjusting to a new environment. She probably thought no one else could possibly hurt as much as she did. I knew words were useless, because nothing I could say would change her mind. When she was ready she would learn, as I had, that we must get over our hurts if we are ever going to grow.

. . .

Just before Christmas, 1984, Naim received word of his early admission to Harvard. This good news made me realize for the first time how fortunate we were to be back in America, where my husband could find work and provide for our well-being. And I remembered Grandmother Catherine's words when she had tried to discourage me from moving to Beirut in 1969: 'America's the most glorious place on earth, Cathy, and don't you ever forget it.'

Bless her Irish heart, she was right. In Beirut, Michel used to ask me at least once a month what I wanted most in the world, and I always answered: to be able to afford to give our children a good education. If Michel and I had stayed in Lebanon, we would never have been able to send Naim to such a fine university. The fulfillment of my long-standing desire was bittersweet; I was forced to compromise one dream in order to realize another.

. . .

I fell in love with a house just outside the Eau Claire city limits. While it was not particularly beautiful, its vista reminded me of the view we had sitting on the terrace watching sunsets in Cornet Chehouan. When I had satisfied myself I could redesign the interior to fit our needs, I decided on the changes I could afford to make, negotiated with the owners, and went to the bank to apply for a mortgage.

Every time I asked Michel anything having to do with the house, he invariably replied, "Don't ask me. I slept in a bathtub in Beirut for three months. I don't care where I live."

When I got annoyed at his lack of interest, he would insist, "This is your house, Cathy. You do what you want."

My immediate reaction was that Michel had unfairly dumped an enormous burden on my shoulders. I only reevaluated my resentment when my friend Eileen pointed out how lucky I was to be making decisions on my own. She had to ask her husband's approval for every part of her recent remodeling job, until one day he said, "I bet you wish you were Cathy Sultan so you wouldn't have to run everything by me."

At once I saw things more clearly. I had interpreted Michel's apparent indifference as a reproach, when in fact by letting me do as I saw fit he was showing complete confidence in my ability to do things right. Such respect said more about his love for me than any 'I love you.'

. . .

Nayla could have attended Boston University or New York University, but chose the University of Minnesota instead, an hour and a half drive west of Eau Claire. She lived on campus for a year before getting her own apartment.

In universities across America in the late 1980s, students were talking about the School of the Americas, and about CIA involvement in Guatemala and elsewhere in Central America. Nayla was already distrustful of the world, a war veteran who could relate to oppressed peoples in conflict. So it was perfectly natural for her to be drawn into a student movement at the University of Minnesota. This new sense of purpose seemed to have a healthy effect on her. I could not remember her ever being so energized.

Nayla came home most weekends, and tried to discuss her new

political opinions with her father. She wanted to share what she was learning about America's foreign policy, and tell him about the despots it supported. No matter how incisive her analysis, or how intelligent she was in presenting her case, her father refused to believe a word she said. It was absurd. Now that he was an American citizen, it was as though he had transferred his loyalties from Bachir and his Christian militia to the Republican cause, and any kind of dissent had become a criminal offense.

Looking back, I wish I had understood what I do now, and been able to say to him, 'Let Nayla make her own discoveries, let her be overly enthusiastic about something that may or may not be true. You're not always right.'

Michel was very argumentative, and when Nayla challenged him, or voiced an opinion contrary to his, he took offense. Imagine how bad it was when Nayla literally beat him at every stage of an argument. For every one of his comments, she had a better one; for every historical reference he offered, she found another which proved him wrong. This struck deeply at his pride. Suddenly we were back to playing war across the dining table.

Eventually, Michel did learn to concede he was not always right, and he did learn to respect each of us for our own opinions. It did not happen overnight.

With Nayla going to the University of Minnesota, I had time to work part-time in Michel's office. His practice was growing rapidly and his secretary could not keep up with the paperwork, so he was enormously relieved when I offered to pick up the slack. The next thing I knew, I was enrolling in a computer course at the local technical college, and six months later we had a computer system installed in his office.

Little by little I felt myself begin to recuperate from the effects of war. It was probably a combination of being out of the chaos of Beirut, of taking on new and stimulating challenges, and of having a more nurturing relationship with our daughter, which made me feel more confident and less emotional.

One day Michel said, "Tell your daughter ..." I interrupted him and said flatly, "Tell her yourself. I am not doing that anymore," and walked out of the room.

He was quiet for a moment while he decided whether to be angry or let my comment slide.

He surprised me when he asked in a calm tone, "What kind of an attitude is that?"

"A new one," I replied, walking back into the room. "It's time things changed around here."

"Explain what you mean."

"Look, your daughter is exactly like you. Not only is she like you, she's an exact duplicate, with the same anxieties, the same stubborn streak, the same pride, the same intellect. When you can acknowledge all of those things, you'll start getting along much better with her, and until then your wars won't be over."

He looked at me and smiled roguishly. It was the first breakthrough.

· · ·

At first I attended daily Mass just as I had in Beirut. Despite my good intentions I still felt spiritually adrift. The priest's sermons sounded trite and out of touch with my realities. Adherence and commitment to long-established ritual practices are integral parts of daily worship in Beirut. In Eau Claire I have found no connection with an adaptation of Catholicism that has discarded Latin in favor of English, so I have stopped going to Mass. I still pray in the small chapel at Sacred Heart Hospital, and while I can meditate in this quiet place, uninterrupted by a congregation reciting a version of The Lord's Prayer I no longer recognize, I do not necessarily feel the presence of God. But when the organist in my Beirut church plays Bach's *Toccata & Fugue in d minor*, it makes the hair on my arms stand up, and my spine tingle, and I know I am in the presence of God.

· · ·

As Nayla's second year at the University of Minnesota was coming to a close in 1989, the Palestinian *intifada* in Israel had already begun. She volunteered to go to the West Bank as an official observer for a Washington-based Palestinian organization. One weekend, when she and I were sitting in our kitchen, she told me what she wanted to do. The kitchen was similar to the one in Beirut, and I still hung my apron behind the door. It felt strange to be sitting there in Eau Claire and be reminded of our association with the Palestinians in Beirut, and have our daughter wanting to go to Israel to defend their rights. The crazy part was that I understood completely, that I agreed with her and that I wanted to go myself.

After my earlier conversation with Michel, not only had he begun talking to Nayla, he had begun listening to the things she said. So when Nayla told him that she wanted to go to Israel, not only did he hear her, he agreed it was a good idea.

Nayla spent six weeks in the West Bank and Gaza, and after she returned she was restless. In Israel she had met several people from the French observer team, and she wanted to move to Paris to be with them. Nayla attended one more semester at the University of Minnesota while she figured out how to organize her move. When she came to me for suggestions, I found a possible solution.

"You're majoring in Women's Studies, Middle Eastern Studies and French. Find a study-abroad program in Paris in one of your majors."

Although I was not opposed to Nayla's move, I was concerned for her mental well-being. Paris was far away; what could I do from Eau Claire if she had a major crisis there? I brushed aside my concerns, and began to discuss her plans with Michel. We had missed out on a normal married life with young children and the pleasures that included. We had grown into a strong couple, but in a distorted, abnormal way. We had dodged bullets and put our lives on the line each day. In a situation where many couples we knew fell apart, somehow we had managed to survive, no doubt because along the way Michel had come to rely on me and respect my judgment. When I argued Nayla's case, insisting it would be very therapeutic for her, he acquiesced.

Nayla's time in France was not without its problems. She called home often; her depression flared up again; she did not like her roommate; she was lonely. I found something to say in each telephone call, some chord to strike which seemed to give her comfort. Shortly after she met Frédérique things began to change for the better. 'Fred,' as Nayla called her, had her own apartment, and asked Nayla to move in with her. Nayla applied to, and was accepted at, the University of Paris. Her credits from the University of Minnesota transferred, and at last everything seemed to be falling into place for her.

I continued to work part-time in Michel's office; once a week I entertained, mostly colleagues of Michel's and their spouses; I took French Literature courses at the local university; I gave the outward appearance of being fully acclimated to my new life; in reality I was simply applying the survival skills I learned in Beirut. There, it was largely physical survival; in Eau Claire, I was fighting for my mental stability. If I kept busy enough, I did not have to think about what I had left behind. I still dreamed of retiring to Lebanon and living in an old stone house with a red tile roof and a spectacular view of the sea, like the one in Cornet Chehouan. I longed for that future time when I would once again make bouillabaisse or paella, uncork good wines and entertain my friends at my table.

. . .

Michel's political epiphany occurred in 1990, when six Jesuit priests were murdered in El Salvador. Although the American government made a great show of public outrage at the atrocity, it continued to fund the same government which was believed to have been responsible for the murders. This tragedy radically changed the way Michel thought about American foreign policy. Everything Nayla had been saying suddenly made sense. Now he, too, would delve below the surface every time he listened to the news, and examine more closely which regimes the American government was supporting and why.

A few days after the news from El Salvador surfaced, I suggested Michel call Nayla in Paris.

"After all," I said, "you two have been arguing about Central America for a long time. Tell her what you've learned."

He thought about it for a moment, while he tried to decide whether to be offended by what I suggested or to act rationally. Then that lovely roguish smile of his spread across his face.

He picked up the telephone and dialed Nayla's number. As soon as he heard her voice, he said, "I presume you've heard what happened to the Jesuits? You were right all along, Nayla, and I just wanted to tell you."

He laughed when she made him repeat the 'you were right' part a second time. "Yes, I know," he said, responding to some comment. "Everything you said about America's involvement in Central America is true. I don't know why I never saw it."

. . .

Nayla got drawn into politics again in Paris, this time involving Algerian students and their right to remain in France. I put up a brave front, and applauded my daughter's concern, but on the inside I was still terribly worried. Every time the telephone rang I dreaded answering it.

The call I had feared came one evening at eight o'clock. Michel had just been called into the hospital for an emergency. It was an odd time for Nayla to be calling since it was three in the morning in Paris.

"Darling, it's the middle of the night there," I said. "Are you all right?" She did not answer. "Nayla, what's the matter? I hear that awful sound. It's an ambulance, isn't it? Were you in an accident? Speak to me, tell me you're not hurt."

Finally she said, "Yes, they're sounding an alarm for someone."

"What's the matter, Nayla? Something is terribly wrong, isn't it? I hear it in your voice. You don't sound well."

In that same dazed voice, she answered, "Not very well, Mommy."

"What are you saying? What's the ..."

"I'm giving up Middle Eastern Studies," she said. "I don't want to do that anymore."

"What are you talking about? You're not making any sense. You love the subject. What made ..."

"No, I'm giving it up. I hate Arabs now. I don't want to deal with them anymore. I'm changing my major to History."

"When did that ... Nayla, please tell me what happened."

"It'll be okay, Mommy. I just have to work this out."

I wanted to do something for her, but all I could do was to give her privacy, just as Grandmother Catherine would have done. She would have known she was dealing with a strong, determined young woman.

. . .

The first year I could safely return to Beirut was 1992. I traveled via Rome; one of my favorite places there is the Coliseum.

Once in Beirut, as I drove down Damascus Street from Sodeco toward the center of town with my friend Fay, I was struck by the odd similarity of ruins everywhere. These buildings had nowhere near the grandeur or size of the Coliseum, but there was a resemblance in the way they had been stripped bare of everything on the outside so that only the concrete skeletons remained. I felt as though the same thing had happened to me. After the war I was left a hollow shell and it has taken many years to rebuild myself into who I am today.

In the midst of such desolation, I was surprised at how well Nature had resisted the war. Yellow sunflowers grew where Martyrs' Square and the ancient *souks* had once stood, where Cleopatra had strolled and merchants had haggled over gold. Fuchsia bougainvillea and purple wisteria crept up the walls of shelled-out buildings. Despite broken water mains, smoldering mounds of garbage and the charred remains of cars, trees were blooming, lush with green leaves, their canopies shading tired, bullet-riddled façades from the summer sun.

War-damaged buildings were being demolished to make way for a multi-billion dollar redevelopment project, and archaeologists had been given six months to study Beirut's past. They discovered an eight-thousand-year-old Phoenician city buried beneath Martyrs' Square, which proved conclusively Beirut was Phoenician. In the summer of 1994, I toured the site amidst bulldozers tearing down buildings and dump trucks hauling off mountains of masonry and rock. Somewhere in this desolation, buried deep beneath the rubble, lay the spirit of my former lover Beirut. It was fitting that I should be there to see it laid to rest alongside its distinguished forefathers.

The archaeologists' pleas for more time did not sway the developers, who had a city waiting to be rebuilt. To their credit they did remove several important Roman ruins before beginning reconstruction in early 1995. One of the pieces stands in the Foch-Allenby District in front of the Parliament building, in a section of Beirut which has been meticulously restored in French Mandate style. The new, crisp, yellow sandstone façades will take a long time to blend in with the adjoining buildings still in dire need of repair.

Several blocks away, in the banking district, developers unearthed an elaborate system of Roman baths, wisely choosing to include them in their restoration, the ruins now surrounded with exquisite gardens lined with fragrant rosemary bushes. In the late nineties the redevelopment project succumbed to financial difficulties, leaving Lebanon with a staggering twenty-one billion dollar debt.

In 1999 the National Museum, which had sustained extensive damage, was reopened to the public. At the onset of war, in order to preserve the antiquities, the curator and his staff poured cement over every large piece. The smaller objects were boxed, labeled and stored in the basement. They filmed the tedious three-year restoration project, showing how carefully they chiseled away the cement, how they restored objects they had mistakenly thought safe from extensive water damage in the basement, and how they refurbished each piece. Today this video is shown to museum visitors. When, with tears streaming down my face, I saw the collapsed walls, the fallen Roman columns and the general condition of the neighborhood – which had been my own – our apartment was two blocks away – I wondered how my family and I ever survived such devastation.

On a visit in 2001, I peered from the recently reopened Phoenicia Hotel, in all its splendor, at the charred remains of the Holiday Inn next door, where Michel and I had often danced in the ballroom. As a news announcer I had been forced to lie about the hideous battles in the hotel sector, and so I never got to tell the story of the young *Kataeb* fighter whose feet had been tied to the back of a Jeep by rival militiamen in front of the Holiday Inn. They drove up and down the street jeering as his head bounced about like a ball on the pavement.

. . .

That same year, 2001, I revisited our old apartment for the first time. I understood that the squatters living there had no reason to keep up appearances; nonetheless, I was shocked by what I saw. The pitiful state of disrepair, the reckless way my walnut dining room table was thrown outside to wither in the hot sun, and the apparent poverty of those living there, sadly mirrored what was happening all over a city trying to recover from twenty years of civil war.

Spearheaded by then-Prime Minister, Rafic Hariri, Lebanon's massive reconstruction project has been geared to the revival of tourism. There is only so much money, which means more urgent needs like failing power grids, water shortages, inadequate telecommunications, an economy in shambles resulting in high unemployment, the continued use of leaded gasoline causing dangerously high levels of lead poisoning and air pollution – things that dramatically affect the well-being of all the Lebanese people – are being neglected.

Hariri was assassinated on February 14, 2005, when his motorcade was attacked with a bomb near the waterfront in Beirut. Hariri had worked tirelessly with France and the U.S., calling for the withdrawal of Syrian troops from Lebanon.

. . .

The lives of my family members and friends have stayed pretty much the same since 1984. Wadia is now ninety-two, and unable to travel. She still lives with Nademe in Achrafieh, where her quiet neighborhood has given way to a major thoroughfare. The incessant honking of the massive traffic jams – so intense as to prevent conversation on the balcony – bother her no more than the Israeli bombing did, since she hears nothing when she removes her hearing aid.

My parents moved to Florida after they retired, and enjoyed it for some fifteen years until two years ago, when my father passed away and my mother moved to New York.

My brother-in-law Jacques and Joe Soussou and their families still live in Boston.

Edith tends her gardens in Cornet Chehouan, while Fouad manages a large business just outside Tripoli in northern Lebanon.

Naim has recovered from the war, and is even able to write about it; he is compiling a collection of short stories and including several about his childhood in the war. After he graduated from Harvard Magna Cum Laude, with a major in Comparative Study of Religion, he and his friend and business partner Kevin bought a piece of land in Costa Rica, learned Spanish from the *campesinos* while clearing away jungle, and planted a hundred thousand teak trees. In the years since, one farm has grown to three. He loves nothing more than being immersed in nature, where his gentle soul seems to find great peace. He and his lovely wife Maria Teresa live on ninety acres overlooking the Pacific in Oaxaca, Mexico.

When I had bi-lateral total knee replacements in January, 1994, Naim came to be my nurse for five months. He carried me in and out of the house, drove me to physical therapy every day, grocery shopped and cooked, and constantly encouraged me with massive doses of moral support.

Romantic interests took Nayla to Rome after she graduated from the University of Paris in 1992. Fluent in Italian, she taught English as a second language for a number of years. She, her husband Adriano, and their beautiful daughter Caterina live in Rome.

After all these years it is such a relief not to worry about her. The strength she has acquired has instilled in her a tremendous sense of self-confidence. I laugh at her spunk and feistiness even when it is directed at me. Recently, in Rome, she gave me a good talking-to when I suggested she not get so upset about something.

"If you would just learn to ignore people's silly remarks you would be much better off," I said.

Hands on her hips, Nayla looked carefully at me. "Mom," she said, "would you please stop? It's not enough that I've come around ninety-nine percent, is it?"

"I wasn't being critical," I said, "I'm extremely proud of what you've accomplished."

"Yeah, yeah," she said, smiling. "But I know you only too well. You're still looking for that additional one percent. You try to do everything well, and you expect everyone else to do the same."

"But I have good intentions."

"I know that, Mom," she said, wrapping her arms around me and planting a kiss on my cheek. "You don't even realize you're doing it."

Of course she was right. How many times over the years had I given her a good talking to, and a lot of advice over the telephone? Now it was her turn to give me some back. I have to smile when I think how much she is like me. Nor was I offended at being bested, and that pleases me even more.

. . .

In Beirut, I found my place to grow. My commitment to stay there through the war was a consequence of a deep love affair. I had married into a family which was for the most part loving and accepting, and it was exciting to wake up every day as a foreigner embraced by a Lebanese family. This is the kind of love which develops a loyal Beirut heart, one which never dissolves.

Here I am, some twenty years later, still filled with this love for a city that continues to struggle to recover from civil war. Until recently, the Syrians maintained a presence there, and the Israelis still occasionally knock out power stations and bomb villages in southern Lebanon, just as they have been doing for twenty-five years.

After being forced to retreat to the Bekaa Valley during the 1982 Israeli invasion, Syrian troops re-entered West Beirut on July 4, 1986. By mid-1987, the Syrian Army appeared to have settled into Beirut for a protracted stay. The prevailing anarchy in Lebanon was regarded by Syrian officials as an unacceptable risk to Syrian security. The senior Syrian military commander in Lebanon, Brigadier General Ghazi Kanaan, announced that the Lebanese militia's role in Lebanon had ended and that the Syrian intervention was 'open-ended,' implying Syria would occupy West Beirut indefinitely.[30]

In October, 1989, Lebanese leaders agreed on a charter of national reconciliation known as the Taif Agreement. Syria made sure the agreement read: 'Syrian forces were to stay in place for a full two years, assisting the Lebanese government to extend its authority.' The agreement gave no timetable for a Syrian withdrawal, stipulating only that all withdrawals would be negotiated at the appropriate time by the governments of Lebanon and Syria.

After twenty-nine years of military occupation, corruption on a massive scale, political domination, and a long list of assassinations to its credit, the Syrian military formally withdrew its forces from Lebanon in March, 2005. However, no one doubts that its infamous intelligence units are still present and firmly in control. In addition, the Palestinians in Lebanon are still armed, as are the Hezbollah, and the Israelis continue to occupy the Shabba Farms in south Lebanon.

· · ·

I think about dodging snipers and running into shelters, about aprons with bullet holes, and about rescuing children from school. In my memory I can still see my frail Nayla and her despair.

---

30 Cedarland: The Lebanese War, www.cedarland.org/war. 1994–2005, Cedarland.org.

I think back to the time when we were hit by the rocket, to the bodies in the street and to poor Bachir. I think about the frightened stork, of the times when I was so depressed I nearly gave up hope, and I rejoice that I chose instead to enjoy life in all its incredible passion and beauty.

Michel and I live with our dog Churchill[31] on fourteen acres, just outside the city limits of Eau Claire. I must confess that I am still something of a romantic, and I enjoy living among my most prized possessions from Beirut, the Roman artifacts, the Persian carpets, the Phoenician amphorae, our five hundred French comic books – all things which Gisèle was able to ship to us several years ago.

I cannot help that my heart still beats to the rhythms of a city which no longer exists. I have lovely friends in Eau Claire, for whom I still love to cook and give dinner parties. Thanks to my new knees, I can dance again. There are no fancy nightclubs in Eau Claire, but Michel and I roll up a carpet, put on our LPs and pretend we are back at the Retro or the Caves du Roi.

I still take a siesta in the middle of the day, and I still speak like a Lebanese, casually drifting from English to French to Arabic, depending on what I want to say or whichever comes first. My heart is loyal: loyal to my wonderful Michel, and to our children who shared and survived the experience of war, and loyal to a country still in crisis. My adopted country, that dysfunctional old lover I've driven you mad talking about, is always in trouble. Finally, a popular swell of nationalism and world opinion has sent the Syrian occupation force packing. But bombs are going off again, and politicians are being murdered and here we go again! I cannot go back there to stay and risk my hard-won sanity, and I have finally accepted that. While there is sadness in this acceptance, I feel a sense of liberation in being able to acknowledge it at long last. With war finally cleaned out of me, my Beirut heart can enjoy the peacefulness of Eau Claire.

---

31 Churchill is a year-and-a-half-old golden retriever.

Glossary

Baba Ganouj – an eggplant dip seasoned with tahini, lemon juice and garlic. Hummus is the other traditional dip. This uses chickpeas instead of eggplant but, otherwise, uses the same ingredients listed above.

Baksheesh – a tip if given to a waiter who seats you at the best table or a porter for carrying your luggage. If it is given to the President to buy a favor, it is a bribe.

Corniche – a promenade along the sea. As in most Mediterranean coastal cities, it is a large walkway where the public strolls along the sea, often in the evening, to catch a glimpse of the sun setting.

Couscous – traditional Moroccan dish made with meat and vegetables and served with either a very spicey hot sauce or an aioli, a garlic mayonnaise.

Hakeme – A wise person, more commonly used when addressing a physician.

Hawaja – In Muslim countries, this is an honorary title bestowed on a Christian man, taken from the Turkish "Khadja." A Muslim man would be called Sayed, meaning master. The Christian would call his priest or bishop Sayedna, which means my master.

Kibbeh – Lebanese traditional dish. In its most classic form, it is made with ground lamb, bulgur and a variety of spices and nuts. There are over 50 different ways of making Kibbeh. I have two personal favorites: Fish Kibbeh, served with a tahini sauce, and Pumpkin Kibbeh with spinach, chickpeas and walnuts.

Kibbeh nyeh – another form of the traditional kibbeh but in this dish raw meat is mixed with the bulgur, onions and spices

Minaret – the tall, slender tower on a mosque with one or more projecting balconies from which the muezzin summons the faithful to prayer

Mougrabia – Lebanese couscous with meat or chicken. The Mougrabia grain is white and much larger than the traditional small yellow couscous. It is slowly cooked in the chicken or meat broth and spiced with cumin and traditional Syrian peppers.

Souk – ancient marketplace, still found in many Middle East cities like Cairo, Damascus and Jerusalem. The 3000-year-old souks in Beirut were, regrettably, destroyed during the war. When Beirut's center was restored, a semblance of the old traditional souks were added. However, nothing can replace the musty smells of the ancient walkways that dated back to biblical times.

Tabouli – traditional Lebanese salad. The primary ingredient is parsley to which tomatoes, green onions, mint and lemon juice are added.

Wasta – a person who does something for you. In Beirut, we had a man who did our car inspections, another one who took care of our residency papers. He is essentially a man who renders you a service and is, in turn, paid for whatever it is he does.

Bibliography

Bamford, James: *Body of Secrets: Anatomy of the Ultra-Secret National Security Agency*, Doubleday, New York, 2001.

David, Ron: *Arabs & Israel for Beginners*, Writers and Readers, New York, 1996.

Fisk, Robert: *Pity the Nation: The Abduction of Lebanon*, Atheneum, New York, 1990.

—— "Travels in a Land Without Hope," *The Independent*, August 29, 2001.

Fox, Robert: *The Inner Sea: The Mediterranean and Its People*, Alfred A. Knopf, New York, 1993.

Fromkin, David: *A Peace to End All Peace: The Fall of the Ottoman Empire and the Creation of the Modern Middle East*, Avon Books, New York, 1989.

Randall, Jonathan C.: *Going All the Way: Christian Warlords, Israeli Adventurers and the War in Lebanon*. Vintage, 1984.

Questions for Discussion

1. Cathy Sultan attempts to explain why she stayed in Beirut, why she kept her children in a war zone. Were you satisfied with the reasons she gave? What would you have done under similar circumstances?

2. Women are the unsung heroes in war. The author believes women should raise their collective voices to protest war at any cost. She stands with the Women in Black in her community. Around the world, WIB stand in silent vigil to protest war, rape as a tool of war, ethnic cleansing and human rights abuses. Would you consider starting a WIB group in your community?

3. Whether catalyst or cause, the Palestinian presence in Beirut was a major factor in the Lebanese civil war. Does the author explain this adequately? Do you think Arafat was justified in using Lebanon to attack Israel and if not, what should he have done differently?

4. If you lived in South Lebanon, how would you have dealt with the Palestinian presence on your land? Were the Israelis justified in retaliating the way they did?

5. Israel illegally occupied South Lebanon for twenty-two years. Some Lebanese chose to collaborate with the Israelis. Those who refused were thrown into the Israeli-run Khiam prison. What would you have done?

6. Hezbollah fought Israel's illegal occupation of South Lebanon, eventually forcing the Israeli Army to withdraw. Were they right to resist occupation? Would you have joined them?

7. The author has given an in-depth look at the various militias involved in the Lebanese civil war. Can you explain how otherwise civilized men can turn into cold-blooded killers seemingly overnight?

8. The author conducted herself, at times, irresponsibly. Did you sympathize with her or did you find her behavior outrageous?

9. In 1982–1983, the U.S. Marines in Beirut were on a peace-keeping mission. They were not allowed to carry weapons. Should they have been allowed to defend themselves?

10. In Spring 1983, another suicide bomber destroyed the American Embassy in Beirut. Do you think the U.S. government learned any lessons from that tragedy?

11. Lebanon, like other countries in the Middle East, was emerging as a place where centuries of Arab resentment toward the West were beginning to find voice and direction. Is America's behavior in Iraq encouraging stability or turmoil in the area?

12. In February, 2004, Lebanon's former Prime Minister, Rafic Hariri, was assassinated. If it was the Syrians who killed him, what did they hope to gain? If it was not the Syrians, who else stood to gain from continued turmoil in Lebanon and why?

13. After living war first-hand, the author now promotes peace. She sits on the Board of the National Peace Foundation, a Non-Governmental Organization in Washington, D.C. where she coordinates programs that educate people about the Middle East conflict. Would you be interested in working with the author on one of her projects? She can be reached at npf@ nationalpeace.org.